Volume XXXI

New World Medievalisms

ISSN 2043–8230

Series Editors
Karl Fugelso
Chris Jones

Medievalism aims to provide a forum for monographs and collections devoted to the burgeoning and highly dynamic multi-disciplinary field of medievalism studies: that is, work investigating the influence and appearance of 'the medieval' in the society and culture of later ages. Titles within the series investigate the post-medieval construction and manifestations of the Middle Ages – attitudes towards, and uses and meanings of, 'the medieval' – in all fields of culture, from politics and international relations, literature, history, architecture, and ceremonial ritual to film and the visual arts. It welcomes a wide range of topics, from historiographical subjects to revivalism, with the emphasis always firmly on what the idea of 'the medieval' has variously meant and continues to mean; it is founded on the belief that scholars interested in the Middle Ages can and should communicate their research both beyond and within the academic community of medievalists, and on the continuing relevance and presence of 'the medieval' in the contemporary world.

New proposals are welcomed. They may be sent directly to the editors or the publishers at the addresses given below.

Professor Karl Fugelso	Professor Chris Jones	Boydell & Brewer Ltd
Art Department	Department of English	PO Box 9
Towson University	University of Utah	Woodbridge
3103 Center for the Arts	LNCO, Room 3500	Suffolk IP12 3DF
8000 York Road	255 S Central Campus Drive	UK
Towson, MD 21252-0001	Salt Lake City, UT 84112	
USA	USA	
kfugelso@towson.edu	chris.s.jones@utah.edu	

Previous volumes in this series are printed at the back of this book

New World Medievalisms

The Middle Ages in the American Cultural Imaginary

Scott Corbet Riley

D.S. BREWER

© Scott Corbet Riley 2025

All Rights Reserved. Except as permitted under current legislation
no part of this work may be photocopied, stored in a retrieval system,
published, performed in public, adapted, broadcast,
transmitted, recorded or reproduced in any form or by any means,
without the prior permission of the copyright owner

The right of Scott Corbet Riley to be identified as
the author of this work has been asserted in accordance with
sections 77 and 78 of the Copyright, Designs and Patents Act 1988

First published 2025
D.S. Brewer, Cambridge

ISBN 978 1 84384 678 9

D.S. Brewer is an imprint of Boydell & Brewer Ltd
PO Box 9, Woodbridge, Suffolk IP12 3DF, UK
and of Boydell & Brewer Inc.
668 Mt Hope Avenue, Rochester, NY 14620–2731, USA
website: www.boydellandbrewer.com

A CIP catalogue record for this book is available
from the British Library

The publisher has no responsibility for the continued existence or accuracy of
URLs for external or third-party internet websites referred to in this book, and
does not guarantee that any content on such websites is, or will remain, accurate
or appropriate

Contents

Acknowledgement		vi
Introduction		1
1	The New World Crusades: British Colonial Charters, Pilgrim-Crusaders, and the Transatlantic Captivity Narrative	17
2	Errant in the Wilderness: The Naming of California, *Don Quixote*'s America, and Other Geographic Fantasies	35
3	*Mad Trist*: American Anglo-Saxonism, James Fenimore Cooper's *Leatherstocking Tales*, and Edgar Allan Poe's Subversive Medievalism	55
4	The Time Machine in the Garden: Frontier Medievalisms, Owen Wister's *The Virginian*, and Mark Twain's Apophatic America	74
5	The Persistent Medieval: T.S. Eliot's *The Waste Land*, Ezra Pound's *The Cantos*, and William Faulkner's Organic Medievalism	98
6	The Spectacle of the Medieval: America's New Feudalism, HBO's *Game of Thrones*, and Ursula K. Le Guin's Hainish Novels	120
Conclusion		140
Bibliography		155
Index		177

Acknowledgement

A portion of Chapter 2 was published in *The Medieval Globe* 4:2 (2018) as "Anachronous Antipodes: The Island of California, The Medieval Mediterranean and the Modern Pacific."

Introduction

Historical periodization, like geographic territorialization, has been indispensable to the discourse of colonialism.[1] The division of history into discrete periods supports the "deliberate destruction of the past" that colonialism enacts, for such periodization reduces historiography's complexity and polyvocality into uniform, unequivocal "grand narratives."[2] The entire notion of a nation's "development" relies upon such periodizing schemata, according to which nations undergo similar historical processes – especially that of Western European nation-states' supposed shift from a "Dark Age" to modernity.[3] Popularized during the European Enlightenment of the seventeenth and eighteenth centuries, this periodizing schema defines modernity in direct antithesis to the Middle Ages – understood as an epoch of disease, warfare, and ignorance – then overlays that schema onto various colonial contexts, portraying non-Europeans as unmodern and Europeans as modern.[4] This "medieval/modern divide," as Kathleen Davis has deemed it, is inscribed within colonialism's network of binary oppo-

---

[1] Kathleen Davis, *Periodization and Sovereignty: How Ideas of Feudalism and Sovereignty Govern the Politics of Time* (Philadelphia, PA: University of Pennsylvania Press, 2008), 6–20.

[2] Robin D.G. Kelly, "A Poetics of Anticolonialism," in Aimé Césaire, *Discourse on Colonialism*, trans. Joan Pinkham (New York, NY: Monthly Review Press, 2000), 9. On "grand narratives," see Jean-Francois Lyotard, *The Postmodern Condition: A Report on Knowledge*, trans. Geoff Bennington and Brian Massumi (Minneapolis, MN: University of Minnesota Press, 1979), xxiii–xxiv.

[3] For more on the formulation of the concept of the Dark Ages, see Davis, *Periodization and Sovereignty*, 9, 42. On Eurocentrism in development studies, see Ziauddin Sardar, "Development and the Location of Eurocentrism," in *Critical Development Theory: Contributions to a New Paradigm*, eds. Ronaldo Munck and Denis O'Hearn (London: Zed Books, 1999), 44–62.

[4] For more on the rupture of modernity from the unmodern, see Carol Symes, "When We Talk about Modernity," *The American Historical Review* 116:3 (2011), 715. On Enlightenment renderings of the Middle Ages, see Alicia Montoya, *Medievalist Enlightenment: From Charles Perrault to Jean-Jacques Rousseau* (Cambridge: D.S. Brewer, 2013), 43–7.

sitions, with modernity being associated with industrial society, secularism, democracy, and civilization and the medieval with developing countries, religion, monarchy, and barbarism.[5]

The Enlightenment's rendering of the Middle Ages as a Dark Age, meanwhile, was amended in the late eighteenth and early nineteenth centuries by European Romanticism, which continued to rely upon a binary opposition between modernity and the medieval but now connected modernity with disorientation, confusion, ennui, and superficiality and the medieval with purity, clarity, and passion.[6] Twentieth- and twenty-first-century American cultural productions are riddled through with these antithetical historiographies; while Disney films portray medievalized worlds of authenticity, love, and beauty, replete with majestic castles, princesses, and tales of derring-do, political discourses across the political spectrum often rely upon a historical myopia according to which, for instance, the United States was, after the American Revolutionary War (1775–83), radically divorced from its pre-national past – as if with the surrender of Lord Cornwallis at Yorktown the nation were born *ex nihilo*, "out of nothing."[7]

Since the 1970s, an insightful conversation has been developing between medieval studies and postcolonial studies that interrogates this medieval/modern divide. This scholarship has taken up a wide range of cultural contexts – from Nadia Altschul's study of the Venezuelan–Chilean politician and writer Andrés Bello and South American independentist movements to Michelle R. Warren's analysis of francophone Réunion – but little research has yet been conducted upon either British-American colonial or U.S. contexts.[8] Indeed, medievalism studies – that is, the inter-

---

[5] Davis, *Periodization and Sovereignty*, 2–4.

[6] For more on Romanticism's fascination with the medieval, see Elizabeth Fay, *Romantic Medievalism: History and the Romantic Literary Ideal* (New York, NY: Palgrave Macmillan, 2002), 2. For a thorough history of Romanticism, see Carmen Casaliggi and Porscha Fermanis, *Romanticism: A Literary and Cultural History* (New York, NY: Routledge, 2016). For more on the exoticization of the medieval, see Amy Burge, *Representing Difference in the Medieval and Modern Orientalist Romance* (New York, NY: Palgrave Macmillan, 2017), 15–16.

[7] On Disney's use of the Middle Ages, see Tison Pugh and Susan Aronstein, eds. *The Disney Middle Ages: A Fairy-Tale and Fantasy Past* (New York, NY: Palgrave Macmillan, 2012). For more on the historical myopia of U.S. historiography, see Amy Kaplan and Donald Pease, eds., *Cultures of U.S. Imperialism* (Durham, NC: Duke University Press, 1993), as well as Maria O'Malley and Denys Van Renen, eds., *Beyond 1776: Globalizing the Cultures of the American Revolution* (Charlottesville, VA: University of Virginia Press, 2018).

[8] Nadia Altschul, *Geographies of Philological Knowledge: Postcoloniality and the Transatlantic National Epic* (Chicago, IL: University of Chicago Press, 2012); Michelle R. Warren, *Creole Medievalism: Colonial France and Joseph Bédier's Middle Ages* (Minneapolis, MN: University of Minnesota Press, 2011).

disciplinary field that takes as its subject matter the representation of the Middle Ages in modern contexts – has had little sway on American Studies at all, and those few texts that have connected the fields have largely focused on the U.S. Civil War and its aftermath without considering how the medieval/modern divide has affected U.S. cultural productions throughout the nation's history, let alone throughout British-American colonial history.[9] Americanist Ritchie Devon Watson, Jr., for instance, has demonstrated convincingly how the U.S. South's plantation society was "founded on a medieval sense of social gradation and order and a modern sense of precise and scientific racial distinctions," but Watson does not grapple with the question of why we associate either "social gradation and order" with the Middle Ages or scientific precision with modernity.[10] T.J. Jackson Lears, meanwhile, has emphasized the extent to which the Middle Ages existed for late-nineteenth- and early-twentieth-century U.S. Northern writers, artists, architects, and politicians as an "escape from the rigors of bourgeois adulthood," especially the increasing industrialization of the post-Civil-War United States.[11] Like their Southern counterparts, who considered their loss in the Civil War to be the death knell of a "medieval-inspired" social order, these Northern writers turned to the Middle Ages for a bygone epoch of "purity and honor" that dramatized and clarified a particular conception of the present as inferior to that imagined medieval past.[12] Like Watson, however, Lears does not consider the literary, political or historiographical discourses that associated the medieval with purity and honor and modernity with industrialization, let alone the

---

[9] For a concise introduction to the field of medievalism studies, see David Matthews, *Medievalism: A Critical History* (Cambridge: D.S. Brewer, 2015), 1–10.

[10] Ritchie Devon Watson, Jr., *Normans and Saxons: Southern Race Mythology and the Intellectual History of the Civil War* (Baton Rouge, LA: Louisiana State University Press, 2008), 71.

[11] T.J. Jackson Lears, *No Place of Grace: Antimodernism and the Transformation of American Culture, 1880–1920* (Chicago, IL: University of Chicago Press, 1981), 146.

[12] Watson, *Normans and Saxons*, 51. Lears, *No Place of Grace*, 101. Other examples of scholars associating American Studies and medieval studies include: Peter Williams, "The Varieties of American Medievalism," *Studies in Medievalism* 1:2 (Spring 1982), 7–20; Kathleen Verduin, ed., *Studies in Medievalism VI: Medievalism in North America* (Cambridge: D.S. Brewer, 1994); Bernard Rosenthal and Paul E. Szarmach, eds., *Medievalism in American Culture* (Binghamton, NY: Center for Medieval and Early Renaissance Studies, 1989); Gordon Hutner, ed., *American Literary History* 22:4 (2010); Kim Ileen Moreland, *The Medievalist Impulse in American Literature: Twain, Adams, Fitzgerald, and Hemingway* (Charlottesville, VA: University Press of Virginia, 1996); and Tison Pugh and Susan Aronstein, eds., *The United States of Medievalism* (Toronto: University of Toronto Press, 2021).

broader connections among European colonization of the New World, U.S. western expansionism, and the European Middle Ages.

American Studies scholarship concerned explicitly with medievalism studies has maintained this focus on the late nineteenth and early twentieth centuries. Elizabeth A. Emery, for instance, interprets the postcolonial Gothic style of two Episcopal cathedrals – the National Cathedral in Washington and the Church of St. John the Divine in New York City, both built at the turn of the twentieth century – as emblematic of the fraught relationship between the United States and its imagined medieval past, illustrating how, as Henry James famously declares in *The American Scene* (1907), "the multitudinous sky-scrapers [that] like extravagant pins in a cushion already overplanted" had come to supersede cathedrals as the prototypical American architecture.[13] Tison Pugh, meanwhile, has outlined the extent to which the U.S.'s "myth of southern masculinity" relies fundamentally upon a "medieval chivalric ideal," which Pugh rereads as not only a "historical myth" but "a queer one at that."[14] Engaging with the recognition, famously discussed by Mark Twain in *Life on the Mississippi* (1883), that "[t]he South has not yet recovered from the debilitating influence of [Sir Walter Scott's] books," Pugh sees this U.S. Southern medieval chivalric ideal as a decidedly homoerotic figuration, surreptitiously reframing the South's "appropriation of medieval chivalry" as disclosures of "queer anxieties" underlying these exaggeratedly masculine narratives and images.[15]

This attention to the U.S.'s North/South divide resembles the way late nineteenth-century and early twentieth-century U.S. historians often framed U.S. history itself in terms of the Civil War, and it was precisely this dialectic that Frederick Jackson Turner's seminal "frontier thesis" served to dismantle.[16] Turner's controversial "frontier thesis," first posed

[13] Elizabeth A. Emery, "Postcolonial Gothic: The Medievalism of America's 'National' Cathedrals," in *Medievalisms in the Postcolonial World: The Idea of "The Middle Ages" outside Europe*, eds. Nadia Altschul and Kathleen Davis (Baltimore, MD: Johns Hopkins University Press, 2009), 237–64. Henry James, *The American Scene* (New York, NY: Harper Brothers, 1907), 74.

[14] Tison Pugh, *Queer Chivalry: Medievalism and the Myth of White Masculinity in Southern Literature* (Baton Rouge, LA: Louisiana State University Press, 2013), 102.

[15] Mark Twain, *Life of the Mississippi* (New York, NY: Harper Brothers, 1883/1917), 333. Pugh, *Queer Chivalry*, 6. For more on the U.S. South's fascination with the medieval, see Richard Utz, "Three Vignettes and a White Castle: Knighthood and Race in Modern Atlanta" in *The United States of Medievalism*, eds. Tison Pugh and Susan Aronstein (Toronto: University of Toronto Press, 2021), 111–29.

[16] Frederick Jackson Turner, "The Significance of the Frontier in American History" in *Proceedings of the Forty-first Annual Meeting of the State Historical Society of Wisconsin* (Madison, WI: State Historical Society of Wisconsin, 1894),

in 1894, contended that it was not the Civil War but the eradication of a western frontier to colonize and exploit that would prove crucial to the twentieth-century United States, and since Lynn White, Jr., first noted how U.S. "frontiersmen [...] were particular beneficiaries of the Middle Ages" and that theirs "was very largely the culture of the mediaeval lower classes," a similar reframing of American medievalisms has occurred, with a handful of scholars since the mid-1960s noting the extent to which representations of the U.S.'s western frontier regularly associate that territory with the Middle Ages.[17] In the only book-length study of these "frontier mediaevalisms," as White deems them, medievalist Milo Kearney and Latin Americanist Manuel Medrano have outlined how the U.S.–Mexico border "cannot be fully understood without knowledge of [the] medieval underpinnings in both Castile and in England."[18] While Kearney and Medrano's research constructs a persuasive genealogical argument focused on tracing the medieval "roots" and "influences" shared by Mexican and U.S. cultures, scholarship that critiques the entire medieval/modern divide would see these transnational North American medievalisms as indicative of a shared colonial historiography – namely, one that situates the Middle Ages, in the paradoxical logic of colonialism, as both "the cradle of Europe and its nations" and "the barbaric past that [those nations] left behind."[19]

Since the late 1980s, scholars of postcolonial studies and American Studies have considered the extent to which postcolonial theory might be applied to U.S. contexts.[20] After all, "[w]hile the U.S. defined itself as

---

199–227. For more on how Turner's frontier thesis disrupted American Studies' focus on the Civil War, see Henry Nash Smith, *Virgin Land: American West as Myth and Symbol* (New York, NY: Vintage Books, 1950), 250.

[17] Lynn White, Jr., "The Legacy of the Middle Ages in the American Wild West," *Speculum* 40:2 (April 1965), 193. Also, see Luis Weckmann, *The Medieval Heritage of Mexico*, trans. Frances M. López-Morillas (New York, NY: Fordham University Press, 1992) and Owen Ulph, "The Legacy of the American Wild West in Medieval Scholarship," *American West* 3:4 (1966), 50–2, 88–91.

[18] White, "The Legacy of the Middle Ages in the American Wild West," 199. Milo Kearney and Manuel Medrano, *Medieval Culture and the Mexican American Borderlands* (College Station, TX: Texas A&M University Press, 2001), 1–2.

[19] Kathleen Davis and Nadia Altschul, "The Idea of 'The Middle Ages' outside Europe," in *Medievalisms in the Postcolonial World: The Idea of "The Middle Ages" Outside Europe*, eds. Kathleen Davis and Nadia Altschul (Baltimore, MD: Johns Hopkins University Press, 2009), 1.

[20] Early considerations of the connections between postcolonial theory and U.S. literature include Bill Ashcroft, Gareth Griffiths and Helen Tiffin, *The Empire Writes Back: Theory and Practice in Post-Colonial Literatures* (New York, NY: Routledge, 1989), Lawrence Buell, "American Literary Emergence as a Postcolonial Phenomenon," *American Literary History* 4:3 (1992), 411–42, and Amritjit Singh and Peter Schmidt, *Postcolonial Theory and the United States: Race, Ethnicity and Literature* (Jackson, MS: University Press of Mississippi, 2000).

the world's first independent and anti-colonial nation-state[,] it simultaneously incorporated many of the defining features of European colonial networks – including the color line – into its economic and cultural life."[21] Indeed, U.S. medievalisms, including American Anglo-Saxonism, which uses the medieval European cultural groups of the Angles and Saxons to depict the quintessential American, tend to resemble European colonial rather than anti-colonial discourses, for these figurations invoke the European Middle Ages as a means of buttressing the racial and ethnic hierarchies endemic to European colonialism and Euro-American settler colonialism.[22] If our goal is to interrogate the medieval/modern divide, however, the medievalisms of a nation-state, such as the United States, that purports to exemplify European colonial conceptions of development and yet remains preoccupied by an anachronous and geographically displaced space-time – i.e., the European Middle Ages – reveal not only the arbitrary nature of the medieval/modern divide but also the racial, linguistic, historiographical, and cultural contentions embedded within and perpetuated by that preoccupation.[23]

After all, the question of how precisely to define "medievalism," not to mention the medieval period itself, is of long-standing debate in medievalism studies and medieval studies alike.[24] "It is simple enough," writes David Matthews in *Medievalism: A Critical History* (2015), "to say that medievalism is the study of the Middle Ages after the Middle Ages, but very difficult to discern a precise method. Like cultural studies, medievalism has proved difficult to house within traditional disciplines."[25]

[21] Singh and Schmidt, *Postcolonial Theory and the United States*, 5.

[22] As is discussed in more detail in Chapter 3, settler colonialism involves "the outward migration of settlers from a metropolitan center to establish colonial outposts on the periphery of empire," Adam Dahl, *Empire of the People: Settler Colonialism and the Foundations of Modern Democratic Thought* (Lawrence, KS: University of Kansas Press, 2018), 11. The term "Anglo-Saxon" has itself been brought into question recently for its association with white supremacist ideologies and the ways it has been historically employed to justify exclusionary practices and racial hierarchies. The problematic nature of the term has led scholars to critically re-evaluate its use, considering the implications it carries in both academic and popular discourse. For more, see Nell Irvin Painter, *The History of White People* (New York, NY: W.W. Norton, 2010), 184–90.

[23] On "periodization and historiography" with respect to U.S. history and development theory, see Martin J. Sklar, *The United States as a Developing Country: Studies in U.S. History in the Progressive Era and the 1920s* (Cambridge: Cambridge University Press, 1992), 1–36.

[24] On the matter of defining the Middle Ages themselves, see Johannes Fried, *The Middle Ages*, trans. Peter Lewis (Cambridge, MA: Belknap Press, 2015), vii–ix.

[25] Matthews, *Medievalism*, 9. For more on the establishment of medievalism studies as a research field, as well as for a discussion of possible distinctions between "medievalism" and "neomedievalism," see Ionut Costea, "Medievalism.

Scholars working in medievalism studies have tended to define the field in contradistinction to medieval studies, itself understood as the "study of the *actual* Middle Ages."[26] In the last several decades, however, with journals such as *Studies in Medievalism* (1979–) and, more recently, *postmedieval* (2010–) serving as primary sites of scholarship, this binary opposition has been brought into question, for, "[w]hile medieval studies might be concerned with the medieval period, *all* such study of the Middle Ages (by definition) has gone on after the Middle Ages."[27] "[M]edievalism," in this sense, "inhabits medieval studies as an abiding trauma," and in order to "mov[e] beyond the purview" of this opposition of medieval studies and medievalism studies, scholars such as Matthews have promoted an "extended medieval studies" that includes not only the study of the process of creating the Middle Ages as a modern historiographical periodization but also "global histories that extend to the European Middle Ages and beyond."[28]

Such collaboration between medievalism studies and medieval studies underscores both the extent to which medieval studies is riddled through with medievalism and the importance of critical engagement with the

---

Historiographic Markers," *Studia Universitatis Babeș-Bolyai Historia* 68:1 (June 2023): 131–60. For more on the challenge of placing medievalism studies within traditional academic disciplines, as well as on its penchant for Anglocentrism, see Richard Marsden, "Medievalism: New discipline or scholarly no-man's land?" *History Compass* 16:2 (2018): https://onlinelibrary.wiley.com/doi/10.1111/hic3.12439.

[26] Matthews, *Medievalism, A Critical History*, 1. Italics his own.

[27] Matthews, *Medievalism: A Critical History*, 172. Italics his own. For more on the history of contemporary medievalism studies, see Richard Utz and Tom Shippey, *Medievalism in the Modern World: Essays in Honour of Leslie Workman* (Turnhout: Brepols Publishers, 1998), 1–6, and Berit Kjærulff, "Medievalism and the Post-medieval Middle Ages: A Review of Anglophone Medievalism Studies," *Orbis Litterarum* 73 (2018), 458–70.

[28] Kathleen Biddick, *The Shock of Medievalism* (Durham, NC: Duke University Press, 1998), 11. Matthews, *Medievalism: A Critical History*, 180. Other definitions of medievalism have associated the term with the postcolonial scholar Edward Said's concept of "Orientalism," which Said defines as "a Western style for dominating, restructuring, and having authority over the Orient" (Edward Said, *Orientalism* (New York, NY: Pantheon Books, 1978), 3). Sharon Kinoshita, for example, argues that Said's "trenchant critique of Orientalism […] is bought at the price of what we might call 'Medievalism' – itself a widespread phenomenon"; for Kinoshita, "Medievalism" – she capitalizes the term, echoing Said's capitalization of Orientalism – is synonymous with the infantilizing and othering of the medieval period by modernity (Sharon Kinoshita, "Deprovincializing the Middle Ages" in *The Worlding Project: Doing Cultural Studies in the Era of Globalization*, eds. Rob Wilson and Chris Connery (Berkeley, CA: North Atlantic Books, 2007), 67). For more on the relationship between medievalism and Orientalism, see John M. Ganim, *Medievalism and Orientalism* (London: Palgrave Macmillan, 2005).

Middle Ages by scholars of medievalism studies, lest that historical period continue to be subjected to the "recurring cycles of demonization, romanticism, gothicization, obfuscation, and dismissal" that it has for so long endured.[29] In an effort to reckon with this complexity, scholars of medievalism studies have regularly pluralized the term, thinking of "medievalisms" as "disparate" and "polyphonic," surreptitiously echoing the pluralism of the term "Middle Ages" itself, and such a pluralized conception clarifies, in particular, the multitudinous and often contradictory ways in which modernity has conceived of and portrayed the Middle Ages.[30]

The question of how to define "America" is also, of course, quite fraught. The term, which refers to the continents of both South and North America, is regularly used synonymously with the United States of America, occluding the term's inherent transnationality and multiculturalism. Indeed, just as Matthews has espoused an "extended medieval studies," scholars of American Studies have argued for an "extended American Studies" that thinks broadly about the diverse and interconnected cultures of the Americas.[31] "Since 'America' names the entire hemisphere from the Yukon to Patagonia," Kirsten Silva Gruesz writes, "its common use as a synonym for the United States of America is technically a misnomer, as Latin Americans and Canadians continually (if resignedly) point out," and Gruesz has promoted the "worlding" of American Studies as a means of considering America not only as a plural, multicultural, and transnational territory but also in terms of the transoceanic cultural exchanges that continue to affect and, in part, define it.[32]

---

[29] Carol Symes, "When We Talk about Modernity," *The American Historical Review* 116:3 (2011), 718. On the medievalism endemic to medieval studies, see Matthews, *Medievalism: A Critical History*, ix–xiv.

[30] Paul Murphy, "Disparate Medievalisms in Early Modern Spanish Music Theory," in *Studies in Medievalism XIII: Postmodern Medievalisms*, eds. Richard Utz et al. (Cambridge: D.S. Brewer, 2004), 17–19. For more on the pluralizing of "medievalism," see Karl Fugelso, ed., *Studies in Medievalism XVII: Defining Medievalism(s)* (Cambridge: D.S. Brewer, 2009); Tison Pugh, *Medievalisms: Making the Past in the Present* (New York, NY: Routledge, 2013); and Martin Aurell, Florian Besson, Justine Breton, and Lucie Malbos, "Introduction," in *Les médiévistes face aux médiévalismes*, eds. Martin Aurell, Florian Besson, Justine Breton, and Lucie Malbos (Rennes: Presses Universitaires de Rennes, 2023), 7–11.

[31] Winfried Fluck, "Men in Boats and Flaming Skies: American Painting and National Self-Recognition," in *Re-framing the Transnational Turn in American Studies*, eds. Winfried Fluck, Donald E. Pease, and John Carlos Rowe (Hanover, NH: Dartmouth University Press, 2011), 143.

[32] Kirsten Silva Gruesz, "America," in *Keywords for American Cultural Studies*, 2nd edn, eds. Bruce Burgett and Glenn Hendler (New York, NY: New York University Press, 2014), 21. For more on the "worlding" of American Studies, see Susan Gillman, Kirsten Silva Gruesz, and Rob Wilson, "Worlding American Studies," *Comparative American Studies: An International Journal* 2:3 (2004),

Such a transnational and transoceanic American Studies, however, can be supplemented by transhistorical frameworks that "thread America[n] texts into the topical events of other cultures, while also threading the long durations of those cultures into the [relatively] short[er] chronology of the United States."[33] After all, while the term "America" is clearly a construct of European colonialism – derived as it is from the Christian name of the Italian merchant and sailor Amerigo Vespucci – the diverse cultures to which it refers are certainly not defined solely by either European colonization or any single American nation-state.[34] Studies of Indigenous cultures throughout the Americas serve as primary sites of scholarship for this transhistorical conception of American Studies, for such research can emphasize how the Americas "remained overwhelmingly Indigenous well into the nineteenth century" and, therefore, "rather than a 'colonial America,' we should speak of an *Indigenous America* that was only slowly and unevenly becoming colonial."[35] Studies of the ways in which non-American cultural imaginaries – such as those of Europe or East Asia – have shaped the cultures of the Americas can also, however, serve to emphasize how this purportedly "New World" has been and continues to be deeply inflected by cultural imaginaries that extend far beyond the Americas and that long predate Columbus's arrival upon the shores of Guanahaní, and it is with such broader, more global and transhistorical conceptions of medievalism studies, medieval studies, and American Studies alike that this project embarks.

Each of the chapters in this book, in turn, takes up a period of British colonial or U.S. cultural history with an eye to how authors of that period depict, refer to, and imagine the medieval. The first chapter, for instance, explores the connections between British colonial and Christian crusader charters, especially pointing out the colonial charters' attention to Christianizing non-Christian lands and the crusader charters' attention

---

259–70; as well as Rob Sean Wilson, "Worlding as Future Tactic," in *The Worlding Project: Doing Cultural Studies in the Era of Globalization*, eds. Rob Sean Wilson and Christopher Leigh Connery (Berkeley, CA: North Atlantic Books, 2007), 209–23. With respect to the fixation on the United States in American Studies, see Amy Kaplan and Donald Pease, eds., *Cultures of U.S. Imperialism* (Durham, NC: Duke University Press, 1993), 11–13.

[33] Wai Chee Dimock, *Through Other Continents: American Literature across Deep Time* (Princeton, NJ: Princeton University Press, 2006), 3.

[34] Gruesz, "America," 22–4.

[35] Pekka Hämäläinen, *Indigenous Continent: The Epic Contest for North America* (New York, NY: Liveright Publishing, 2022), 1. Italics his own. For more on how colonialism produces "uneven" spatialities, see Smith, *Uneven Development*, 92–131.

to "financial arrangements."[36] This problematizing of distinctions between the medieval Christian Crusades and New World colonization connects the latter with the history of medieval Europe and recasts European colonization of the New World, including British-American colonization, as the logical extension, or even "culmination," of a medieval Christian crusader ideology.[37] At the close of this chapter, meanwhile, I demonstrate how the captivity narrative, one of the canonical genres of British colonial literature, is directly linked to the medieval Barbary captivity narrative, itself a means of justifying the medieval Christian Crusades against the Ottoman Empire. In British colonial captivity narratives such as Mary Rowlandson's, it is not Moors but Native Americans who capture and imprison Christians, and such an adaptation of the Barbary captivity narrative further demonstrates how British colonists were utilizing a medieval Christian crusader ideology to make sense of their experiences in this (so-called) New World.[38]

Entwined with this colonialist discourse that links New World conquest and colonization with the medieval Christian Crusades, meanwhile, is a subversive medievalism that mocks that very association. The remarkable popularity throughout American literary history of Miguel Cervantes's *Don Quixote* (1605, 1615) – often deemed the first modern novel and which tells of a Spanish nobleman's obsession with medieval chivalric romances – functions as a starting place for exploring the complicated relationship that American medievalisms maintain with the medieval/modern divide.[39] In the second chapter, therefore, I outline the linkages between the New World and *Don Quixote*, which not only repeatedly mentions the Americas but also was transported to the Americas within the first years of its publication.[40] An account of *Quixote*'s early reception history throughout the Americas, when juxtaposed with a reading that situates New World colonization as allied with the medieval Christian Crusades, serves to outline how American medievalisms simultaneously

---

[36] Corliss Konwiser Slack, *Crusader Charters 1138–1270* (Tempe, AZ: Arizona Center for Medieval and Renaissance Studies, 2001), xxix.

[37] Eduardo Subirats, *El continente vacío: la conquista del Nuevo Mundo y la conciencia moderna* (México D.F.: Siglo XXI, 1994), 81.

[38] Mary Rowlandson, "Narrative of the Captivity and Restoration," in *Racism: A Global Reader*, eds. Kevin Reilly et al. (London: M.E. Sharpe, 2003), 94–103.

[39] Miguel de Cervantes Saavedra, *The Indigenous Hidalgo Don Quixote de la Mancha*, trans. John Rutherford (New York, NY: Penguin Books, 2000). For more on the contradictions of medievalism, see Warren, *Creole Medievalism*, xxix, and Davis, *Periodization and Sovereignty*, 26–8.

[40] Irving A. Leonard, *Books of the Brave: Being an Account of Books and of Men in the Spanish Conquest and Settlement of the Sixteenth-century New World* (Berkeley, CA: University of California Press, 1992), 289.

canonize and critique European colonialism. Meanwhile, the fascinatingly complex history of the place-name of "California," which derives from a chivalric romance entitled *Las sergas de Esplandián* (itself featured in *Don Quixote*), affords a salient instance of how medieval European cultural productions survive in oblique, seemingly innocuous ways throughout the Americas.[41] If New World colonization was begun in the spirit of a medieval Christian crusade, as Perry Miller observed in his study of second- and third-generation Puritans, that quest quickly devolved into a "fool's errand," a quixotic sally that would function not only to colonize the Americas but also to "Americanize" the colonists.[42]

Keeping the connection between the medieval Christian Crusades and New World colonization in mind, the third chapter turns to the crucial role that the Norman Conquest of Britain played in the British-American colonial cultural imaginary. The Magna Carta, as it was understood by British American colonists such as Thomas Jefferson, existed as a pre-Norman constitution that protected citizens from an oppressive regime and, in turn, was used by British American colonists as a model upon which to base the U.S. Constitution.[43] The notion of the U.S. citizenry as constituted of Anglo-Saxons, rather than Normans, allowed writers such as Thomas Jefferson to portray the United States as an oppressed people opposed to monarchy, even as this discourse buttressed both slavery and the genocide of Indigenous Americans. In this chapter, I explore the complex interplay between anti-monarchism and racism endemic to American Anglo-Saxonism by taking up James Fenimore Cooper's *Leatherstocking Tales* (1823–41), which features the hybrid figure of Natty Bumppo as an "errant Grail knight."[44] I contrast this American Anglo-Saxonism, meanwhile, with the medievalisms of Edgar Allan Poe, who, in short stories such as "The Gold-Bug" (1843) and "Fall of the House of Usher" (1839), associates the Middle Ages with texts that are reproduced within the contexts of his short stories and so utilizes a subversive medievalism, similar

---

[41] Cervantes, *The Indigenous Hidalgo Don Quixote*, 53.
[42] Perry Miller, *Errand into the Wilderness* (Cambridge, MA: Belknap Press, 1956), 11.
[43] Roger L. Kemp, ed., *Documents of American Democracy: A Collection of Essential Writings* (New York, NY: McFarland & Co., 2010), 12.
[44] Louis Owens, *Mixedblood Messages: Literature, Film, Family, Place* (Norman, OK: University of Oklahoma Press, 2001), 66. For Jefferson's American Anglo-Saxonism, see Thomas Jefferson, *A Summary View of the Rights of British Americans* (Brooklyn: Historical Printing Club, 1892), 27. On James Fenimore Cooper's medievalisms and Anglo-Saxonism, see George Dekker, *James Fenimore Cooper: The American Scott* (New York, NY: Barnes & Noble, 1967). On Natty Bumppo's hybrid nature, see Jason Richards, *Imitation Nation: Red, White, and Blackface in Early and Antebellum Literature* (Charlottesville, VA: University of Virginia Press, 2017), 89–107.

to Cervantes's, that embeds the Middle Ages within the modern contexts of his stories.[45] Poe's medievalisms blur the medieval/modern divide by treating the medieval as a textually constructed space-time, epitomized by the appearance, in his short story "Fall of the House of Usher", of an invented medievalized chivalric romance, *Mad Trist*, that the narrator reads aloud to Roderick Usher as the House of Usher collapses.[46] The medieval, for Poe, haunts modernity, and such an understanding portrays American Anglo-Saxonism in particular as a continuation of European colonialism's crusader ethos, yet another ideological justification for New World colonization.

Chapter 4 continues to explore the medievalisms latent within American Anglo-Saxonism by outlining the extent to which, as Owen Wister, the author of the first Western novel, proclaimed, "the knight and the cowboy are nothing but the same Saxon of different environments."[47] In this chapter, I interpret Frederick Jackson Turner's frontier thesis as an early enunciation of what Gloria Anzaldúa would theorize in the last decades of the twentieth century as a "borderlands" region, and I use Anzaldúa's theoretical concept of the borderlands to propose a comparative model that defies the historiographical tenets of European colonialism.[48] An understanding of western expansionism as both a temporal and spatial contestation recasts Turner's notion of the closing of the western frontier as the occlusion of the "spatio-temporal fix," which David Harvey has argued is central to market capitalism as a whole, for it involves the

---

[45] Edgar Allan Poe, *The Collected Tales and Poems* (New York, NY: Modern Library, 1992), 42–70, 231–45.

[46] Poe, *Collected Tales and Poems*, 182.

[47] W.M. Verhoevan, *James Fenimore Cooper: New Historical and Literary Contexts* (Amsterdam: Rodopi, 1993), 84; Owen Wister, "The Evolution of the Cow-Puncher," *Harper's* (September 1895): 606. Wister's contention that "the knight and the cowboy are nothing but the same Saxon" occludes the hybridity of not only Anglo-Saxon ancestry itself but also the figure of the cowboy as a transnational and transhistorical cultural production – not to mention the fact that medieval knight-errantry itself is by no means solely, or even primarily, a European practice, but derives from the "Davidic ethic," shared among Norman, Frankish, Moorish, Hebraic, and Spanish cultures, among others (John France, *Mercenaries and Paid Men: The Mercenary Identity in the Middle* Ages (Boston, MA: Brill, 2008), 24). Nevertheless, this ideological concatenation of the knight with the Anglo-Saxon frontiersman has had profound and lasting effects, casting the violent invasion and cooptation of Native American lands as not only necessary but chivalrous. For more on Cooper's "Anglo-American Novels," see D.H. Lawrence, *Studies in Classic American Literature*, Vol. 2, eds. Ezra Greenspan, Lindeth Vasey, and John Worthen (Cambridge: Cambridge University Press, 2003), 204–14.

[48] Gloria Anzaldúa, *Borderlands/La Frontera: The New Mestiza* (San Francisco, CA: Aunt Lute, 1987). Turner, "The Significance of the Frontier in American History," 199–227.

construction of both spatial markets, beyond the purview of central economies, and future markets, for which capital, in the form of profits, is saved or to which capital, in the form of debts, is pledged.[49] Exemplified by the *corrido* genre of the U.S.–Mexico borderlands and Western novels such as Wister's *The Virginian* (1902), frontier medievalisms serve to explore non-chronological temporalities and displaced spatialities; they conjure what happens to space and time when this spatio-temporal frontier is occluded, highlighting in particular how the closure of the U.S.'s western frontier is coeval with the closure of a colonialist historiography that rends the modern from the medieval.[50] The latter portion of this chapter, meanwhile, turns to the medievalisms of Mark Twain, with an eye to how Twain slyly mocks the U.S.'s fascination with medieval Europe, especially the chivalric romance tradition, all the while canonizing that displaced and anachronous space-time within the oeuvre of one of the most iconic of U.S. authors. Twain's medievalisms, present in nearly all of his novels and many of his short stories, become particularly apparent in the conclusions of his novels, and this association allows Twain to reckon both with what the quintessential U.S. citizen becomes when the nation no longer has a coherent western frontier and with the limits of Realism itself – the literary and aesthetic movement of the late nineteenth and early twentieth centuries that, in response to Romanticism, presented the world in detailed, unembellished, "realistic" fashion.[51] The turn to the medieval in the final chapters of his novels affords Twain the opportunity to simultaneously mock and reproduce the chivalric romance tradition within American contexts, and I link Twain's ambivalent conception of the Middle Ages with contemporary analyses of the medieval Christian apophatic tradition; like Twain's medievalisms, medieval apophatic theologians' definitions of the divine emphasize their own ignorance, and such a comparative reading speaks to the ways in which Twain's representations

---

[49] David Harvey, *The New Imperialism* (Oxford: Oxford University Press, 2005), 65. For more on the spatial fix, see Neil Smith, *Uneven Development: Nature, Capital, and the Production of Space* (Athens, GA: University of Georgia Press, 1984), 177–80.

[50] Owen Wister, *The Virginian* (New York, NY: Macmillan Co., 1902). On the *corrido* form, see Américo Paredes, *"With His Pistol in His Hand": A Border Ballad and its Hero* (Austin, TX: University of Texas Press, 2004).

[51] Luc Herman, *Concepts of Realism* (Columbia, SC: Camden House, 1996), 195–6. On Realism's relationship to Romanticism, see Erich Auerbach, *Mimesis: The Representation of Reality in Western Thought* (Princeton, NJ: Princeton University Press, 1953).

of the Middle Ages suggest the essential unknowability of not only that historical period but also U.S. national identity itself.[52]

In the fifth chapter, I turn to the medievalisms present in works of U.S. literary Modernism, the movement of the late nineteenth and early twentieth centuries that looked to enact "a major revolt [...] against the prevalent literary and aesthetic traditions of the Western world."[53] Modernist medievalisms, such as those present in T.S. Eliot's *The Waste Land* (1922) and Ezra Pound's *The Cantos* (1925), portray the Middle Ages as a linchpin for a cohesive conception of history and, therefore, continue to deploy the medieval/modern divide by portraying the medieval as the site of an esoteric knowledge without which true understanding of modernity is impossible. I contrast these pedagogical medievalisms with the medievalisms present in the novels of William Faulkner.[54] As opposed to the Modernist medievalisms of Pound and Eliot, Faulkner does not refer to the Middle Ages as a totalizing lens with which he can make sense of modernity but integrates a romanticized image of the medieval into the very psyches of his characters and so explores the effect that the "myth of southern masculinity," undergirded by a "medieval chivalric ideal," has had in buttressing racism, sexism, and anti-Semitism throughout the Americas, and especially in the United States.[55]

In the sixth chapter, I discuss contemporary U.S. medievalisms with respect to their role as spectacles in a capitalist market economy.[56] Late twentieth- and early twenty-first-century medievalisms have been leveraged in support of remarkably profitable brands and franchises, and I take up HBO's *Game of Thrones* (2011–19), a rendering of George R.R. Martin's *A Song of Ice and Fire* (1996–), as a prototypical example of these spectacular medievalisms, which serve to codify class distinctions within a purportedly egalitarian society such as the United States.[57] The medievalisms of Ursula K. Le Guin's Hainish novels, meanwhile, interrogate this spectacular medievalism and intersect well with Jane Chance's analysis of

---

[52] See Andrew Louth, "Apophatic and Cataphatic Theology," in *The Cambridge Companion to Christian Mysticism*, eds. Amy Hollywood and Patricia Z. Beckman (Cambridge: Cambridge University Press, 2012), 140.

[53] Astradur Eysteinsson, *The Concept of Modernism* (Ithaca, NY: Cornell University Press, 1990), 2.

[54] T.S. Eliot, *The Waste Land: A Facsimile and Transcript of the Original Drafts, Including the Annotations of Ezra Pound* (New York, NY: Harvest Book, 1971); Ezra Pound, *The Cantos* (New York, NY: New Directions, 1996), 3.

[55] Pugh, *Queer Chivalry*, 102.

[56] Guy Debord, *Society of the Spectacle*, trans. Ken Knabb (London: Rebel Press, 2002).

[57] *Game of Thrones*, television series, created by David Benioff and D.B. Weiss (2011–19; Los Angeles, CA: HBO). George R.R. Martin's *A Song of Ice and Fire* includes *A Game of Thrones* (New York, NY: Bantam Spectra, 1996), *A Clash of*

medieval women writers such as Catherine of Siena, Hildegard of Bingen, and Marie de France.[58] For Chance, the "subversive" European literary tradition is present in works such as Christine de Pizan's *The Book of the City of Ladies* (1405) and Julian of Norwich's *Revelations of Divine Love* (c. 1390), and I use her reading of *The Book of the City of Ladies*, which emphasizes de Pizan's foregrounding of the materiality of the text, as a means of making sense of Le Guin's own foregrounding of the materiality of texts in her Hainish novels.[59] In turn, this chapter theorizes that the connections developed between literary texts and the Middle Ages – such as Don Quixote's obsession with medieval chivalric romances and Miss Sophonsiba's tacit obsession, in Faulkner's *Absalom! Absalom!* (1936), with the romances of Sir Walter Scott – speak to how literary texts function as tools for suturing the medieval/modern divide.[60]

In the Conclusion, meanwhile, I critique the use of the Enlightenment/Romanticism historiographical divide (outlined in the opening paragraphs of this Introduction) to understand New World medievalisms, emphasizing how this framework utilizes a dialectical methodology with roots in medieval Christian scholasticism – with all of its Islamophobic, anti-Semitic, and patriarchal ideologies.[61] Instead, I turn to Walter Benjamin's historiography, especially his focus on "involuntary memory," as a means of understanding the crucial difference between ethnonationalist medievalisms and subversive medievalisms.[62] While U.S. ethnonationalist medievalisms strive for historical continuity with an imagined medieval past, U.S. subversive medievalisms revel in anachronism and displacement, foregrounding the arbitrary and often comical American preoccupation with medieval Europe. Similarly, in an effort to move beyond

---

Kings (New York, NY: Bantam Spectra, 1998), *A Storm of Swords* (New York, NY: Bantam Spectra, 2000), *A Feast of Crows* (New York, NY: Bantam Spectra, 2005), and *A Dance with Dragons* (New York, NY: Bantam Spectra, 2011)

[58] Jane Chance, *The Literary Subversions of Medieval Women*, 15. Ursula K. Le Guin, *The Left Hand of Darkness* (New York, NY: Penguin Books, 1969/2016); Ursula K. Le Guin, *The Dispossessed* (New York, NY: Harper & Row, 1974).

[59] Chance, *The Literature Subversions of Medieval Women*, 10.

[60] On Don Quixote's obsession with medieval chivalric romances, see Cervantes, *The Indigenous Hidalgo Don Quixote*, 52–8. On Miss Sophonsiba's obsession with Sir Walter Scott, see William Faulkner, *Faulkner in the University* (Charlottesville, VA: University of Virginia Press, 1959/1995), 135.

[61] Here, I rely especially on contemporary research on Thomas Aquinas: John Y.B. Hood, *Aquinas and the Jews* (Philadelphia, PA: University of Pennsylvania Press, 1995); Zulfiqar Ali Shah, *St. Thomas Aquinas and Muslim Thought* (Milpitas, CA: Claritas Books, 2022); and Susanne M. Decrane, *Aquinas, Feminism and the Common Good* (Washington D.C.: Georgetown University Press, 2004).

[62] Walter Benjamin, *Illuminations*, trans. Harry Zohn (New York, NY: Schocken Books, 2007), 211.

the use of European historiographical concepts to understand American cultural productions, I turn to Leslie Fiedler's fourfold geographic system for interpreting U.S. literature as a means of analyzing American medievalisms.[63] In particular, I briefly examine the medievalisms of twentieth-century novelists Theodore Dreiser, Erskine Caldwell, Jack Kerouac, and Henry James – each connected, respectively, with the American North, South, West, and East[64] – and so demonstrate how the medievalisms of the American South and North, in particular, engage deeply with questions of social stratification, especially the difference between feudalism and capitalism, while the medievalisms of the American East and West grapple with the nature of transnational cultural exchange. American medievalisms, I conclude, afford a set of allusions and references that allow these authors to consider how a purportedly egalitarian nation-state stratifies its citizenry and how U.S. national identity in particular is often constructed, counterintuitively, in transnational terms. For all four regions, moreover, the medieval exists as a "sedentary space," juxtaposed with the "nomad space" of modernity, and I contend that it is the disruption of such a correspondence between the medieval and the sedentary that more fundamentally distinguishes subversive medievalisms from ethnonationalist medievalisms.[65]

---

[63] Leslie Fiedler, *The Return of the Vanishing American* (New York, NY: Stein and Day, 1976), 16.

[64] Gilles Deleuze and Félix Guattari, *A Thousand Plateaus: Capitalism and Schizophrenia*, trans. Brian Massumi (New York, NY: Continuum, 1987), 571n18.

[65] Deleuze and Guattari, *A Thousand Plateaus*, 458.

1

The New World Crusades: British Colonial Charters, Pilgrim-Crusaders, and the Transatlantic Captivity Narrative

That Christopher Columbus's arrival in the New World occurred the same year (1492) as both Muhammed XII's surrender of Granada to the Catholic Monarchs Queen Isabella I and King Ferdinand II, which concluded Nasrid rule of the Iberian peninsula, and the "Alhambra Decree," which ordered the expulsion of non-Christians from Spain, has long been recognized in postcolonial theory as a salient synchronism for demonstrating the Janus-faced nature of European colonialism.[1] The retreat of the Moors from Western Europe precipitated a two-pronged Christian mission to "purify" Western Europe of non-Christians (Jews, Muslims, and Romanies alike) and to conquer non-Christian lands – internal and external colonialism, respectively – and the discovery of the New World afforded a particularly alluring territory in which to deploy the latter. In U.S. historiography, however, this linkage between New World colonization and the medieval Christian Crusades has largely been overlooked in favor of U.S.-focused contexts that too often treat the United States as a special case – exceptional, if you will – that, in 1776, was irreconcilably rent from medieval Europe.[2] According to a broader, transhistorical and transnational historiography, however, the American

---

[1] For more on 1492 and the birth of the modern world-system, see Felipe Fernandez-Armesto, *1492: The Year the World Began* (New York, NY: Bloomsbury Publishing, 2011). The Spanish *Reconquista* refers to the Christian "Reconquest" of the Iberian Peninsula from the Muslim Moors – a war that lasted from the eighth century to 1492. The "Alhambra Decree" was a marked intensification of the Spanish Inquisition – the persecution of non-Christians, especially Jews and Muslims, throughout Spain – that began in 1478 with the establishment of the Tribunal of the Holy Office of the Inquisition and lasted well into the nineteenth century.

[2] For more on U.S. exceptionalism in American Studies, see Kaplan and Pease, eds., *Cultures of United States Imperialism*, 11–13.

Revolution, U.S. western expansionism and contemporary U.S. ethnonationalism can be seen as direct descendants of European external colonialism, while ethnonationalist programs, especially African American slavery and the genocide of Native Americans, closely resemble European internal colonializing projects.[3] Such a conception of British colonial and U.S. history draws a through-line from the medieval Christian Crusades, including the Spanish *Reconquista*, to the conquest and colonization of the New World, understood broadly as encompassing not only the Age of Exploration and early colonial history but also nineteenth-century U.S. western expansionism and twentieth-century U.S. imperialism.

The medieval Christian crusades, after all, were a loosely linked series of religious wars initiated and supported by the Latin Christian Church, aimed at reclaiming holy lands and defending Christendom from perceived external threats.[4] These campaigns spanned several centuries and were characterized by a complex interplay of religious fervor, political ambition, economic interests, and social dynamics – a description that might also be applied to the colonization of the New World. Indeed, in tracing the correlation between the Crusades and British-American colonization, one need look no further than the opening paragraphs of the "First Charter of Virginia," signed by King James I of England in 1606:

> JAMES, by the Grace of God, King of England, Scotland, France and Ireland, Defender of the Faith, &c. WHEREAS our loving and well-disposed Subjects, Sir Thorn as Gales, and Sir George Somers, Knights, Richard Hackluit, Clerk, Prebendary of Westminster, and Edward-Maria Wingfield, Thomas Hanharm and Ralegh Gilbert, Esqrs. William Parker, and George Popham, Gentlemen, and divers [sic] others of our loving Subjects, have been humble Suitors unto us, that We would vouchsafe unto them our License, to make Habitation, Plantation, and to deduce a colony of sundry of our People into that part of America commonly called VIRGINIA, and other parts and Territories in America, either appertaining unto us, or which are not actually possessed by any Christian Prince or People.[5]

---

[3] On the connections between African American slavery and the genocide of Native Americans, see Kyle T. Mays, *An Afro-Indigenous History of the United States* (Boston, MA: Beacon Press, 2021).

[4] For more on the Crusades, including the complexities and varying definitions, see Jonathan Riley-Smith, *The Crusades: A History* (New Haven, CT: Yale University Press, 2005); Christopher Tyerman, *God's War: A New History of the Crusades* (Cambridge, MA: Belknap Press, 2006); Thomas Asbridge, *The Crusades: The Authoritative History of the War for the Holy* Land (New York, NY: Ecco, 2010).

[5] Virginia House of Burgesses, *Charters of the Colony of Virginia* (Philadelphia, PA: Dalcassian Publishing, 2018), 5.

James begins his charter, echoing Pope Urban II's "Letter of Instruction to the Crusades" (1095), with a reference to his divine right and overtly portrays the Virginia Colony as "the providence of Almightie God."[6] The colonists are given permission to colonize any territories "not actually possessed by any Christian Prince or People," and James refers to several of the colonists explicitly as "Knights" and "Esqurs." (i.e., Esquires) whose work is the "propagating of Christian religion."[7] The "Charter of Virginia" is, moreover, no outlier. The opening lines of the "Charter of the Massachusetts Bay Company" (1691) read:

> WILLIAM & MARY by the grace of God King and Queene of England Scotland France and Ireland Defenders of the Faith &c. To all to whome these presents shall come Greeting. Whereas his late Majesty King James the First Our Royall Predecessor by his Letters Patents under the Greate Seale of England bearing date at Westminster the Third Day of November in the Eighteenth yeare of his Reigne did Give and Grant unto the Countill established at Plymouth in the County of Decon for the Planting Ruleing Ordering and Governing of New England in America to the Successors and Assignes all that part of America lying and being in Breadth from Forty Degrees of Northerly Latitude from the Equinoctiall Line to the Forty Eighth Degree aforesaid throughout all the Main Lands from Sea to Sea together alsoe with all the firme Lands Soiles Grounds Havens Ports Rivers Waters Fishings Mines and Mineralls as well Royall Mines of Gold and Silver as other Mines and Mineralls Pretious Stones Quarries and all and singular other Comodities Jurisdiccons Royalties Priveleges Franchises and Preheminences both within the said Tract of Land upon the Main and the said Lands Islands and Seas adjoyning *Provided* always that the said Lands Islands or any the premises by the said Letters Patents intended or meant to be Granted were not then actually possessed or Inhabited by any other Christian Prince or State.[8]

While the "Charter of Carolina" (1663) begins:

> CHARLES the Second, by the grace of God, king of England, Scotland, France, and Ireland, Defender of the Faith, &c., To all to whom these present shall come: Greeting:

---

[6] For an English translation of Urban II's "Letter of Instruction to the Crusaders," see August C. Krey, *The First Crusade: The Accounts of Eyewitnesses and Participants* (Princeton, NJ: Princeton University Press, 1921), 42–3.
[7] Virginia House of Burgesses, *Charters of the Colony of Virginia*, 5.
[8] Francis Newton Thorpe, ed., *The Federal and State Constitutions, Colonial Charters, and other Organic Laws of the States, Territories and Colonies Now Heretofore Forming the United States of America*, Vol. III (Washington D.C.: Government Printing Office, 1909), 1870.

1st. Whereas our right trusty, and right well beloved cousins and counsellors, Edward Earl of Clarendon, our high chancellor of England, and George Duke of Albemarle, master of our horse and captain general of all our forces, our right trusty and well beloved William Lord Craven, John Lord Berkley, our right trusty and well beloved counsellor, Anthony Lord Ashley, chancellor of our exchequer, Sir George Carteret, knight and baronet, vice chamberlain of our household, and our trusty and well beloved Sir William Berkley, knight, and Sir John Colleton, knight and baronet, being excited with a laudable and pious zeal for the propagation of the Christian faith, and the enlargement of our empire and dominions, have humbly besought leave of us, by their industry and charge, to transport and make an ample colony of our subjects, natives of our kingdom of England, and elsewhere within our dominions, unto a certain country hereafter described, in the parts of America not yet cultivated or planted, and only inhabited by some barbarous people, who have no knowledge of Almighty God.[9]

These charters portray British colonization of the New World as a decidedly Christian undertaking – a connection that will be of no surprise to scholars of either Latin American Studies or Muslim American Studies, who have long pointed out how a Christian crusader ideology has been regularly applied to New World colonization.[10] As philosopher and cultural theorist Eduardo Subirats summarizes, "[H]istorically, the conquest of America signifies the culmination of the *Reconquista* and employs its same ethico-military ideals, its same ideology of repressive universalism, and its same rationality," while literary scholar and cultural theorist Anouar Majid has pointed out the extent to which the image of the Moor was transposed directly onto any number of non-European peoples, including Africans and Native Americans, to justify European colonialism: "[t]he conquest of the Indians," Majid concludes, "was simply an extension of

---

[9] Francis Newton Thorpe, ed., *The Federal and State Constitutions, Colonial Charters, and other Organic Laws of the States, Territories and Colonies Now Heretofore Forming the United States of America*, Vol. V (Washington D.C.: Government Printing Office, 1909), 2590.

[10] See Ella Shohat, "The Sephardi-Moorish Atlantic," in *Sajjilu Arab American: A reader in SWANA Studies*, eds. Louise Cainkar, Pauline Homsi Vinson, and Amira Jarmakani (Syracuse, NY: Syracuse University Press, 2022), 86–92; Edwin Williamson, *The Penguin History of Latin America, Revised Edition* (New York, NY: Penguin, 2009), 3–76; Christina Civantos, *The Afterlife of Al-Andalus: Muslim Iberia in Contemporary Arab and Hispanic Narratives* (Albany: SUNY Press, 2017), 165–220. The connections between the surrender of Granada and Columbus's "discovery" of the New World are also an important historical allusion to Salman Rushdie's *The Moor's Last Sigh* (New York, NY: Random House, 1995).

the Crusades launched against Muslims in earlier centuries, culminating in the surrender of Granada in 1492."[11]

While American Studies scholarship has overlooked these connections, the persistent presence of allusions and references to, as well as studies of, the Middle Ages throughout colonial British and U.S. cultural history reveals that these linkages between New World colonization and the medieval Christian Crusades are often hiding in plain sight. These New World medievalisms demonstrate not only the clear corollaries between New World conquest and the Crusades but also the extent to which New World cultural productions grapple continuously with the medieval/modern divide, understood as the "universal traumatic change" that dislocates modernity from the "un-Modern."[12] This divide functions as "a regulating principle" for modern historiography, a means of "postulat[ing] historical breaks as fully 'achieved' and outside politics," a rupturing of history into discrete periods that creates the abiding trauma that medievalism studies diagnoses.[13] Attentive analysis of medievalisms, in turn, "becomes the method for countering a colonial politics of knowledge precisely because this politics instantiates the medieval/modern divide as a form of territorialization."[14] Medievalisms, in short, disrupt the medieval/modern divide and draw our attention to the repressed trauma enacted by a colonialist historiography that rends history into discrete, homogeneous periods and modernity, specifically, from its deep past.

The relationship between nationalism and modern representations of the medieval serves as a salient wellspring for medievalism studies, for modern nation-states and territories have often constructed their identities in terms of an imagined medieval past.[15] Nationalist discourses that present Anglo-Saxons or Carolingian Franks as central to a given nation-state's identity avoid recognizing that such communities were cobbled together of indigenous populations that, over time, came to consider themselves descended from a single, often mythological or mythologized figure.[16] In turn, these nationalist discourses frame their imagined national ethnicities as incommensurate gestalts, often leveraging those representations in support

---

[11] Subirats, *El continente vacío*, 81. Translation my own. Anouar Majid, *We Are All Moors: Ending Centuries of Crusades against Muslims and Other Minorities* (Minneapolis, MN: University of Minnesota Press, 2009), 65.

[12] James Muldoon, "Introduction," in *Bridging the Medieval–Modern Divide: Medieval Themes in the World of the Reformation*, ed. James Muldoon (New York, NY: Routledge, 2016), 7. Symes, "When We Talk about Modernity," 715.

[13] Muldoon, *Bridging the Medieval–Modern Divide*, 7.

[14] Davis, *Periodization and Sovereignty*, 117.

[15] See Patrick Geary, *The Myth of Nations: The Medieval Origins of Europe* (Princeton, NJ: Princeton University Press, 2003), 37.

[16] Geary, *The Myth of Nations*, 37.

of regressive, ethnonationalist projects. While the preponderance of this research on nationalism and medievalism focuses, predictably, on European nation-states, a similar methodology of national identity construction has been observed in non-European territories.[17] Historian Michelle R. Warren, for instance, has discussed how Joseph Bédier (1864–1938), a scholar of medieval French who grew up in Reúnion, developed a "creole medievalism" that "challenges the traditional binarisms of imperial discourse [...] join[ing] a myriad of [...] strategies for representing postcolonial society."[18] As figurations and narratives that inscribe European history and cultures onto colonial territories, these creole medievalisms "can never veer too far from the[ir] imperial conditions," but, at the same time, these "creative claims on the Middle Ages hold out the possibility of moving beyond colonial dualities (civilization/savagery, inclusion/exclusion, etc.)."[19] In a study of Chilean-Venezuelan grammarian and scholar Andrés Bello (1787–1865), meanwhile, Nadia Altschul "argue[s] for the simultaneous presence of both creole Occidentalism and creole resistance in Bello's work."[20] Borrowing Warren's term, Altschul sees Bello's creole medievalism – especially his interpretation of the medieval poem that would become, during the long nineteenth century, Spain's national epic, *Song of El Cid* – as framing Hispanic America simultaneously as an extension of Europe and as a territory in its own right, free to pursue its own interests.[21]

With respect to the British-American colonies, we can enact a subversive rereading of this reception history by remembering that the Christian Crusades were intimately entwined, within the medieval European cultural imaginary, with the concept of pilgrimage. As Giles Constable has written, "In addition to being sanctified soldiers and, in a sense, secular monks, crusaders were pilgrims, who were both called *peregrini* ['pilgrims'] and regarded themselves as pilgrims and their expeditions as pilgrimages."[22] Indeed, the precise distinction between a crusade and a

[17] On medievalism and European nationalism, see Geary, *The Myth of Nations*; Michael S. Richardson, *Medievalism and Nationalism in German Opera* (New York, NY: Routledge, 2021); Richard Utz, "Academic medievalism and nationalism," in *The Cambridge Companion to Medievalism*, ed. Louise d'Arcens (Cambridge: Cambridge University Press, 2016), 119–34; Kathy Lavezzo, ed., *Imagining a Medieval English Nation* (Minneapolis, MN: University of Minnesota, 2004).
[18] Warren, *Creole Medievalism*, xii.
[19] Warren, *Creole Medievalism*, xii.
[20] Altschul, *Geographies of Philological Knowledge*, 136.
[21] On the definition of the "long nineteenth century," see Trevor R. Getz, *The Long Nineteenth Century, 1750–1914: Crucible of Modernity* (New York, NY: Bloomsbury Publishing, 2018).
[22] Giles Constable, *Crusaders and Crusading in the Twelfth Century* (New York, NY: Routledge, 2016), 155.

pilgrimage in the medieval European imaginary remains a point of contention among medievalists:

> Despite a considerable historiography on the crusades, there are still flickers of division among historians as to the definition of a crusade, or rather, divisions as to when all the features of a crusade become established. The First Crusade suffers the most from this tendency. [...] Some of this tension arises because modern terms to define a crusade come with accumulated inferences and meanings which are anachronistic when applied retrospectively. The term 'pilgrimage' is such a contentious term, given its implications of an unarmed endeavour, and it is often qualified. The crusade was, therefore, an 'armed pilgrimage' or a 'crusade-pilgrimage'; the crusaders were 'warrior pilgrims.' Although a seemingly contradictory impulse, the term 'pilgrimage' became associated with the crusade because the Latin *peregrinatio* was frequently used by contemporaries for these expeditions. The crusades also shared a number of features with pilgrimages; participants often took a vow before setting off; each was considered an act of penance which would count against the individual's sins in the soul's reckoning after death; canon law protected the property and position of both crusaders and pilgrims during their absence from home.[23]

If we, with U.S. historiography in mind, recall the extent to which a crusade and a pilgrimage are bound together in the medieval European imaginary, we can also recognize that the portrayal of the Plymouth colonists as "pilgrims" subtly links New World conquest with the medieval Christian Crusades.[24] The nineteenth-century U.S. historian Alexander Young, reading William Bradford's "Of Plymouth Plantation," noted Bradford's reference to Hebrews 11 – "they were strangers and pilgrims on the earth" – and, in turn, titled his republication of "Of Plymouth Plantation" and other primary documents of early British colonists *Chronicles of the Pilgrim Fathers of the Colony of Plymouth from 1602 to 1625* (1844).[25] This appellation, over the ensuing decade, became remarkably popular, with publications such as Joseph Barnyard's *Plymouth and the Pilgrims* (1851), George Barrell Cheever's *The Pilgrim Fathers* (1849), and William Hendry Stowell's *A*

---

[23] Léan Ní Chléirigh, "Nova Peregrinatio: The First Crusade as a Pilgrimage in Contemporary Latin Narratives," in *Writing the Early Crusades*, eds. Marcus Bull and Damien Kempf (Woodbridge: Boydell Press, 2014), 63–4.

[24] For more on the representation of the Plymouth colonists as pilgrims, see John G. Turner, *They Knew They Were Pilgrims: Plymouth Colony and the Contest for American Liberty* (New Haven, CT: Yale University Press, 2020), 1–6.

[25] Alexander Young, *Chronicles of the Pilgrim Fathers of the Colony of Plymouth from 1602 to 1625* (Boston, MA: Charles C. Little, 1844).

History of the Puritans and the Pilgrim Fathers (1849).[26] Such a portrayal of the Plymouth colonists as "pilgrims" was, after all, useful to a nation in the midst of rampant western expansionism, for it framed that nation as a persecuted people seeking land upon which to peacefully subsist – rather than as invaders violently conquering that land. If we recall, however, the linkage between pilgrimage and crusade, that nineteenth-century portrayal becomes more complex. No longer are the "pilgrim fathers" pitiable figures in search of peace from oppression, but they are themselves crusaders murderously attacking those whom they deem heretic, savage, or infidel.

This is not to say that British colonial charters were solely religious documents, but neither were crusader charters. The Charter of the Massachusetts Bay Company, after all, declares possession of "all the Main Lands from Sea to Sea together alsoe with all the firme Lands Soiles Grounds Havens Ports Rivers Waters Fishings Mines and Mineralls as well Royall Mines of Gold and Silver as other Mines and Mineralls Pretious Stones Quarries and all and singular other Comodities Jurisdiccons Royalties Privileges Franchises and Preheminences," while the First Virginia Charter claims possession of "all the Lands, Woods, Soil, Grounds, Havens, Ports, Rivers, Mines, Minerals, Marshes, Waters, Fishings, Commodities, and Hereditaments, whatsoever."[27] Modern distinctions between economics and religion are simply inadequate for the consideration of possible motivations of these British colonial charters, and something quite similar has been said about medieval crusader charters. The charter of Enguerran II de Coucy (d. 1147), for instance, written by the abbot of Prémontré, is focused primarily on offering tax exemptions to the abbey of Prémontré:

> In the name of the holy and undivided Trinity. I, Barthélemy, by God's grace bishop of Laon, wish it to be known to those to come and to those present that Enguerran, son of Thomas de Coucy, for the salvation of his soul and for those of his father, his mother, and of their ancestors, gives perpetually to the church of Prémontré exemption from the taxes (*wionage* and *naule*) levied on the transport of wine by road and water in all of his land where they are collected from non-residents, except on that which is bought so that it may again be transported and sold. This concession was made in the year of the Incarnate Word 1138, epact 7,

---

[26] Joseph Barnyard, *Plymouth and the Pilgrims* (Boston, MA: Gould and Lincoln, 1851); George Barrell Cheever, *The Pilgrim Fathers* (London: T.W. Collins, 1849); William Hendry Stowell, *A History of the Puritans and the Pilgrim Fathers* (New York, NY: R. Carter and Bros., 1849).

[27] Thorpe, ed., *The Federal and State Constitutions*, Vol. III, 1870. Virginia House of Burgesses, *Charters of the Colony of Virginia*, 5.

indication 1, concurrent 5, in the choir of that same church of Prémontré on the day on which Enguerran left on pilgrimage for Jerusalem.[28]

Similarly, in a charter issued by Bishop Barthélemy of Laon, the primary objective of the charter is to settle "a long-standing quarrel between Radulph Canis and the canons of Prémontré over part of the tithe of the parish of Brancourt":

> In the name of the holy and undivided Trinity. I, Barthélemy, by God's grace Bishop of Laon, wish it to be known to those to come and to those present that for the Lord Norbert – a man of outstanding religious life who was the first to go to Prémontré to settle there – and for his brethren, I by my episcopal authority freed the nearby valleys surrounding that place both from tithes and from other customary duties from all who seemed to possess such rights there by hereditary right, just as it was ratified by me in their privileges [...] He was about to set out for Jerusalem, so he sought and received pardon; and what he had forfeited from there to the abbot and church, he granted that the aforesaid church could freely possess in perpetuity for the remedy of his soul and the souls of those attending him there.[29]

Financial arrangements, in other words, were "a key [...] motivation" for Christian crusaders, for "[i]t will be remembered that there were two ways [crusader] charters could be used to comment on crusade motivation: through the choice of religious house and through the financial arrangements made to pay for the crusade."[30] Like New World colonial charters, crusader charters do not clearly distinguish between economics and religion, and "a reading of the charters leaves a fairly clear picture of financial and political advantage from participation in the crusades."[31]

With these linkages between New World conquest and the medieval Christian Crusades in mind, the fact that a canonical genre of British-American colonial literature – the captivity narrative – is also a canonical genre of medieval Christian crusader literature makes sense. Captivity narratives such as Jonathon Dickinson's *God's Protecting Providence* (1699) and Cotton Mather's account of the captivity of Hannah Dustin (1702), both of which tell of British colonists who were taken captive by Native Americans, were reimagining the Barbary captivity narratives of the fifteenth and sixteenth centuries within their own

---

[28] Slack, *Crusader Charters*, 1.
[29] Slack, *Crusader Charters*, 13–14.
[30] Slack, *Crusader Charters*, xxix.
[31] Slack, *Crusader Charters*, xxix.

non-Mediterranean contexts.[32] Often deemed the first captivity narrative, Johann Schiltberger's *Reisebuch* (c. 1460), for instance, tells of Schiltberger's adventures throughout the Eastern Mediterranean and the Near East in the mid-fifteenth century and includes a description of his captivity at the hands of the Ottoman Empire.[33] Indeed, "[a]mong the earliest Western representations of the Muslim world," Charles Sabatos argues, "were those written by Central European authors [such as Schiltberger] who had survived captivity in the Ottoman Empire," and Sabatos argues that these captivity narratives should be thought of as "a largely unexplored genre" – namely, "Ottoman captivity narratives."[34] In making this claim, Sabatos is rethinking how the more oft-studied genre of Barbary captivity narratives is entrenched within a broader, more general social project – namely, the medieval Christian crusades.[35] These texts, which utilize overtly anti-Islamic rhetoric and Christian theological notions of salvation, clearly play upon a Christian crusader ideology that simultaneously demonizes Muslims and presents Christians as a sinless, persecuted people in need of redemption. In *Reisebuch*, for instance, Schiltberger's account begins by stating that he began his voyage "at the time that King Sigismund of Hungary left for the land of the Infidels," clearly situating himself as both a pilgrim and crusader:

> I, JOHANNS SCHILTBERGER, left my home near the city of Munich, situated in Payren, at the time that King Sigismund of Hungary left for the land of the Infidels. This was, counting from Christ's birth, in the thirteen hundred and ninety-fourth year, with a lord named Leinhart Richartingen. And I came back again from the land of the Infidels, counting from Christ's birth, fourteen hundred and twenty seven. All that I saw in the land of the Infidels, of wars, and that [which] was wonderful, also what chief towns and seas I have seen and visited, you will

[32] Jonathon Dickinson, *Jonathan Dickinson's Journal, or God's Protecting Providence. Being the Narrative of a Journey from Port Royal in Jamaica to Philadelphia between August 23, 1696 and April 1, 1697* (Philadelphia, PA: 1699); Cotton Mather, *Magnalia Christi Americana* (London: Thomas Parkhurst, 1702), 550–2.
[33] Johann Schiltberger, *The Bondage and Travels of Johann Schiltberger, a Native of Bavaria, in Europe, Asia, and Africa, 1396–1427*, trans. Karl Friedrich Neumann (London: Hakluyt Society, 1879).
[34] Charles Sabatos, "The Ottoman Captivity Narrative as Transnational Genre in Central European Literature," *Archiv Orientální* 83:2 (2015), 233.
[35] The Barbary captivity narrative, canonized by Miguel de Cervantes himself in his captive's tale featured at the close of Part I of *Don Quixote* – based, like many narratives in the genre, upon his own experience – focuses on the capture of Christians by Barbary pirates, who then sell the captives either for ransom or as slaves into the Ottoman slave markets (see Cervantes, *The Indigenous Hidalgo Don Quixote*, 360–95).

find described hereafter, perhaps not quite completely, but I was a prisoner and not independent.[36]

Compare this opening with the lengthy title that British colonial author Mary Rowlandson gives to her wildly popular – and now canonical – British colonial captivity narrative that dramatizes her capture by Native Americans during King Philip's War (1675–78):

> The sovereignty and goodness of GOD, together with the faithfulness of his promises displayed, being a narrative of the captivity and restoration of Mrs. Mary Rowlandson, commended by her, to all that desires to know the Lord's doings to, and dealings with her. Especially to her dear children and relations. The second Addition Corrected [sic] and amended. Written by her own hand for her private use, and now made public at the earnest desire of some friends, and for the benefit of the afflicted. Deut. 32.39. See now that I, even I am he, and there is no god with me, I kill and I make alive, I wound and I heal, neither is there any can deliver out of my hand.[37]

If either of these is the more religious, it is not the narrative set during the medieval Christian Crusades, yet both frame their first-person narrators as allied with Christianity, itself presented as a persecuted religion, and this sense of persecution continues to be asserted in the ensuing paragraphs. Immediately after these opening remarks, both Rowlandson and Schiltberger turn to their abduction narratives. Rowlandson writes, in her characteristically plain-spoken style:

> On the tenth of February 1675, came the Indians with great numbers upon Lancaster: their first coming was about sunrising; hearing the noise of some guns, we looked out; several houses were burning, and the smoke ascending to heaven. There were five persons taken in one house; the father, and the mother and a sucking child, they knocked on the head; the other two they took and carried away alive. There were two others, who being out of their garrison upon some occasion were set upon; one was knocked on the head, the other escaped; another there was who running along was shot and wounded, and fell down; he begged of them his life, promising them money (as they told me) but they would not hearken to him but knocked him in head, and stripped him naked, and split open his bowels. Another, seeing many of the Indians about his barn, ventured and went out, but was quickly shot down.[38]

[36] Schiltberger, *The Bondage and Travels of Johann Schiltberger*, 1.
[37] Rowlandson, "Narrative of the Captivity and Restoration," 94.
[38] Rowlandson, "Narrative of the Captivity and Restoration," 94–5.

Rowlandson wastes no time in portraying the "Indians," as she deems the Narragansett, Wampanoag and Nipmuc tribes who had allied themselves against the British in King Philip's War, as merciless and violent; no mention here is made about how this attack was part of a larger war, for such a portrayal would necessarily require that Rowlandson grapple with how the Massachusetts colonists had, over the last century, brutally invaded and colonized the region. Indeed, Rowlandson's description of the diverse group of Native Americans is decidedly more disparaging than Schiltberger's description of the Ottoman "Infidels." After Schiltberger's "Message to the Reader," he begins with a description of "the first combat between King Sigismund and the Turks":

> From the first, King Sigismund appealed in the above-named year, thirteen hundred and ninety-four, to Christendom for assistance, at the time that the Infidels were doing great injury to Hungern. There came many people from all countries to help him; then he took the people and led them to the Iron Gate, which separates Ungern from Pulgery and Walachy, and he crossed the Tunow into Pulgary, and made for a city called Pudem. It is the capital of Pulgery. Then came the ruler of the country and of the city, and gave himself up to the king; then the king took possession of the city with three hundred men, good horse and foot soldiers, and then went to another city where were many Turks. There he remained five days, but the Turks would not give up the city; but the fighting men expelled them by force, and delivered the city to the king. Many Turks were killed and others made prisoners. The king took possession of this city also, with two hundred men, and continued his march towards another city called Schiltaw, but called in the Infidel tongue, Nicopoly. He besieged it by water and by land for XVI days, then came the Turkish king, called Wyasit, with two hundred thousand men, to the relief of the city. When the king, Sigismund, heard this, he went one mile to meet him with his people, the number of whom were reckoned at sixteen thousand men. Then came the Duke of Walachy, called Werterwaywod, who asked the king to allow him to look at the winds. This the king allowed, and he took with him one thousand men for the purpose of looking at the winds, and returned to the king and told him that he had looked at the winds, and had seen twenty banners, and that there were ten thousand men under each banner, and each banner was separate from the other.[39]

---

[39] Schiltberger, *The Bondage and Travels of Johann Schiltberger*, 2.

While the place-names Schiltberger uses are certainly instances of Orientalism, his description of the "Infidels" is relatively benign.[40] He presents them as an enemy army that drastically outnumbers his own, and the defeat of the Christian forces is presented as a valiant but ultimately ill-fated venture. Indeed, if there is a primary villain in this opening chapter it is not the Turks but the Duke of Burgundy, who disobeys King Sigismund's orders and rashly leads his men against the Ottoman forces, only to quickly surrender. As the Christian forces are overwhelmed, Schiltberger does not, as Rowlandson does, describe the atrocities of the rout but actually focuses on the cruelty of the Christian forces as they push each other overboard in an effort to flee.

In any case, both captivity narratives turn, after these descriptions of military defeat, to the author's own capture. Rowlandson writes:

> At length they came and beset our own house, and quickly it was the dolefulest day that ever mine eyes saw. The house stood upon the edge of a hill; some of the Indians got behind the hill, others into the barn, and others behind anything that could shelter them; from all which places they shot against the house, so that the bullets seemed to fly like hail; and quickly they wounded one man among us, then another, and then a third. About two hours (according to my observation, in that amazing time) they had been about the house before they prevailed to fire it (which they did with flax and hemp, which they brought out of the barn, and there being no defense about the house, only two flankers at two opposite corners and one of them not finished); they fired it once and one ventured out and quenched it, but they quickly fired it again, and that took.[41]

Both Rowlandson's and Schiltberger's truncated syntax and unembellished description of events, as well as their attention to specific materials and place-names (e.g., "flax and hemp" and "Pulgery and Walachy"), function, via verisimilitude, to subtly corroborate their respective authority.[42] The awkwardness of their narration style is by no means an obstacle to their accounts but is integral to it, for that style, centuries before Realist fiction would come into fashion – not to mention that Roland Barthes's essay "The Reality Effect" (1968) would coin the phrase "effect of reality" – endears us to these tongue-tied, not-altogether-trustworthy narrators, whom we are,

---

[40] On Orientalism, see Said, *Orientalism*, 3.
[41] Rowlandson, "Narrative of the Captivity and Restoration," 95.
[42] On the role of verisimilitude in literature, see Roland Barthes, *The Rustle of Language*, trans. Richard Howard (Berkeley, CA: University of California Press, 1989), 141–8, as well as Roman Jakobson, *Language in Literature*, eds. Krystyna Pomorska and Stephen Rudy (Cambridge, MA: Belknap Press, 1987), 20–4.

paradoxically, somehow more willing to trust because of their admissions of possible misapprehension.[43] Rowlandson reminds us that this is all "according to my observation, in that amazing time," suggesting that she may not remember everything exactly "as it happened," while Schiltberger confesses that he has described events "perhaps not quite completely" – overt admissions of their narrators' unreliability.[44] Rowlandson continues:

> Now is the dreadful hour come, that I have often heard of (in time of war, as it was the case of others), but now mine eyes see it. Some in our house were fighting for their lives, others wallowing in their blood, the house on fire over our heads, and the bloody heathen ready to knock us on the head, if we stirred out. Now might we hear mothers and children crying out for themselves, and one another, "Lord, what shall we do?" Then I took my children (and one of my sisters'[sic], hers) to go forth and leave the house: but as soon as we came to the door and appeared, the Indians shot so thick that the bullets rattled against the house, as if one had taken an handful of stones and threw them, so that we were fain to give back. We had six stout dogs belonging to our garrison, but none of them would stir, though another time, if any Indian had come to the door, they were ready to fly upon him and tear him down. The Lord hereby would make us the more acknowledge His hand, and to see that our help is always in Him. But out we must go, the fire increasing, and coming along behind us, roaring, and the Indians gaping before us with their guns, spears, and hatchets to devour us.[45]

The description of the "Indians" as preparing to "devour" Rowlandson's family is particularly poignant with respect to Geraldine Heng's scholarship on the anthropophagic atrocity of the medieval chivalric romance.[46] According to Heng, the medieval romance *Richard Coer de Lyon* (c. 1275) and Geoffrey of Monmouth's pseudo-historical chronicle *History of the Kings of Britain* (1136) "materialize [...] as a form of cultural rescue" in response to the Third and First Crusades, respectively, "during which the Latin Christian crusaders did the unthinkable – committing acts of cannibalism on infidel Turkish cadavers."[47] The medieval romance tradition, Heng maintains, is an attempt to justify these atrocities by "dehumaniz[ing]" the Moors and other foes to the extent that it would be acceptable to slaughter

---

[43] Barthes, *The Rustle of Language*, 141–8.
[44] Rowlandson, "Narrative of the Captivity and Restoration," 95; Schiltberger, *The Bondage and Travels of Johann Schiltberger*, 1.
[45] Rowlandson, "Narrative of the Captivity and Restoration," 95.
[46] Geraldine Heng, *Empire of Magic: Medieval Romance and the Politics of Cultural Fantasy* (New York, NY: Columbia University Press, 2003), 29.
[47] Heng, *Empire of Magic*, 2.

and consume them.[48] Rowlandson's own portrayal of Native Americans, then, as "devour[ing] us" serves as a reminder not only of this shared motif between chivalric romances and captivity narratives but also that European colonists took part in similarly unthinkable atrocities, including cannibalism. Bartolomé de las Casas famously compares Spaniards "to wild animals, feasting on the flesh of the innocent Amerindians," while the engravings of Theodore de Bry present "conquistadors retailing human flesh."[49] Within a British colonial context, archeological studies of Jamestown skeletons have found "'incontrovertible evidence that a girl, whom [the researchers] came to call Jane, had been cannibalized' during the Starving Time," the winter of 1609–10, while John Smith himself, the famed English explorer featured in Disney's *Pocahontas* (1995), described how the colonists murdered, buried, disinterred, and cannibalized the corpse of a Native American.[50] Rowlandson's narrative, meanwhile, continues:

---

[48] Heng, *Empire of Magic*, 123.
[49] Rebecca Earle, "Spaniards, Cannibals, and the Eucharist in the New World," in *To Feast on Us as Their Prey: Cannibalism and the Early Modern Atlantic*, ed. Rachel B. Herrmann (Fayetteville, AR: University of Arkansas, 2019), 91.
[50] Rachel B. Herrmann, "Introduction," *To Feast on Us as Their Prey: Cannibalism and the Early Modern Atlantic*, ed. Rachel B. Herrmann (Fayetteville, AR: University of Arkansas, 2019), 9–10. With respect to the genre of captivity narratives, Olaudah Equiano's *The Narrative of the Life of Olaudah Equiano* (1789), a description of Equiano's capture in Africa and enslavement in America, describes how a British captain remarked, during a passage from North America to Britain, "jocularly that he would kill me to eat" (Olaudah Equiano, *The Interesting Narrative of the Life of Olaudah Equiano* (Boston, MA: The Floating Press, 2009); Rachel B. Herrmann, "The Black People Were Not Good to Eat," *To Feast on Us as Their Prey: Cannibalism and the Early Modern Atlantic*, ed. Rachel B. Herrmann (Fayetteville, AR: University of Arkansas, 2019), 201). Equiano, who had been captured as a child, continues: "Sometimes he would say to me – the black people were not good to eat, and would ask me if we did not eat people in my country. I said, No: then he said he would kill Dick (as he always called [a fellow slave]) first, and afterwards me. Though this hearing relieved my mind a little as to myself, I was alarmed for Dick and whenever he was called I used to be very much afraid he was to be killed" (Herrmann, "The Black People Were Not Good to Eat," 201). Equiano's own captivity narrative, as well as later variations on the genre such as Frederick Douglass's *Narrative of the Life of Frederick Douglass* (1845), Harriet Jacobs's *Incidents in the Life of a Slave Girl* (Boston, 1861) and Zitkala-Ša's *American Indian Stories* (1921), amounts to yet another reframing of the captivity genre by African Americans and Native Americans alike – instances of what in Chapter 2 I will discuss as the subversive tradition of American medievalism (Frederick Douglass and Harriet Jacobs, *Narrative of the Life of Frederick Douglass and Incidents in the Life of a Slave Girl* (New York, NY: Random House, 2000); Zitkala-Ša, *American Indian Stories* (Mineola, NY: Dover Publication, 2012)). On the medievalisms in *Pocahontas*, see Pugh and Aronstein, *The Disney Middle Ages*, 179–81.

> No sooner were we out of the house, but my brother-in-law (being before wounded, in defending the house, in or near the throat) fell down dead, whereat the Indians scornfully shouted, and hallowed and were presently upon him, stripping off his clothes, the bullets flying thick, one went through my side, and the same (as would seem) through the bowels and hand of my dear child in my arms. One of my elder sisters' [sic] children, named William, had then his leg broken, which the Indians perceiving, they knocked him on [his] head. Thus were we butchered by those merciless, standing amazed, with the blood running down to our heals. My eldest sister being yet in the house, and seeing those woeful sights, the infidels hauling mothers one way, and children another, and some wallowing in their blood: and her elder son telling her that her son William was dead, and myself was wounded.[51]

Rowlandson is definitely biased; she describes the "Indians," engrossed in a war for their very survival, as "infidels," "merciless," and bloodthirsty "butcher[s]" – yet another allusion to cannibalism – before turning to her actual capture:

> When we are in prosperity, Oh the little that we think of such dreadful sights, and to see our dear friends, and relations lie bleeding out their heart-blood upon the ground. There was one who was chopped into the head with a hatchet, and stripped naked, and yet was crawling up and down. It is a solemn sight to see so many Christians lying in their blood, some here, and some there, like a company of sheep torn by wolves, all of them stripped naked by a company of hell-hounds, roaring, singing, ranting, and insulting, as if they would have torn our very hearts out; yet the Lord by His almighty power preserved a number of us from death, for there were twenty-four of us taken alive and carried captive. I had often before this said that if the Indians should come, I should choose rather to be killed by them than taken alive, but when it came to the trial my mind changed; their glittering weapons so daunted my spirit, that I chose rather to go along with those (as I may say) ravenous beasts, than that moment to end my days; and that I may the better declare what happened to me during that grievous captivity, I shall particularly speak of the several removes we had up and down the wilderness.[52]

The remainder of Rowlandson's narrative revolves around these "removes," and in this her work also resembles Schiltberger's, whose narrative revolves around his own capture at the hands of the Turks and the various voyages

---

[51] Rowlandson, "Narrative of the Captivity and Restoration," 95–6.
[52] Rowlandson, "Narrative of the Captivity and Restoration," 96.

that this abrupt removal from Christian society initiates. More interesting, though, at least with respect to Rowlandson's narrative, is Schiltberger's description of his own capture, which, while not short-winded, is certainly more direct than is Rowlandson's:

> And now when the King Weyasat had had the battle, he went near the city where King Sigismund had encamped with his army, and then went to the battle-field and looked upon his people that were killed; and when he saw that so many of his people were killed, he was torn by great grief, and swore he would not leave their blood unavenged, and ordered his people to bring every prisoner before him the next day, by fair means or foul. So they came the next day, each with as many prisoners as he had made, bound with a cord. I was one of three bound with the same cord, and was taken by him who had captured us. When the prisoners were brought before the king, he took the Duke of Burgony that he might see his vengeance because of his people that had been killed. When the Duke of Burgony saw his anger, he asked him to spare the lives of several he would name; this was granted by the king. Then he selected twelve lords, his own countrymen, also Stephen Synüher and the lord Hannsen of Bodem. Then each was ordered to kill his own prisoners, and for those who did not wish to do so the king appointed others in their place. Then they took my companions and cut off their heads, and when it came to my turn, the king's son saw me and ordered that I should be left alive, and I was taken to the other boys, because none under xx years of age were killed, and I was scarcely sixteen years old.[53]

Schiltberger's narrator is surprisingly aware of King Weyesat's grief, framing the murder of the captives as itself "vengeance."[54] The portrayal shows a remarkable ability to sympathize with the Turks who took Schiltberger captive, and such sympathy demands a recognition of the Ottoman captivity narrative genre as a response to the chivalric romance tradition, at least as Geraldine Heng conceives it.[55] If the chivalric romance tradition serves to dehumanize non-Christians in order to justify the atrocities of the Christian Crusades, then Ottoman captivity narratives serve to undermine, or at least nuance, that dehumanization. After all, the entire premise that captives escape from captivity and return to their homelands to tell of their adventures requires a rethinking of their captors as, if not good-hearted, at least not all-powerful. The paradox of Rowlandson's dehumanization of her captors is that they choose to preserve the lives of her and

---

[53] Schiltberger, *The Bondage and Travels of Johann Schiltberger*, 4.
[54] Schiltberger, *The Bondage and Travels of Johann Schiltberger*, 4.
[55] Heng, *Empire of Magic*, 4–10.

her twenty-three fellow colonists. This is a trope of captivity narratives as a whole: they serve not so much as impetuses to but justifications for vengeance, and it is in this sense that we can see how the captivity genre is a fitting corollary to the colonial charter genre itself. While colonial charters serve as juridical documents for pilgrim-crusades to be undertaken, captivity narratives serve as historico-literary texts that either bolster support in anticipation of or serve as *post hoc* justifications for those pilgrim-crusades. In either case, these transatlantic texts – captivity narratives and colonial charters alike – rely necessarily upon a medieval Christian crusader ideology that insists upon an unequivocal distinction between Christian and infidel, as well as between civilization and barbarism.[56]

---

[56] For more on distinctions between civilization and barbarism as a central theme of European and Euro-American conceptions of the New World, see Juliet Hooker, *Theorizing Race in the Americas: Booker, Sarmiento, Du Bois, and Vasconcelos* (Oxford: Oxford University Press, 2017), 67–112.

2

Errant in the Wilderness: The Naming of California, *Don Quixote*'s America and Other Geographic Fantasies

> As it happened some ages before to be the fashion to saunter to the Holy Land, and go upon other Quixote adventures, so it was now grown the humour to take a trip to America. The Spaniards had lately discovered rich mines in their part of the West Indies, which made their maritime neighbours eager to do so too. This modish frenzy being still more inflamed by the charming account given of Virginia, by the first adventurers, made many fond of removing to such a paradise.
>
> —William Byrd II, *History of the Dividing Line* (1728)[1]

If, as New World charters such as the First Charter of Virginia and the Charter of Carolina suggest, Europeans first conceived of New World colonization as a chivalric quest akin to a Christian crusade, they quickly realized that such a quest was decidedly unrealistic. As Americanist Perry Miller famously asserts in his now canonical work of American Studies, *Errand into the Wilderness* (1952), the first generation of Puritans settling in New England conceived of their "medieval pilgrimage" to the New World as an "errand," "an essential maneuver in the drama of Christendom."[2] The second and third generation of Puritans, however, largely forgotten by Europe and enduring the arduous task of surviving in the New World, recognized that quest as a "fool's errand" and bemoaned both their forefathers' idealism and their own inability to complete that quest.[3] This growing pessimism was not exclusive to New England Puritans,

---

[1] William Byrd, II, *History of the Dividing Line and Other Tracts*, Vol. 1 (Richmond, VA: 1866), 3.
[2] Miller, *Errand into the Wilderness*, 101, 11.
[3] Miller, *Errand into the Wilderness*, 11.

however, nor even to British colonists more generally; while early Spanish, Italian, and Portuguese explorers such as Christopher Columbus and Peter Martyr of Angleria "bind the New World to pastoral images of fertility and innocence that have a biblical air and associate the pastoral New World with terrestrial Paradise or with a lost Golden Age," the Spanish Baroque period of the late seventeenth century depicted a "dystopian New World," highlighting the persecution of Native Americans and "assail[ing] the arrogance, depravity, and heterogeneity gone terribly wrong [in] a New World more akin to Babel than to St. Augustine's earthly city."[4]

This dystopian rendering of the New World is, in fact, legible long before the Spanish Baroque, especially in place-names applied to the New World such as the Amazon – named after the mythical land of the Amazons, foes of Classical Greece – and California, a place-name derived from an early modern Spanish chivalric romance entitled *Las sergas de Esplandián* (1510). Indeed, *Las sergas* connects this dystopian rendering of the New World with what has come to be known as the "first modern novel" – namely, Miguel de Cervantes's *Don Quixote* (1605, 1615), which tells of a Spanish hidalgo obsessed with medieval chivalric romances like *Las sergas* and *Amadís de Gaula* and who endeavors to embark on his own chivalric quest in early modern Spain. A critical reading of the place-naming of California juxtaposed with a discussion of the connections between New World colonization and Cervantes's novel, then, emphasizes how New World colonization can be understood as not only a medieval Christian crusade but also a quixotic sally, akin to those of Don Quixote and his faithful servant, Sancho Panza.[5]

Like Don Quixote interpreting his lived experience through the lens of medieval chivalric romances, European explorers and colonists interpreted the Americas through the cultural productions available to them, especially Marco Polo's *Book of Marvels* (c. 1300), the Bible, and chivalric romances like *Las sergas de Esplandián* and *Amadís de Gaula* (c. 1508) – as well as Islamic cultural productions such as the concept of a caliphate.[6] To recognize those explorers and colonists as akin to Don Quixote rather than a traditional Christian crusader or pilgrim casts New World colonization itself as an unfeasible, quixotic task that would ultimately result, as the second and

---

[4] Stephanie Merrim, *The Spectacular City, Mexico, and Colonial Hispanic Literary Culture* (Austin, TX: University of Texas Press, 2012), 84, 252–3.

[5] Simone Pinet, *Archipelagoes: Insular Fictions from Chivalric Romances to the Novel* (Minneapolis, MN: University of Minnesota Press, 2011), 141. For more on the application of the myth of the Amazons to the New World, see Candace Slater, *Entangled Edens: Visions of the Amazon* (Berkeley, CA: University of California Press, 2010), 84–6.

[6] Pinet, *Archipelagoes*, xxv.

third generation Puritans themselves realized, not in the colonization of the Americas but in the "Americanization" of the colonists.[7]

Edward Everett Hale, in an 1862 article published in *The Atlantic*, noticed the connection between the place-name "California" and *Las sergas de Esplandián*, which was the Castilian author Garcí Rodriguez de Montalvo's sequel to his own rendition of the popular Iberian medieval chivalric romance *Amadís de Gaula*.[8] *Las sergas* tells of the adventures of Amadís's son, Esplandián, and can be counted among the "infinite progeny" of *Amadís* imitations that Miguel Cervantes would lampoon in the opening paragraphs of *Don Quixote* (*Las sergas*, in fact, is the first book the barber and priest burn in Part I's book-burning).[9] *Amadís*, the latter portions of which are set on the high seas, was especially popular among the early explorers of the New World; when he first saw Tenochtitlan, for instance, Bernal Diaz del Castillo (c. 1496–1584), the chronicler of Cortéz's conquests, declared that it was "like the enchantments they tell of in the legend of Amadís."[10] Likewise, one of Cortéz's footmen was reportedly nicknamed "Argyares" because of his resemblance to a character of that same name in *Amadís de Gaula*.[11] When Spanish explorers traveled along the western shores of North America and came upon what they thought was a long, narrow island off the coast of the New World (but which turned out to be the peninsula that still to this day bears the name "Baja California"), the explorers purportedly declared it the "Island called California," described in Montalvo's *Las sergas*.[12]

Far from innocuous, the allegorical mapping of *Las sergas* onto North America promoted a specific sociopolitical end. The "island called California," described in *Las sergas*, alludes directly to another crusading era – namely, the *Reconquista*, the Christian "reconquest" of the Iberian peninsula from the Moors.[13] Montalvo's description of California appears toward the end of *Las sergas*; once Esplandián and his crew arrive at the island, it becomes clear that the ruler of California, Queen Calafia, plans

---

[7] Miller, *Errand into the Wilderness*, 9.
[8] Edward Everett Hale, "The Queen of California," *The Atlantic* 13:77 (March 1864), 265–80. This essay was reprinted in Hale's collected stories, *His Level Best, and Other Stories* (Boston, MA: Roberts Brothers, 1872), 234–80.
[9] Cervantes, *The Indigenous Hidalgo Don Quixote*, 703, 53.
[10] Dora Polk, *The Island of California: A History of the Myth* (Lincoln, NE: University of Nebraska Press, 1995), 128.
[11] Charles E. Chapman, *A History of California: The Spanish Period* (New York, NY: Macmillan, 1921), 62.
[12] Garcí Rodriguez de Montalvo, *Las sergas de Esplandián* (1526), 108. Translation my own.
[13] For a discussion of the *Reconquista* as a medieval Christian crusade, see Joseph F. O'Callaghan, *Reconquest and Crusade in Medieval Spain* (Philadelphia, PA: University of Pennsylvania Press, 2003).

to attack the city of Constantinople in order to aid the Turkish invaders who are laying siege to the city. Mounted on the backs of armored griffins, Queen Calafia and her fellow Californians soar to Constantinople, where they come close to defeating the Christian defenders of the city. However, when Esplandián and his father, Amadís, arrive, the Christian knights are able to halt the siege. Amadís eventually battles Queen Calafia in single combat – albeit chivalrously avoiding ever striking her outright – and Esplandián defeats one of the Turkish lords to end, once and for all, the onslaught. By way of denouement, Queen Calafia is converted to Christianity and, while she wishes to marry Esplandián, marries Esplandián's cousin, Talanque, who, in turn, becomes king of California.[14] Applying the name to the western shores of the Americas, the Spanish explorers (or whoever mapped the toponym of California onto the region[15]) were casting the New World in the image of Montalvo's speculative, overtly fantastical history and, in so doing, implying that the New World was the property of a Christian king. By 1510, Constantinople – or Istanbul – had been under the rule of the Ottoman Empire for over fifty years; to tell of the Turkish siege of Constantinople – and to rewrite that siege as unsuccessful – was to undermine the Ottoman claim to the city and to fantasize about how an expansion of the *Reconquista* beyond Iberia might have kept the Ottoman Empire from coalescing in 1453.

Moreover, the representation of the peninsula of Baja California as an island is illustrative of a medieval and early modern European cosmography through which the Spanish explorers were interpreting the New World. Early modern European cultures, trying to make sense of what sociologist Eviatar Zerubavel deems the "cosmographic shock" dealt to medieval notions of the cosmos by the discovery of the New World, began by imagining the New World as Asia itself.[16] They then began to see this "New World" as an archipelago between Asia and Europe, before finally recognizing the Americas as de facto continents. This "insular imaginary"

---

[14] Montalvo, *Las sergas*, 109–25.
[15] The specific individual who first applied that appellation to the region remains unknown. When Hale rediscovered Montalvo's "California" in 1862, he declared that it was Cortéz himself who named the island "California." Charles Chapman argued that such a claim is unfounded and that Cortéz himself had in fact only written of the "island" (Baja California) as "Santa Cruz." Instead, Chapman asserts, it was likely Fortún Jimenez who first applied the name to the region. Jimenez, who had led a mutiny against – and eventually murdered – Cortéz's confidante and kinsman, Francisco de Becerra, was not in Cortéz's good graces. Chapman, therefore, suggests that it would have been unlikely for Cortéz to honor Jimenez's chosen name for the region. See, Polk, *The Island of California*, 121–9.
[16] Eviatar Zerubavel, *Terra Cognita: The Mental Discovery of America* (New Brunswick, NJ: Rutgers University Press, 1992), 25.

can be seen as a lens through which European cultures were grappling with this cosmographic shock, and the place-name of California exists as a survival of this colonial cartography, when the explorers were trying to "force the new evidence into the old dogma."[17] Indeed, depictions of California underwent a similar geo-temporal transformation to those of the New World itself. Montalvo's description of California noted that it was "on the right-hand side of the Indies" and early maps and descriptions of North America famously depict California as an island off the western coast of North America.[18] Indeed, while the earliest maps of the region rendered the peninsula of Baja California properly as a peninsula, when the name "California" was applied to the region, that peninsula began to be rendered consistently as an island, a mismapping that persisted throughout the seventeenth and eighteenth centuries.[19]

That Montalvo may have been translating the Old French "Califerne," described in the Old French chanson de geste *Song of Roland* (c. 1040), into Spanish – as Americanist Ruth Putnam has argued – further illustrates the extent to which this place-naming was an act of medieval Christian cartography.[20] While mourning his fallen nephew, Roland, Charlemagne declares:

> "Roland, my friend, man of honor, noble youth,
> When I shall be at Aix, in my chapel,
> Men will come, they will ask for news.
> I shall tell them the awesome and cruel facts:
> 'My nephew, through whom I conquered so much, is dead.'
> The Saxons will rebel against me,
> The Hungarians, the Bulgars, and so many infidel peoples,
> The Romans, the Apulians, and all the men of Palermo,
> The men of Africa and those of Califerne."[21]

Putnam assumes that Montalvo would have been familiar with *Roland* and was playing imaginatively in *Las sergas* with what and where this land of "Califerne" might have been. The syntactical units of the excerpt support this claim, for they group the various "foes" geographically. The Saxons, Hungarians, and Bulgarians, syntactically, exist as a single unit

---

[17] Pinet, *Archipelagoes*, 25. Eviatar Zerubavel, *Time Maps: Collective Memory and the Social Shape of the Past* (Chicago, IL: University of Chicago Press, 2003), 69.
[18] Montalvo, *Las sergas*, 109.
[19] Montalvo, *Las sergas*, 109. For more on this "mismapping," see Scott Corbet Riley, "Anachronous Antipodes: The Island of California, the Medieval Mediterranean and the Modern Pacific," *The Medieval Globe* 4:2 (2018), 111–12.
[20] Ruth Putnam, *California: The Name* (Berkeley, CA: University of California Press, 1917), 347–8. Also see, Polk, *The Island of California*, 130.
[21] Gerard J. Brault, *The Song of Roland: Oxford Text and English Translation* (University Park, PA: Pennsylvania State University, 1978), 177.

and, in Charlemagne's day, all occupied regions to the east of the Frankish realm; the "Romans, the Apulians and all the men of Palermo" are listed together in line 2923 and all lived either on the Italian peninsula or in Sicily. Finally, in line 2924, the "men of Africa" are grouped with "those of Califerne." If we accept the etymology proposed by Hale – that "California" alludes to the Arabic *khalifa*, "caliphate" – this juxtaposition clearly groups the Muslim "Men of Africa" with the occupants of this mysterious land called Califerne.[22]

Roland can be understood, in part, as propaganda for Charlemagne's claim to all of Christendom, a claim revived by those who claimed to be his successors.[23] The territories of "France" that *Roland* claims for Charlemagne were not part of France either in Charlemagne's day or in the early twelfth century, when the oldest manuscript of *Roland* was copied, nor did France even exist as a sovereign entity, at least in the way we understand sovereignty today.[24] The territories named in the excerpt are fascinating in this regard: Charlemagne had brutally conquered Saxony in his own time, and in the twelfth century – in the immediate aftermath of the First Crusade (1095–99) – Christian knights were calling for crusades against the "pagan" Slavs of Eastern Europe, which included Hungary and Bulgaria.[25] Apulia, meanwhile, a region in the south of the Italian peninsula, and Palermo, a Sicilian port city, had both been Muslim strongholds until the early eleventh century and still had large Muslim populations even after the Norman conquest of southern Italy.[26]

Montalvo would likely not have been aware of all of these connections, but the possibility that he was alluding to the "Califerne" mentioned in *Roland*, imaginatively exploring where that region might have been and who its inhabitants might have resembled, suggests that he was situating Islam as far as possible from the Mediterranean and so challenging its claims to Europe, North Africa, and the Levant. Montalvo's narrative, connecting the Californians with the perennial enemy of medieval Christians, in turn, makes Esplandián and his father emblematic not only of El Cid – the heroic figure of the medieval Spanish epic

[22] Hale, *His Level Best*, 241.
[23] Stephanie Kristin Lohse, *Charlemagne, Roland, and the Islamic Other: Vicarious Reading and Virtual Identity* (Minneapolis, MN: University of Minnesota Press, 2017), 65.
[24] For more on medieval conceptions of sovereignty, see Francesco Maiolo, *Medieval Sovereignty: Marsilius of Padua and Bartolus of Saxoferrato* (Delft: Eburon Academic Publishers, 2007), as well as Davis, *Periodization and Sovereignty*, 1–11.
[25] Ingrid Rembold, *Conquest and Christianization: Saxony and the Carolingian World, 772–888* (Cambridge: Cambridge University Press, 2018), 46–53.
[26] Alex Metcalfe, *Muslims in Medieval Italy* (Edinburgh: Edinburgh University Press, 2009), 2.

poem *The Poem of the Cid* (c. 1140) – and other heroes of the *Reconquista*, fighting the Moors, but also of King Arthur and the heroes of the Crusades, fighting infidel Muslims in the Holy Land and elsewhere.[27]

Montalvo's description of California also imbricates this island within early modern European conceptions of race and gender. Montalvo describes the Californians, who live "without a man among them," as *mujeres negras*, "black women," and compares them to the mythical Amazons.[28] Sixteenth- and seventeenth-century Spain is "critical to the history of Western racism" as a whole because "its attitudes and practices served as a kind of segue between the religious intolerance of the Middle Ages and the naturalistic racism of the modern era."[29] In *Las sergas*, we can see this segue in action, for by describing Californians as "black" and allying them with the Turks, Montalvo conflates race and religion, suggesting that skin pigmentation signifies religious belief – and vice versa – and so reveals how European religious intolerance was, in the early sixteenth century, transforming into a modern naturalistic racism. Montalvo adds gender to this race–religion conflation, illustrating how, as Tessie Liu and other scholars working in the field of intersectional feminism have argued, race and gender can be understood as "consolidated," especially in an early modern European context: "The [*Oxford English Dictionary*] makes clear," Liu writes, "that ideas about descent, blood ties, or common substance are basic to the notion of 'race' [...] 'house,' 'family,' and 'kindred' are synonyms of race."[30] In turn, early modern European notions of race, understood as a synonym of "house" or "family," were inseparable from gender, both terms also functioning as demarcations of social class. Montalvo's description of Queen Calafia and the Californians evidences this interconnected understanding of race, religion, and gender, and the mapping of Montalvo's California onto the landscapes of the New World reveals how New World colonization was informed by these shifting social and political paradigms.[31]

Understood in a medieval Mediterranean context, *Roland*'s Califerne and Montalvo's Island of California, finally, stand as examples of the

---

[27] On the links between King Arthur and the Crusades, see Geraldine Heng, *Empire of Magic*, 21–5.

[28] Montalvo, *Las sergas*, 109.

[29] George Frederickson, *Racism: A Short History* (Princeton, NJ: Princeton University Press, 2002), 40.

[30] Tessie Liu, "Teaching the Differences among Women from a Historical Perspective: Rethinking Race and Gender as Social Categories," in *Unequal Sisters: An Inclusive reading in U.S. Women's History*, eds. Vicki Ruiz and Ellen Carol DuBois (New York, NY: Routledge, 2008), 34.

[31] For more on how America's Indigenous people were treated like Moors, see Majid, *We Are All Moors*, 10.

"different interpretations" of the term "caliphate" itself, both suggesting an "idea of leadership" within Muslim society but framing that concept geographically, treating the term primarily as a place-name.[32] After all, the idea of an Islamic caliphate is by no means monolithic: "The concept of caliphate," historian Hugh Kennedy has written, "has had many different interpretations and realizations through the years [...] but fundamental to them all is that it offers an idea of leadership which is about the just ordering of Muslim society according to the will of God."[33] *Roland*'s "Califerne" and Montalvo's "California," in other words, gesture toward a geographically centered conception of sovereignty that would become central to the modern nation-state – that "revolutionary idea of the pre-eminence of the nation in political and legal life."[34] As literary critic Norman O. Brown has argued, the antecedents of European Romanticism are often lost in Western cultural history because they arrive from the Islamic rather than the Christian tradition.[35] If we understand German Romanticism, regarded as central to "bring[ing] into being the modern nation-state," as connected to Islam, the implications are profound: the modern nation-state becomes the construct of not only German Romanticism but also the Islamic concept of a caliphate, at least as it was interpreted by medieval Christendom, and "California," that place-name with no material referent, becomes an early enunciation of that idea.[36] In turn, "[a]t the very heart of [European] liberalism" is not only the "ugly secret" that "inclusive nationalism is founded on the basis of violent exclusion," as cultural theorist Anouar Majid has observed, but also the perhaps more hopeful notion that modern European nation-states derive their concept of sovereignty, at least in part, from the very religion that Europe continues to exclude and in contrast to which it was largely defined.[37] Even attempts to peripheralize the excluded other – like the association of a distant "island of California" with an Islamic caliphate – memorialize that other, embedding it within the "universal," "fraternal" space of the modern nation-state.[38]

---

[32] Hugh Kennedy, *Caliphate: The History of an Idea* (New York, NY: Basic Books, 2016), 1–5.

[33] Kennedy, *Caliphate*, 1–5.

[34] Maiolo, *Medieval Sovereignty*, 104.

[35] Norman O. Brown, *The Challenge of Islam* (Berkeley, CA: University of California Press, 2009), 44.

[36] Chenxi Tang, *The Geographic Imagination of Modernity: Geography, Literature, and Philosophy in German Romanticism* (Redwood City, CA: Stanford University Press, 2008), 11.

[37] Majid, *We are All Moors*, 47.

[38] On the universalizing quality of the European nation-state, see Charles Taylor, *A Secular Age* (Cambridge, MA: Belknap Press, 2007), 576.

Montalvo's placement of California "to the right-hand side of the Indies" is itself illustrative of this othering discourse. In an extended note appended to "The Queen of California" – the essay that revealed to a U.S. readership the connection between "California" and Montalvo's *Las sergas* – Edward Everett Hale discusses the shared cosmogony of Dante and Columbus in detail, pointing out that "the precise antipodes of Jerusalem, which, according to the cosmogony of Dante, would be the place of the summit of the terrestrial paradise, is just south of Tahiti and southwest of Pitcairn's Island."[39] While he is circumspect about how this relates to a discussion of the place-name of California, Hale implies that, because Montalvo describes the Island of California as "very near the Terrestrial Paradise," Montalvo was thinking in terms of this same medieval European cosmogony.[40] Early modern European cartographies of the Pacific Rim, Hale points out, are deeply inscribed with a medieval Mediterranean cosmography, especially focused on the figure of the antipode. "[E]nthusiasts among modern navigators have fancied that their terrestrial paradise was found" in the South Pacific, Hale points out, and the place-name of "California" overtly maps that cultural production of the medieval Mediterranean onto the Pacific Rim, casting Californians, portrayed as black, matriarchal, and Muslim, as diametrically opposed to Europeans, represented as white, patriarchal, and Christian.[41]

By appending this discussion of medieval European cosmogony to an essay on the naming of the U.S. State of California, moreover, Hale illustrates the extent to which the fascination with this place-name betrays an angst felt by nineteenth-century U.S. western settlers. In the opening paragraphs of the essay, Hale imagines "the excitement which this title ['The Queen of California'] [will] arouse as it flashes across the sierras, down the valley, and into the various reading-rooms and parlors" of San Francisco.[42] "Is [the Queen of California] the blond maiden who took a string of hearts with her in a leash, when she left us one sad morning? Is it the hardy, brown adventuress [...] in her bark-roofed lodge, [...] is it that witch with gray eyes, cunningly hidden?"[43] Hale is noting the anxiety of western settlers unsure of their sovereignty over this recently acquired land, and he predicts that readers will be disappointed that this "queen of California" is "no modern queen."[44] The implication is that, reading *The Atlantic* in San Francisco in 1862, these settlers hope that the queen of

---

[39] Hale, *His Level Best*, 280.
[40] Montalvo, *Las sergas*, 109.
[41] Hale, *His Level Best*, 280.
[42] Hale, *His Level Best*, 242.
[43] Hale, *His Level Best*, 242.
[44] Hale, *His Level Best*, 243.

California will be an exotic and sexually available woman – whether she be "blond" or "brown," a "maiden" or a "witch" – in order to justify and consummate their claim to the region.[45]

The silence surrounding Native Americans in these discussions of the naming of California, like the silence surrounding "crusader cannibalism" in medieval chivalric romances, is blaring; nowhere in the forty-seven pages of Hale's essay are Native Americans mentioned beyond that oblique allusion to a "hardy, brown adventuress."[46] His essay, moreover, is no outlier. Historian A.E. Sokol, in a 1949 essay outlining yet another possible source-text for "California," notes a reference to a woman named "Calefurnia" made in the thirteenth-century German legal code *Sachsenspiegel*, in which a woman named "Calefurnia" is said to have established an unfortunate precedent: "No woman," the excerpt reads, "may be an advocate nor place [a case before the court] without a guardian. This privilege was lost for all women by Calefurnia, who misbehaved before court, being angry because she could not get her will without an advocate."[47] Sokol argues that "Calefurnia" was likely the origin for the "Calefurnia" mentioned in Sebastian Brant's *Ship of Fools* (1497) and that Montalvo "quite conceivabl[y]" drew from Brant's text for his Island of California.[48] Sokol, in other words, casts doubt on the notion that Montalvo's California was an allusion to either *Roland*'s Califerne or the Arabic *khalifa*, instead proposing a thoroughly Northern European etymology. Moreover, his etymology focuses single-mindedly on the gender of Queen Calafia and her fellow Californians, disregarding their religion and racialization by Montalvo and, in so doing, neglecting the intersection of race, religion, and gender in Montalvo's description of Californians. Similarly, following upon Sokol's essay, historian Donald C. Cutter, in an essay published in 1961, points out a passage in *Siete Partidas*, the thirteenth-century Castilian statutory code, in which a woman named Calfurnia, as with the "Calefurnia" of the *Sachsenspiegel*, is forbidden from entering the courtroom because of her angry outbursts.[49] Cutter argues that Montalvo, a counselor for the kingdom of Castille, would have "likely been familiar" with the *Partidas* and, in turn, may have been thinking of this woman named Calfurnia (sometimes translated into English as "Calphurnia") when he

---

[45] Hale, *His Level Best*, 243.

[46] Heng, *Empire of Magic*, 29–30.

[47] A.E. Sokol, "California: A Possible Derivation of the Name," *California Historical Society Quarterly* 28:1 (1949), 23.

[48] Sokol, "California," 30.

[49] Robert I. Burns S.J., ed., *Las Siete Partidas*, Vol. III, trans. Samuel Parsons Scott (Philadelphia, PA: University of Pennsylvania Press, 2001), 598.

imagined the island of California.⁵⁰ The figure of Calfurnia appears in the third *Partida*, which revolves around the "world of law": in a law that considers "who cannot act as advocates for others, but can act as such for themselves," a "woman called Calphurnia" is discussed "who was very learned, and who was so shameless that she annoyed the judges with her speeches, so that they could not do anything with her."⁵¹ Calfurnia (or Calphurnia), then, is used as an example of why "[n]o woman [...] can act as an advocate for others in court."⁵²

As with the *Sachsenspiegel*'s Calefurnia, the figure of Calfurnia in *Siete Partidas* functions as a scapegoat, justifying the law's discrimination against women, and while both Cutter and Sokol are circumspect regarding the implications of their etymologies, one implication would be that Montalvo was mapping this figure of a "shameless" and "annoy[ing]" woman onto the inhabitants of that distant island "on the right hand of the Indies," both feminizing Native Americans and describing them as shameless and annoying. Moreover, if Montalvo happened to be aware that the *Partidas* were, at least in part, derived from Islamic Law, he might have been augmenting the name "Calfurnia" into "California" in order to connect this "shameless" and "annoy[ing]" woman with not only that distant island and its inhabitants but also the Moors and the Umayyad Caliphate. Indeed, even if Montalvo was thinking of the "Calefurnia" mentioned in *Ship of Fools* – who, like those depicted in the *Partidas* and *Sachsenspiegel* is a woman who "misbehaves" in court – Montalvo's shift from "Calefurnia" to "California" can reasonably be seen as alluding to the Arabic *khalifa*.

In any case, no mention is made of Native Americans in either Sokol's or Cutter's essays, which instead trace speculative connections among these various medieval texts, in the same way that, as Geraldine Heng puts it, "public secrets," especially that of crusader cannibalism, are "made visible, while being hidden," in medieval romances.⁵³ That Sokol's and Cutter's essays were published in the postwar era of U.S. history suggests a tendency among U.S. academics during that period, defined, at least in part, by the African American civil rights movement and Black Muslim movements such as the Nation of Islam, to avoid the fact that Montalvo describes Queen Califia and her fellow Californians as "black" and to

---

⁵⁰ Donald Cutter, "Sources of the Name 'California,'" *Arizona and the West* 3:3 (1961), 240. With respect to the medieval Mediterranean, the *Partidas* is of note because of its links to Greek, Roman, Judeo-Christian and Islamic philosophical and juridical traditions.
⁵¹ *Las Siete Partidas*, Vol. III, 598.
⁵² *Las Siete Partidas*, Vol. III, 597.
⁵³ Heng, *Empire of Magic*, 129.

downplay the notion that "California" might derive from the Arabic term *khalifa* – yet another iteration of this history of erasure.[54]

The place-naming of California in the New World can be seen, after all, as an illustration of how "Arabs [and] Africans haunt" the European and Euro-American Christian cultural imaginary well into the modern era.[55] Indeed, the reluctance to mention the Native American Genocide, especially the California Genocide of the early nineteenth century, in these discussions of the naming of California is directly connected to the othering of Muslims in medieval romances in the sense that, when applied to the New World, "California," with its roots in anti-Islamic literature, overtly portrays Native Americans as allied with the Ottoman Empire. The persistent European and Euro-American assertion that Native Americans themselves were cannibalistic can, in turn, be read as a direct overlaying of the anxiety of crusader cannibalism onto the New World and its inhabitants.[56] The fascination among the U.S. public with the place-name of "California," meanwhile, is akin to the popularity of the medieval romance itself; but while the medieval romance is preoccupied with "fantasy" and "magic," these etymologies are preoccupied with geography and history, understood, by the geographer Edward Soja at least, as the fundamental organizing concerns of modernity.[57]

That California was first represented as an island also speaks to the ways that this place-name is a construct of a medieval Mediterranean cosmography. As Simone Pinet argues, the popularity, in early modern Spain, of both the *isolario* or "book of islands" and the medieval chivalric romance points to a general preoccupation with islands: both genres, she explains, "are coeval: that is, they emerge, develop and fade into history at almost exactly the same time," and she sees in both a common "insular imaginary" that fixates upon the figure of the island.[58] The tales of *Amadís* are especially important to Pinet, who sees the latter portions of *Amadís* as indicative of this "insular turn," and notes – albeit not in detail – that this insular imaginary was "bequeathed to the toponymy of the New World in the name of California."[59] The *isolario*, though, was the product of not only late medieval and early modern Spain – the subject of Pinet's work – but

---

[54] Montalvo, *Las sergas*, 109
[55] Heng, *Empire of Magic*, 58.
[56] Heng, *Empire of Magic*, 30; Polk, *The Island of California*, 129.
[57] Edward Soja, *Postmodern Geographies: The Reassertion of Space in Critical Social Theory* (New York, NY: Verso Books, 1989), 10–15.
[58] Pinet, *Archipelagoes*, xi, 25.
[59] Pinet, *Archipelagoes*, 25, 42.

also the medieval and early modern Mediterranean more broadly.[60] Bartolomeo Da Li Sonetti composed his *Isolario* – a collection of maps "mostly of islands but also of coastal areas of the Mediterranean" interspersed with sonnets and charts of the Aegean Sea – in Venice in 1485, while a Turkish *isolario* from 1521 "containing 121 charts of islands and coasts of the Mediterranean Sea" is still housed in the Bodleian Library in Oxford.[61]

The insular imaginary discussed by Pinet, in this sense, can be more broadly understood as a product of the medieval Mediterranean world as a whole and, in turn, Montalvo's Island of California as an example of this insular turn legible in both *Amadís* and late medieval and early modern *isolarios*. As Pinet puts it, analyzing the late medieval tradition of Portolan charts, "Witnesses to the growing knowledge in the fourteenth and fifteenth centuries of the Atlantic and North Atlantic archipelagoes, [Portolan charts] played an important part in the theories of the marvelous and the imaginary islands of Man, Antillia, and Brazil that would find a figured reality in the Americas. Islands, especially from the fourteenth century onward, serve as laboratory for the emergence of 'a new relation between the bookish and the real, between classical space and modern space.'"[62] This "insular imaginary" that dominated early modern Europe was specifically connected with literary texts, not only by means of *isolarios* and late medieval chivalric romances like those of *Amadís* but also because the figure of the island suggested an insularity characteristic of what would become the literary production so central to modernity: the novel. "The structure of the *isolario* itself," Pinet argues, "in its new fragmented yet totalizing effect stands in close relation to the development of the structure of the modern novel," and Pinet specifically notes how *Amadís* influenced the "first modern novel," Miguel Cervantes's *Don Quixote*: "As an exemplar of its kind and as a model for Cervantes's protagonist, the *Amadís* is the privileged pretext for the writing of *Don Quixote*."[63]

Don Quixote, which revolves around a protagonist who, like the Spanish explorers of the New World, is obsessed with medieval chivalric romances, "is very much concerned with a coexistence of modernizing tendencies," as well as "with the medieval past of knight-errantry,

---

[60] John Wyatt Greenlee and Anna Fore Waymack, in their reading of *The Travels of Sir John Mandeville* (c. 1360), for instance, have emphasized the extent to which islands "figure prominently" in the *Travels*' representations of both Asian and European land- and seascapes (John Wyatt Greenlee and Anna Fore Waymack, "Thinking Globally: Mandeville, Memory and Mappaemundi," *The Medieval Globe* (2018), 86–9).

[61] David Woodward, *Cartography in the European Renaissance* (Chicago, IL: University of Chicago, 2007), 268.

[62] Pinet, *Archipelagoes*, 37.

[63] Pinet, *Archipelagoes*, 67, 141.

the latter persisting in the European imagination throughout the modern period," and that the text makes direct reference to *Las sergas* affords a trenchant point of contact between Cervantes's novel and the naming of California.[64] The Americas are, after all, referenced on several occasions in *Don Quixote*. Immediately after their famed encounter with the windmills, Don Quixote and Sancho Panza come across a troop of Benedictine monks escorting a Basque woman to Seville, where she will set out to join her husband in the New World: "Travelling in the carriage, as it turned out, was a Basque woman, who was travelling to Seville, where her husband was preparing to travel to the Indies [*Indias*] in a very honorable position."[65] Later, in the Second Part, Sancho's friend Ricote mentions the Indies, representing them as a site for "rich pickings and certain profits": "I rented a house in a village near Augsburg; then I joined this group of pilgrims [*peregrinos*] – lots of Germans come to Spain each year to visit shrines here, because for them they are what the Americas [*Indias*] are for us, rich pickings and certain profits."[66] The Spanish term "*Indias*," which John Rutherford translates as "the Indies" and "the Americas," exists for Cervantes's Spaniards as a kind of storehouse of treasure, a bank or vault to be plundered by the wealthy when needed (Augsburg, after all, was home to perhaps the wealthiest family in Europe during the fifteenth and sixteenth centuries, the House of Fugger).[67] Cervantes emphasizes the extent to which the Americas had become, in the early seventeenth century, a quintessential example of what modern world-systems theory deems a "peripheral region," and Cervantes adds to this awareness the fact that Spain itself was seen by other Europeans as a peripheral region, a destination, like the Holy Lands, for *peregrinos* (a term, as discussed in Chapter 1, used throughout medieval Europe to describe pilgrims and crusaders alike) – so by at least 1615, Cervantes was grappling with the complex network of power dynamics at play in early modern colonial territorialization, not to mention portraying Iberia, in the tradition of the *Reconquista*, as the proper site of a pilgrim-crusade.[68]

[64] William Childers, *Transnational Cervantes* (Toronto: University of Toronto Press, 2006), 218.
[65] Cervantes, *The Indigenous Hidalgo Don Quixote*, 67.
[66] Cervantes, *The Indigenous Hidalgo Don Quixote*, 855.
[67] Cervantes, *The Indigenous Hidalgo Don Quixote*, 14, 440, 855; Mark Häberlein, *The Fuggers of Augsburg: Pursuing Wealth and Honor in Renaissance Germany* (Charlottesville, VA: University of Virginia Press, 2012).
[68] The New World appears again in Part One Chapter XXIX, when Quixote, Sancho Panza, and Dorotea, along with the barber and priest, set out to restore Dorotea as the Princess of Micomicón: "You must know, sir," the priest says to Don Quixote, "that I was on my way with Master Nicolás, our friend and barber, to Seville to collect some money sent me by a relative who settled in South

It was Hispanist Irving A. Leonard who first traced the appearance of *Don Quixote* in the New World. Tracking the shipment of seventy-two copies of the first edition of *Quixote* to Lima in 1606, Leonard argues that it might well have been in the New World that *Quixote* was first read by a general audience, for "such works were commonly sent to the overseas possessions of the Spanish Crown even before they were generally available to the public in Spain."[69] By 1621, a "guild of silversmiths paraded through the streets of Mexico City in the likenesses of a long line of knights-errant, last and most modern of which was Don Quixote himself, attended by his trusty squire and his ladylove, Dulcinea."[70] In the British colonies of the New World, meanwhile, *Don Quixote* was available by at least 1637, when "the novel [was] deployed, by New England colonists, to satirize English exploits there":

> As early as 1637, barely a generation after Cervantes' death, various figures began to advertise their readings of *Don Quijote*, available to them in English since Thomas Shelton's 1612 translation. John Morton, for example, regards the attack on him by Miles Standish and other Puritan "worthies" as "like don Quixote against the Windmill." And Cotton Mather vilifies Roger Williams – the "first rebel against the divine-church order in the wilderness" – as a violent Don Quixote, a "windmill" whirling in his head with such fury that "a whole country in America" was likely "to be set on fire."[71]

America many years ago – no inconsiderable sum, in fact it was more than sixty thousand pesos in pure silver bars, worth double that amount once alloyed and coined" (Cervantes, *The Indigenous Hidalgo Don Quixote*, 269). Repeatedly, Cervantes associates the New World with almost incomprehensible material wealth. In Chapter XLII, in the captivity narrative, the former captive who has recounted his journey to Quixote – a story that famously mirrors Cervantes's own captivity in Algiers – encounters his long-lost brother, who "was on his way to take up an important position in America, in the Supreme Court of Mexico" (Cervantes, *The Indigenous Hidalgo Don Quixote*, 397). The Americas, again, in this reference, connote success and prestige; they promise not only wealth but also the possibility of social mobility. On peripheral regions and modern world-system theory, see Immanuel Wallerstein, *The Modern World-System II: Mercantilism and the Consolidation of the European World-Economy, 1600–1750* (Berkeley, CA: University of California Press, 1980), xix–xx. On uses of the term *peregrini*, see Constable, *Crusaders and Crusading*, 155.

[69] Leonard, *Books of the Brave*, 289.
[70] Leonard, *Books of the Brave*, 301.
[71] Diana de Armas Wilson, "Editor's Introduction" to *Don Quixote*, trans. Burton Raffel (New York, NY: W.W. Norton & Co., 1995), xv. Cotton Mather, in turn, would be lampooned by Washington Irving as a kind of Don Quixote figure, with the "superstitious schoolmaster" Ichabod Crane, in "The Legend of Sleepy Hollow" (1820), offering a reading of Cotton Mather's account of New

The presence of *Don Quixote* in both the Anglo-American and Hispano-American colonies speaks candidly to the resonances that link Don Quixote to other European explorers of the New World, especially their shared predilection to read the world through the lenses of medieval chivalric romances. As literary critic Jorge Aladro-Font, thinking of Christopher Columbus's famous refusal to accept the fact that he had happened upon a hitherto unknown continent, argues, Columbus and Quixote "share the same dementia, the insanity of reading. Both the hidalgo and the navigator do not see reality[;] they read it. They look at life with the eyes of literature and try to live or see according to literary models; the hidalgo and the navigator read the world to demonstrate the truth of books."[72] Don Quixote and the European explorers and cartographers, including those who mapped the New World in terms of *Las sergas*, demonstrate the absurdity of using European cultural productions to understand the New World, but while the explorers and cartographers, as historical figures, remain seemingly unconscious of this insanity, Quixote, as a literary figure, maintains a tacit comprehension of his own insanity; this self-awareness is significant, for it suggests that the figure of Don Quixote subverts the textual hermeneutic that interprets the world always through the lens of medieval European cultural productions.

Don Quixote itself is, after all, deeply concerned with the slipperiness of reading. Has Quixote misread his chivalric romances, or are the romances themselves, as Don Quixote's niece proclaims, "evil books of misadventure" that "deserve to be put to the flames, like heretics"?[73] The motifs of names and naming in *Don Quixote*, in this sense, afford yet another point of contact between Cervantes's novel and the naming of California. Cervantes's preoccupation with proper names is apparent from the first sentence of the novel, in which the narrator confesses that he "cannot quite recall" the town-name where Quixote (or Quijote) lived, before, four sentences later, stating that the hidalgo's surname was either "Quixada, or Quesada." Indeed, even before this, in the prologue, Cervantes includes several sonnets and an ode, each of which includes at least one proper noun in its title: "Urganda the Unknowable"; "Amadís of Gaul, to Don Quixote de la Mancha"; and "Sir Belianis of Greece, to Don Quixote de la

---

England witchcraft (William Childers, "Reading *Don Quixote* in the Americas," in *Approaches to Teaching Cervantes's* Don Quixote, eds. James Parr and Lisa Vollendorf (New York, NY: Modern Language Association of America, 2015), 279–90; Washington Irving, *The Sketch Book of Geoffry Crayon, Gent.* (New York, NY: Longmans, Green, and Co., 1906), 362, 368).

[72] Jorge Aladro-Font, "*Don Quijote y Cristóbal Colón: O, La sinrazón de la realidad,*" *Lienzo* 15 (1994), 45. Translation my own.

[73] Cervantes, *The Indigenous Hidalgo Don Quixote*, 50.

Mancha."[74] Don Quixote's interpretations of reality amount largely to acts of renaming: after being knighted by the innkeeper in the first chapter of Part One, he takes on the name of "Don Quixote" and renames Aldonza Lorenzo "Dulcinea del Toboso."[75] His fantasies are, rhetorically speaking at least, constructed by the enunciation of such names; when, for instance, in Part One, the priest and barber decide to trick Quixote, they do so by inventing a kingdom named Micomicón, whose princess, Princess Micomicona, is in dire need of a chivalric knight.[76] After the encounter with the windmills, meanwhile, Quixote explains to Sancho that "[a]ffairs of war, even more than others, are subject to continual change. All the more so as I believe, indeed I am certain, that the same sage Frestón who stole my library and my books has just turned these giants into windmills, to deprive me of the glory of my victory, such is the enmity he feels for me."[77] How is Sancho Panza to respond? Frestón, sometimes spelled "Fristón," is the villain in *Belianís de Grecia* (1545), a medieval chivalric romance particularly preoccupied with "deceit and enchantment": "Unlike what we find in *Amadís* and other romances of chivalry, where supernatural intervention is occasional and usually benign, the world of *Belianís* is one dominated by deceit and enchantment. Knights and ladies are sometimes moved about like pawns in a chess game, as magicians (some dating back to the days of the Trojan War) jockey behind the scenes for numerical advantage in a battle, possession of an enchanted sword or ring, to trick and mislead their rivals, or to seek revenge for an old grievance."[78] Don Quixote takes this motif of deceit one step further, contending that his own lived experience is constructed by such enchantments, and his acts of renaming are avenues for dispelling those enchantments – while Cervantes's own inclusion of this complicated fantasy into his novel amounts to an engagement with the "insanity of reading" that, since Columbus's arrival on the shores of Guanahaní, has inflected European conceptions of the New World.[79]

Even Sancho Panza, who is often remembered as the paradigmatic pragmatist, cannot help but deceive himself in this regard, especially with respect to the tradition of a squire receiving the governorship of an island for his faithful service. Don Quixote first recruits Sancho by reminding him that "it was a custom much in use among the knights errant of old to make their squires the governors of islands or kingdoms that they conquered, and

---

[74] Cervantes, *The Indigenous Hidalgo Don Quixote*, 18–24.
[75] Cervantes, *The Indigenous Hidalgo Don Quixote*, 45.
[76] Cervantes, *The Indigenous Hidalgo Don Quixote*, 263.
[77] Cervantes, *The Indigenous Hidalgo Don Quixote*, 64–5.
[78] Howard Mancing, "Bendito sea Alá: A New Edition of Belianís de Grecia," *Bulletin of the Cervantes Society of America*, Vol. XXI, Issue II (2001), 113.
[79] Aladro-Font, "*Don Quijote y Cristóbal Colón: O, La sinrazón de la realidad*," 45.

I have determined that such an ancient usage shall not lapse through my fault," and in Part Two, the Duke and Duchess convince Sancho to mount the wooden steed Clavileño the Swift – and so, blindfolded, fly to the aid of the "bewitched" Countess Trifaldi – by promising him the governorship of that island.[80] After Don Quixote and Sancho successfully free Countess Trifaldi from her "enchantment" (the Countess, who is, in fact, the Duke's steward in disguise, has been cursed with a beard for abetting an affair between a princess and a knight), the Duke and Duchess arrange for Sancho's fantasy to come true, and he is made to believe that he has been appointed – similar to Esplandián's cousin Talanque, who is made king of California after the defeat of Queen Calafia – the governor of an island named, in this case, Barataria (which, again like California, is not an island at all but a landlocked town near the Duke and Duchess's residence and whose place-name would, yet again like California, be eventually applied directly to the New World in the Bayou of Barataria in the U.S. State of Louisiana).[81]

Cervantes's "subversive discourse" not only lampoons Quixote's obsession with names and his fantasy of medieval knight-errantry – as well as Sancho's fantasy of a governorship of an island – but also questions the centrality of Christianity itself to early modern Spain: "When the Spanish monarchy began its conquest and colonization of the New World, a parallel process of internal colonization was also beginning, leading eventually to the imposition of a centralized authority and state-sanctioned culture on a heterogenous population."[82] Indeed, in large part, the ideology of the *Reconquista* was transferred wholesale to the New World. As Anouar Majid succinctly puts it: "The West's minorities, whether Native Americans, enslaved Africans, Jews, or non-European, particularly Hispanic, immigrants (legal or illegal), would become indispensable for the expanding European and American, or Euro-American, sense of self after 1492, just as the Moor had been for Christian Europe up to that time."[83] The anti-Islamic rhetoric of medieval Europe, in other words, became a means of justifying the genocide of Native Americans, the enslavement of Africans, and the persecution of non-Christians in Europe and abroad.

---

[80] Cervantes, *The Indigenous Hidalgo Don Quixote,* 62, 756–7.

[81] That U.S. Forty-Niners would, with the mid-nineteenth century's famed California Gold Rush, cast California itself as the site for yet another New World crusade-pilgrimage demonstrates the extent to which California continued well into the modern era to serve as a kind of "Barataria" for European immigrants to the New World, an imagined island that promised incomprehensible wealth and power to even the most plebian.

[82] Childers, *Transnational Cervantes,* 4. On Cervantes's "subversive discourse," see James A. Parr, *Don Quixote: An Anatomy of Subversive Discourse* (Newark, DE: Juan de la Cuesta, 1988).

[83] Majid, *We Are All Moors,* 5.

Cervantes's own engagement with Islamic-Christian relations in *Quixote* is of long-standing critical debate, but recently a "scholarly consensus has emerged around the notion that Cervantes, in Part One of *Don Quixote* at least, depicts Spain's Muslim past and present Mediterranean relationships in such a way that Islam is understood as a permanent, integral part of Iberian experience."[84] Cervantes's parody of the chivalric romance tradition is also necessarily a parody of the anti-Islamism endemic to that tradition with, in particular, the figure of Cide Hamete – the fictional Muslim historian who, according to *Quixote* itself, is the author of *Don Quixote* – placed at "the heart of what eventually became the greatest classic of Spanish literature."[85] This presence of Iberia's Islamic heritage in *Quixote* functions implicitly as a critique of the internal colonization at play throughout early modern Spain in the same way that the text's engagement with European colonization – as in Sancho's musings about becoming governor of an island – subtly critiques Spain's external colonization of non-European territories, including those of the New World. Cervantes's novel, in this way, subverts the modern European colonial world-system even as its textual distribution and canonization – including in the Americas – depends upon that colonial system.

Such a contradiction makes engagement with the novel, especially with respect to its reception in non-European territories such as the New World, a fruitful exercise for investigating the contradictions endemic to European colonialism. As Hispanist Eric Clifford Graf argues, *Don Quixote* "anticipate[s] many of today's fashionable academic deconstructions of the ideological discourses that support political power": "Cervantes's worldview may be inescapably Eurocentric," he continues, "but far from reproducing an uncritical endorsement of the rise of the imperialistic, ethnocentric, and religiously conformist institution known as the early modern nation-state, [Cervantes] writes about it in dissenting and disorienting ways."[86] The novel defies placement within the strict categories of Christian/Muslim, imperial/republican, modern/medieval, colonial/anticolonial, and romance/novel, and the presence of *Don Quixote* in the New World, then, speaks both to the central role that European colonialism has played in the construction of the Americas as a geographical territory (or territories) and to the anticolonial, revolutionary response to that colonialism.

---

[84] David Thomas and John Chesworth, eds. *Christian–Muslim Relations: A Bibliographical History* (Boston, MA: Brill, 2017), 233.

[85] Thomas and Chesworth, *Christian–Muslim Relations*, 233.

[86] Eric Clifford Graf, *Cervantes and Modernity* (Lewisburg, PA: Bucknell University Press, 2007), 22.

As sociologists Immanuel Wallerstein and Aníbal Quijano have argued, "the creation of this geosocial entity, the Americas, is the constitutive act of the modern world-system," for the Americas afforded two of the three fundamental needs of the capitalist world-economy: "an expansion of the geographical size of the world in question and the development of variegated methods of labor control for different products and different zones of the world-economy."[87] The third need, meanwhile, "the creation of relatively strong state machineries in what would become the core-states of this capitalist world-economy," is, if not the primary theme of *Quixote*, at least one of the novel's central motifs.[88] As Childers puts it, thinking of Quijano's concept of "coloniality of power," "Coloniality of power was operative at all levels of sixteenth-century Spanish society, and among all groups. Although the Moriscos and *conversos* are the most obvious examples, it is important to recognize that the cultural identity of *Cristiano Viejo* peasants was also reshaped during this period, and that a vastly transformed society emerged from this process by the century's end," a transformation that *Quixote* both diagnoses and critiques.[89] The work of "decolonizing Cervantes" involves the recognition that "the Spaniards themselves were multicultural, intercultural […] to us their culture was a single whole that they imposed, denying differences, denying interculturality. However, they were denying their own reality […] [T]his just demonstrates that humanity has no other destiny than the recognition of its own diversity. Not that diversity is a product of the present because we are discussing it now, but rather because for thousands of years it has been and is today the richness of civilizations."[90]

The subversive discourse that Cervantes develops in *Don Quixote*, then, becomes a useful literary tool, especially in the remarkably diverse world of the Americas, and while the colonialist discourse that would portray colonization of the New World as a chivalric quest continues unabated well into the modern era, it is entwined with a subversive discourse that lampoons or bemoans such a contestation. This is the "dystopian New World" that Miller notices portrayed in the writings of second- and third-generation Puritans, and the ensuing chapters turn to the complicated entwining of these two seemingly contradictory discourses in canonical U.S. texts with the intention of demonstrating how the movement between colonialism and anticolonialism, between uniformity and diversity, is central to the process of U.S. national identity formation.[91]

---

[87] Quijano and Wallerstein, "Americanity as a concept," 549.
[88] For a summary of the capitalist motif in *Don Quixote*, see David Quint's introduction to James H. Montgomery's translation of *Don Quixote* (Indianapolis, IN: Hackett Publishing Company, 2009), xxx–xxxiii.
[89] Childers, *Transnational Cervantes*, 5–6.
[90] Childers, *Transnational Cervantes*, 1.
[91] Merrim, *The Spectacular City*, 84. Miller, *Errand into the Wilderness*, 9.

3

Mad Trist: American Anglo-Saxonism, James Fenimore Cooper's *Leatherstocking Tales*, and Edgar Allan Poe's Subversive Medievalism

> A curious exemplification of the power of a single book for good or harm is shown in the effects wrought by *Don Quixote* and those wrought by *Ivanhoe*. The first swept the world's admiration for the medieval chivalry silliness out of existence; and the other restored it. As far as our South is concerned, the good work done by Cervantes is pretty nearly a dead letter, so effectually has [Sir Walter] Scott's pernicious work undermined it.
>
> —Mark Twain, *Life on the Mississippi*[1]

On the title page of the proceedings of the first Constitutional Congress is an image of twelve arms – signifying the twelve British colonies – reaching to support a column, at the base of which is scrawled "Magna Carta."[2] The Magna Carta, throughout the American Revolution, played an outsized role in the Founders' thinking about how to assert their rights against an oppressive regime, and the language of the Magna Carta is invoked in a number of state constitutions, as well as in the Bill of Rights itself.[3] A charter written by the archbishop of Canterbury in 1215 to appease an assembly of barons who believed themselves to be unfairly treated by King John (1166–1216), the Magna Carta promoted neither democracy nor universal liberty: "The charter was a feudal document

---

[1] Twain, *Life on the Mississippi*, 314. Walter Scott, *Ivanhoe* (New York, NY: E.P. Dutton & Co., 1942).

[2] *Journal of the Proceedings of the Senate of the United States of America* (Philadelphia, PA: William and Thomas Bradford, 1789), accessed April 1, 2024, https://archive.org/details/journalofproceed00unit.

[3] David Starkey, *Magna Carta: The True Story Behind the Charter* (London: Hodder and Stoughton, 2015), 10–12.

and meant to protect the rights and properties of the few powerful families that topped the rigidly structured, feudal system."[4] In sixteenth- and seventeenth-century Britain, however, through what historian Anthony Musson has deemed the "Magna Carta effect" (i.e., "the appropriation of widely revered legal documents as symbolic of fundamental law"), the Magna Carta came to represent an imagined English constitution that delineated individual freedoms, such as the freedom from unlawful seizures or the right to a speedy trial, and which predated the Norman Conquest of England (1066) – itself directly connected to the various other Christian crusades of the eleventh and twelfth centuries, including the First Crusade of 1096.[5] This conception of the Magna Carta as symbolic of fundamental law was shared among British colonists, and by the eighteenth century, "[t]o an astonishing extent, the American colonists printed, distributed, invoked and formally enacted passages from Magna Carta."[6]

British colonists, including Thomas Jefferson, added to this conception the assertion that the individual liberties promoted by the Magna Carta "were legacies of the Anglo-Saxons."[7] According to this historiography, "The Normans imposed feudalism and temporarily deformed these rights, but the ancient rights were restored in Magna Carta. The constitutional battles of the seventeenth century were further examples of the English asserting their rights against tyrants. American[s] saw themselves in a continuation of this struggle to preserve the ancient rights of Englishmen against usurpers."[8] The Magna Carta existed, in the minds of eighteenth-century English reformers and English colonists alike, as a constitution that would protect an individual against a repressive regime. In turn, the colonists' interest in the Magna Carta, imagined as the restoration of a pre-Norman constitution, speaks to a vision of history directly connected to the then nascent ideology of American Anglo-Saxonism – a racial belief system, developed by eighteenth- and nineteenth-century British American intellectuals who believed individuals of English or Anglo-Saxon ancestry to be necessarily superior

---

[4] Roger L. Kemp, ed., *Documents of American Democracy: A Collection of Essential Writings* (New York, NY: McFarland & Co., 2010), 12.

[5] Anthony Musson, *Medieval Law in Context: The Growth of Legal Consciousness from Magna Carta to the Peasants' Revolt* (Manchester: Manchester University Press, 2001), 254. For more on the connections between the Norman Conquest of Britain and other Norman crusades, as well as on the relationship between crusading and pilgrimage in the Norman world, see Kathryn Hurlock and Paul Oldfield, eds., *Crusading and Pilgrimage in the Norman World* (Woodbridge: Boydell Press, 2015).

[6] Renée Lettow Lerner, "The Troublesome Inheritance of Americans in Magna Carta and Trial by Jury," in *Magna Carta and its Modern Legacy*, eds. Robert Hazell and James Melton (Cambridge: Cambridge University Press, 2015), 81.

[7] Lerner, "The Troublesome Inheritance of Americans in Magna Carta," 81.

[8] Lerner, "The Troublesome Inheritance of Americans in Magna Carta," 81.

to those of other ethnicities.[9] In his "Summary View of the Rights of British America," Jefferson refers on several occasions to "our Saxon ancestors," imagining them as an egalitarian society for which "feudal holdings were certainly altogether unknown": "Our Saxon ancestors held their lands, as they did their personal property, in absolute dominion, disencumbered with any superior, answering nearly to the nature of those possessions which the feudalists term allodial."[10] Jefferson, in fact, lobbied for the inclusion of the brothers Hengist and Horsa, who led the Angles, Saxons, and Jutes in their conquest of early medieval Britain, on the Great Seal of the United States, imagining the British colonists as those first Anglo-Saxons emigrating to – or, alternately, violently invading – Britain.[11] Of course, as much contemporary research in critical race theory has demonstrated, by framing Anglo-Saxons as "our ancestors," Jefferson implicitly withholds citizenship from others – European immigrants of non-Anglo-Saxon ancestry, Native Americans, African Americans and other non-European immigrants, all the while promoting an egalitarianism in which serfs and nobles are purportedly equal, all similarly "Saxon."[12]

Imbued with this paradoxical entwining of egalitarianism and discrimination, American Anglo-Saxonism proved useful to British colonial

---

[9] Reginald Horsman, *Race and Manifest Destiny* (Cambridge, MA: Harvard University Press, 1981), 1–2.

[10] Thomas Jefferson, *A Summary View of the Rights of British Americans* (Brooklyn, NY: Historical Printing Club, 1892), 27.

[11] Charles Adiel Lewis Totten, *The Seal of History, Vol. I* (New Haven, CT: The Our Race Publishing Co., 1897), 26; and note the overt American Anglo-Saxonism in Totten's discussion of Hengist and Horsa.

[12] For more on the term "Anglo-Saxon" and its historical and contemporary implications, see Erik Wade and Mary Rambaran-Olm, "What's in a Name? The Past and Present Racism in 'Anglo-Saxon' Studies?" *Old English to 1200* (YWES), 2022: 135–53. This overtly racist American Anglo-Saxonism endures, of course, to this day. As historian Dino Buenviaje argues, "Anglo-Saxonism is crucial […] to understanding the foreign policy of the United States" throughout the twentieth and into the twenty-first century; "[d]uring the 1920s, Anglo-Saxonists lobbied to restrict immigration to the United States to northern Europeans to prevent American society from becoming diluted by immigrants from southern and eastern Europe, coinciding with the brief revival of the Ku Klux Klan," while that Anglo-Saxonism was also deployed to "justify interventions for less-than-noble reasons in Latin America and other parts of the world throughout the twentieth century […] Even today the unlikely victory of Donald Trump in the 2016 presidential election [is] tied to Anglo-Saxonism [in that] Trump courted disaffected working-class whites by promising them a way of life that they and their ancestors once knew by 'making America great again,'" Dino Buenviaje, *The Yanks Are Coming Over There: Anglo-Saxonism and American Involvement in the First World War* (Jefferson, NC: McFarland & Co., 2017), 6–7. Indeed, in a speech to the National Sheriffs' Association in February 2018, President Trump's Attorney General Jeff Sessions spoke candidly of the "Anglo-American heritage of

and, later, U.S. settler colonialism (i.e., "the outward migration of settlers from a metropolitan center to establish colonial outposts on the periphery of empire").[13] Settler colonies "are characterized by the expropriation of indigenous land," and U.S. western expansionism has regularly utilized Anglo-Saxonism to justify and romanticize that violent expropriation.[14] Moreover, the concept of settler colonialism is an important supplement to the argument, famously made by Americanist Edmund Morgan, that "slavery and liberty existed not in an oppositional or even identical relationship to one another, but in a web of contradictions, giving rise to [...] 'the American paradox of slavery and freedom, intertwined and interdependent, the rights of Englishmen supported on the wrongs of Africans.'"[15]

The medieval/modern divide is a facet of this "web of contradictions" that has bolstered both the territorial dispossession of Native Americans and the enslavement of African Americans. Paul Giles, for instance, has emphasized the extent to which nineteenth-century U.S. writers such as Ralph Waldo Emerson and Henry Wadsworth Longfellow refer to both medieval European cultures and pre-Columbian American cultures in their attempts to forge a cohesive, discrete U.S. national identity:

> Representatives of the new United States frequently tried to compensate for the catastrophic disorientation of suddenly finding themselves without history by reintegrating the English past as their own, such as we see in Washington Irving's tributes to Geoffrey Chaucer and Shakespeare in *The Sketch Book of Geoffrey Crayon, Gent.* (1819–1820) or later in Thomas Bulfinch's widely-read *The Age of Chivalry* (1858), which argued pointedly that Americans "are entitled to our full share of the stories and recollections of the land of our forefathers, down to the time of colonization thence."[16]

---

law enforcement," seeing "the office of sheriff [as] a critical part" of that heritage. Marwa Eltagouri, "Jeff Sessions spoke of the 'Anglo-American heritage of law enforcement.' Here's what that means." *Washington Post*, February 12, 2018.

[13] Dahl, *Empire of the People*, 11.
[14] Dahl, *Empire of the People*, 11.
[15] Dahl, *Empire of the People*, 12, 5. Edmund S. Morgan, *The Challenge of the American Revolution* (New York, NY: W.W. Norton Co., 1978), 172.
[16] Paul Giles, *Global Remapping of American Literature* (Princeton, NJ: Princeton University Press, 2011), 72; Irving, *The Sketch Book*, 98–100, 184, 421–5; Thomas Bulfinch, *Bulfinch's Mythology*, ed. Edward Everett Hale (New York, NY: Review of Reviews Co., 1913), 6; and note, it was Edward Everett Hale, the very same scholar who identified the reference to California in Montalvo's *Las sergas*, who compiled Bulfinch's three volumes – *The Age of Fable, or Stories of the Gods* (Boston, MA: Sanborn, Carter, Bazin and Company, 1855), *The Age of Chivalry; Or Legends of King Arthur* (Boston, MA: Crosby, Nichols, and Company, 1858),

Alongside this interest in medieval Britain, Giles maintains, was a similar interest in Native American cultures. Analyzing Henry Wadsworth Longfellow's *Song of Hiawatha* (1855), Giles writes, "To move backward through time, conjoining the era of national independence with a colonial, pre-colonial, or pre-Columbian history, was equivalent to encompassing the country spatially by superimposing a rational grid on native landscapes that had been the province of many different tribal cultures and so were not naturally susceptible to such linear designs."[17]

This blurring of medieval European cultures with pre-Columbian American cultures supported both settler colonialism's objective of downplaying indigenous claims to the given territory and a colonialist historiography according to which all cultures follow Europe's prescribed "development" from the Dark Ages into industrial capitalism.[18] It is no coincidence, then, that early nineteenth-century U.S. writers, "brooding uneasily on the nation's fractious relationship with the past," developed an American ethnonationalism that deployed the hybrid figure of the "Anglo-American" – part medieval, part modern; part European, part American – to both acclaim and delimit the possibilities of a U.S. national identity.[19] Citing Kathleen Davis's scholarship, Ligia López López has argued, moreover, that the invention of indigeneity itself can be seen as coeval with the development of the medieval/modern divide; along with monolithic terms like "feudalism," "religion," and "undeveloped," López contends, "indigeneity" is similarly connected with the medieval, while "colonizer" and "settler" are connected to the monoliths of "development," "secularity," "capitalism," and "modernity" – the implication being that settler colonialism does not simply utilize this network of binary oppositions but actively creates and propagates them.[20]

---

and *Legends of Charlemagne, or Romance of the Middle Ages* (Boston, MA: Crosby, Nichols, Lee and Company, 1862) – and gave it the moniker of *Bulfinch's Mythology*.

[17] Giles, *Global Remapping*, 77.

[18] On Eurocentrism in development studies, see Sardar, "Development and the Location of Eurocentrism," 44–62.

[19] Giles, *Global Remapping*, 70. On "Anglo-American," see Ralph Waldo Emerson, "The Anglo-American," in *The Selected Lectures of Ralph Waldo Emerson*, eds. Ronald A Bosco and Joel Myerson (Athens, GA: University of Georgia Press, 2005), 186–202.

[20] Ligia López López, *The Making of Indigeneity, Curriculum History, and the Limits of Diversity* (New York, NY: Routledge, 2018), 240n18. Also see: Shona N. Jackson, *Creole Indigeneity: Between Myth and Nation in the Caribbean* (Minneapolis, MN: University of Minnesota Press, 2012), 65; Theodore Allen, *The Invention of the White Race*, vol. 1 (New York, NY: Verso Books, 1994); Aimé Césaire, *The Discourse of Colonialism*, trans. Joan Pinkham (New York, NY: Monthly Review Press, 1972), 50.

On both sides of the Atlantic, and especially with respect to an English-language readership, the reception and adaptations of Walter Scott's *Ivanhoe* (1820) exemplify the use of the medieval/modern divide to construct ethnonationalist identities, for the novel "is not just a reconstruction of the past but a re-visioning of the past that attempts to install a more desirable future," especially one that features "virtuous flaxen-haired Saxon maidens and sturdy, blue-eyed Saxon yeomen."[21] *Ivanhoe*, one of the most widely read English-language novels of the nineteenth century, popularized this alternative history that rendered the Middle Ages as a sentimentalized epoch of honor and virtue to such an extent that Scott's reimagining has often come to stand in for the historical Middle Ages themselves. Scott did not create this alternative history *ex nihilo*; his rendering of the Middle Ages has clear antecedents in Edmund Spenser's *The Faerie Queene* (1590), Torquato Tasso's *Jerusalem Delivered* (1591), and Ludovico Ariosto's *The Frenzy of Orlando* (1532), but *Ivanhoe*'s Romantic medievalism, developed at the same time that history itself was becoming a discrete field of academic study, has, through the novel's popularity and numerous adaptations and imitations, become inextricably linked with Romantic conceptions of the historical Middle Ages themselves.[22]

The popularity of Scott's novels in the United States is difficult to overstate. It gave rise to entirely new textual distribution networks in Boston, New York, and Charleston, while a variety of "Southron reenactments of Scott appropriated the novelist's fascination with ethnic differences and with honour-based aristocratic cultures [...] and used this as an imaginative tool with which to articulate Southern distinctiveness against the background of a growing gap between Northern abolitionists and Southern slave-owners."[23] After the Civil War, meanwhile, the Northern

[21] Fay, *Romantic Medievalism*, 2; Horsman, *Race and Manifest Destiny*, 41. For more on Scott's indebtedness to the medieval romance, see Michael Alexander, *Medievalism: The Middle Ages in Modern England* (New Haven, CT: Yale University Press, 2017), 23–46, 118–36.

[22] For more on the reception history of *Ivanhoe*, see Kwame Anthony Appiah, "Race," in *Critical Terms for Literary Study*, 2nd edn, eds. Frank Lentricchia and Thomas McLaughlin (Chicago, IL: University of Chicago Press, 1995), 281. On Scott's indebtedness to medieval literature, see Jerome Mitchell, *Scott, Chaucer, and Medieval Romance: A Study in Sir Walter Scott's Indebtedness to Medieval Literature* (Lexington, KY: University of Kentucky Press, 2021). On Scott's significant role in Romanticism, see Fiona Robertson, "Romancing and Romanticism," in *The Edinburgh Companion to Sir Walter Scott*, ed. Fiona Robertson (Edinburgh: Edinburgh University Press, 2012), 93–105.

[23] Emily Todd, "Walter Scott and the Nineteenth-Century American Literary Marketplace: Antebellum Richmond Readers and the Collected Editions of the Waverley Novels," *The Papers of the Bibliographical Society of America* 93:4 (1999), 495–517. Also see: Ann Rigney, *The Afterlives of Walter Scott: Memory on the Move* (Oxford: Oxford University Press, 2012), 116.

bourgeoisie took up Scott's Romantic medievalism as a cornerstone of an "antimodernism," creating "a group of overlapping mentalities" associated with this imagined medieval past such as "[p]ale innocence, fierce conviction, physical and emotional vitality, playfulness and spontaneity, an ability to cultivate fantastic or dreamlike states of awareness, [and] an intense otherworldly asceticism."[24] Perhaps it is Henry Adams's *Education* (1907), though, that summarizes the effects of Scott's Romantic medievalism on the American cultural imaginary most succinctly as it describes how, for a young man raised in the nineteenth-century United States, history itself was "less instructive" than Scott's novels.[25]

Throughout the early nineteenth-century United States, moreover, this Romantic medievalism was combined with a pseudo-scientific racial hierarchy espousing "Teutonic greatness": the "burgeoning medievalism," historian Reginald Horsman writes, "which had its immediate origins in the late eighteenth century" blended the "gentle, Romantic medievalism" of Sir Walter Scott's novels with the "German search for racial roots" that relied upon a "new racial interpretation of Anglo-Saxon destiny."[26] This notion of Teutonic greatness, in Germany, England, and the United States throughout the early nineteenth century, was contrived via a complex, often contradictory set of pseudo-scientific, religious, and political contestations, derived in large part from late eighteenth-century German nationalism, itself coeval with German Romanticism.[27] In the United States, these twin strands merged into an American Anglo-Saxonism that was leveraged in support of the slavery of African Americans, the genocide of Native Americans, the Mexican–American War, the exploitation of non-Anglo-Saxon immigrants, anti-Semitic and patriarchal systems and ideologies, and understandings of "Gypsies, the North American Indians, [and] the negroes of St. Domingo [as] wholly incapable of civilization."[28]

Perhaps nowhere is this use of American Anglo-Saxonism to justify U.S. western expansionism more evident, at least with respect to nineteenth-century U.S. literature, than in James Fenimore Cooper's *Leatherstocking Tales* (1823–41). Referred to as "The American Scott," Cooper was an avid reader of Scott's novels and turned especially to

---

[24] Lears, *No Place of Grace*, xvi, 142.
[25] Henry Adams, *Education of Henry Adams* (Boston, MA: Massachusetts Historical Society, 1918), 301.
[26] Horsman, *Race and Manifest Destiny*, 36, 75.
[27] For more on the relationship between German Romanticism and German nationalism, see Chenxi Tang, *The Geographic Imagination of Modernity: Geography, Literature, and Philosophy in German Romanticism* (Redwood City, CA: Stanford University Press, 2008), 11.
[28] Horsman, *Race and Manifest Destiny*, 146.

Ivanhoe when writing his first novel, *Precaution* (1820). Cooper's fascination with Scott is also legible, however, in *Leatherstocking Tales*, a collection of novels that revolve around the figure of Natty Bumppo – also referred to as Deerslayer and Leatherstocking, who, as a white frontiersman raised among the Lenape, uses his resourcefulness and knowledge to survive in the wilds of the U.S.'s western frontier: "Like Scott, Cooper chooses for his novels a time in which an old order is giving way to a new one – in the *Leatherstocking Tales*, the time when the wilderness is giving way to the settlements. Like Scott's heroes, Natty Bumppo is caught between two worlds – that of the pioneer and that of the settler. Like Scott's heroes and heroines, Leatherstocking is the victim of historical progression rather than the author of it."[29]

English novelist D.H. Lawrence, in his own analysis of *Leatherstocking Tales*, argues that Cooper is concerned primarily, albeit obliquely, with death and "the collapse of the white psyche."[30] *Leatherstocking Tales*, for Lawrence, revolves around the "myth of the essential white American": "there is no physical mating for [Cooper] – only the passage and consummation into death. And this is why Deerslayer must live in peril and conflict, live by his death-dealing rifle."[31] Related to this concern with death, moreover, is the death of cultures themselves – the Mohicans in *Last of the Mohicans*, the Pawnee and the frontiersmen in *The Prairie*, the Hurons in *The Deerslayer*, and the complete erasure of African Americans from U.S. cultural history throughout Cooper's oeuvre.[32] Lawrence sees in *Leatherstocking Tales* a recognition that "the great white race in America [is] keenly disintegrating, seething back in electric decomposition,

---

[29] George Dekker, *James Fenimore Cooper: The American Scott* (New York, NY: Barnes & Noble, 1967), 20–32; David Marion Holman, *A Certain Slant of Light: Regionalism and the Form of Southern and Midwestern Fiction* (Baton Rouge, LA: Louisiana State University Press, 1995), 29.

[30] D.H. Lawrence, *Studies in Classic American Literature* (New York, NY: Thomas Seltzer, 1923), 91.

[31] Lawrence, *Studies in Classic American Literature*, 92. The second quote appears in an earlier – and quite divergent – version of the 1923 text: D.H. Lawrence, "Studies in Classic American Literature," *The English Review* 28 (1919), 205. For a summary of the complicated publication history of Lawrence's *Studies in Classic American Literature*, itself now a canonical text of American Studies, see the introductory material to D.H. Lawrence, *Studies in Classic American Literature*, eds. Ezra Greenspan, Lindeth Vasey, and John Worthen (Cambridge: Cambridge University Press, 2002).

[32] For more on the absence of African Americans in Cooper, see Appiah, "Race," 281; Martha Viehmann, "Wests, Westerns, Westerners," in *A Companion to American Literature and Culture*, ed. Paul Lauter (Hoboken, NJ: John Wiley & Sons, Inc., 2020), 394–400. On Cooper's treatment of Native Americans, see Anna Krauthammer, *The Representation of the Savage in James Fenimore Cooper and Herman Melville* (New York, NY: Peter Lang, 2008), 19–60.

back to that crisis where the old soul, the old era, perishes in the denuded frame of man, and the first throb of a new year sets in."[33] American Anglo-Saxonism, Lawrence suggests, is a cultural fantasy enacted by a society fixated upon a notion of premodern ethnic identity, and cultural productions like Cooper's *Leatherstocking Tales* reveal the sense in which, distanced from the unmodern by the medieval/modern divide, citizens of a purportedly modern nation-state like the United States imagine themselves to be severed from any imagined indigenous roots – themselves understood, following the logic of Romantic medievalism, as timeless, eternal, and "authentic."[34]

As Cooper was writing the latter volumes of *Leatherstocking Tales*, Ralph Waldo Emerson, meanwhile, was espousing a more overt form of American Anglo-Saxonism. In a series of lectures from "Permanent Traits of the English National Genius" (1835) to "The Anglo-American" (1855), Emerson, recapitulating Jefferson's Norman/Anglo-Saxon binary, depicts Americans as akin to Anglo-Saxons, understood as Herculean, masculine outdoorsmen, sharply contrasted with the Celts, whom Emerson depicts as tedious and fragile, exhibiting the "slow, sure finish" of the English.[35] In these lectures, particularly "The Anglo-American" (originally titled "The Anglo-Saxon"), Emerson depicts the prototypical American as a frontiersman, grappling with both the hardships and frenzy of western expansionism: "The wild, exuberant tone of society in California is only an exaggeration of the uniform present condition of America in the excessive attraction of the extraordinary natural wealth […] the radiation of character and manners here, the boundless America, gives opportunity as wide as the morning."[36]

Emerson's and Cooper's Anglo-Saxonism, moreover, is part of a larger movement, spanning the early nineteenth century, that portrayed the prototypical U.S. citizen as Anglo-Saxon: "The debates and speeches,"

[33] Lawrence, "Studies in Classic American Literature," 278.
[34] Fay, *Romantic Medievalism*, 8.
[35] Ralph Waldo Emerson, *The Selected Lectures of Ralph Waldo Emerson*, 190. Along with "Permanent Traits of the English National Genius" (1835) and "The Anglo-American" (1855), Emerson's Anglo-Saxon lectures include "The Genius and National Character of the Anglo-Saxon Race" (1843), which he later adapted into "Traits and Genius of the Anglo-Saxon Race" (1852) – see Ralph Waldo Emerson, *Early Lectures*, eds. Stephen E. Whicher and Robert E. Spiller (Cambridge, MA: Belknap Press, 1966), 233–52; Emerson, *Selected Lectures*, 186–202; Ralph Waldo Emerson, *The Later Lectures of Ralph Waldo Emerson, 1842–1871*, Vol. I, eds. Ronald A. Bosco and Joel Myerson (Athens, GA: University of Georgia Press, 2001), 7–18. For more on the history of Anglo-Saxonism, see Nell Irvin Painter, *The History of White People* (New York, NY: W.W. Norton, 2010), 184–90.
[36] Emerson, *The Selected Lectures*, 202.

Reginald Horsman writes, "of the early nineteenth century reveal a pervasive sense of the future destiny of the United States, but they do not have the jarring note of rampant racialism that permeates the debates of mid-century [...] By 1850 the emphasis was on the American Anglo-Saxons as a separate, innately superior people who were destined to bring good government, commercial prosperity, and Christianity to the American continents and to the world."[37] This American Anglo-Saxonism, Horsman contends, was integral to western expansionism as a whole, as it interpreted the western frontier as available specifically to Americans who either were or imagined themselves to be of Anglo-Saxon descent, and such use of a medieval figure – the Anglo-Saxon[38] – to bolster an ethnonationalist project such as western expansionism, it turns out, is a long-standing motif of modern nationalist discourses more generally.

Ethnonationalist discourses of modern European nation-states have turned repeatedly to premodernity, especially the Middle Ages, for figures and narratives that present a given nation-state in monolithic terms: this "pseudo-history," historian Patrick Geary argues, "assumes, first, that the peoples of Europe are distinct, stable and objectively identifiable social and cultural units, and that they are distinguished by language, religion, custom, and national character, which are unambiguous and immutable"; moreover, such pseudo-history – albeit with real, material consequences – suggests that "[t]hese peoples were supposedly formed either in some impossibly remote moment of prehistory, or else the process of ethnogenesis took place at some moment during the Middle Ages, but then ended for all time."[39] While Geary focuses on European nation-states, Nadia Altschul and others interested in postcolonial medievalism studies have recognized the extent to which this ethnonationalist medievalism transfers easily to other, non-European territories' nationalist discourses, especially those of territories colonized by Western European powers. In *Geographies of Philological Knowledge: Postcoloniality and the Transatlantic National Epic* (2012), for instance, Altschul illustrates how nineteenth-century Chilean grammarian Andrés Bello's rendering of the medieval Castilian epic poem *Song of El Cid* (c. 1200) counterintuitively presents the New World as both an adjunct to and an independent region from Europe.[40] That medieval European figures and narratives provide

[37] Horsman, *Race and Manifest Destiny*, 1–2.
[38] For more on the modern conception of the figure of the Anglo Saxon, including the extent to which it is a medievalism, see David Clark and Nicholas Perkins, eds., *Anglo-Saxon Culture and the Modern Imagination* (Cambridge: D.S. Brewer, 2010).
[39] Geary, *The Myth of Nations*, 11.
[40] Altschul, *Geographies of Philological Knowledge*, 136. Andrés Bello, *Obras Completas*, vol. 2 (Santiago: Impreso por Pedro G. Ramírez, 1881).

non-European modern nation-states with a unified sense of national identity speaks particularly clearly to how the medieval/modern divide is central to such ethnonationalist contestations, both in Europe and abroad. After all, such "creole medievalism" necessarily relies upon not geographical but historical contiguity with Europe – the implication being that, even if a nation-state is non-European, it still derives its history and historiography from Europe.[41]

U.S. Anglo-Saxonism exists as a clear instance of this ethnonationalist medievalism, deploying, as it does, the figure of the Anglo-Saxon to represent the prototypical U.S. citizen. Emerson, in contrasting the figure of the "Anglo-American" with the figure of the Celt, emphasizes America's superiority over Britain, all the while using a figure of medieval Europe to do so, just as Thomas Jefferson deploys the figure of the Anglo-Saxon to emphasize British America's separation from Norman England, all the while connecting the soon-to-be nation with Saxon England.[42] American Anglo-Saxonism, then, utilizes figures from European medieval history both to justify European colonization of the New World and to present the prototypical American as "unambiguous and immutable," simultaneously an indigene of premodern Europe (if not Britain) and a settler of the New World, and the ambivalent relationship that American Anglo-Saxonism maintains with Europe mirrors the ambivalent relationship that U.S. nationalist discourses maintain with polyvocal notions of national identity more generally. "Emerson," Horsman writes, "although shunning extreme racial arguments, accepted the idea of inequalities among the different races and saw particular merits in the English race. He thought of this race as 'Saxon,' but he believed it had its origin in a mixture of races and had hybrid strength."[43] American Anglo-Saxonism inherits from Europe not only an imagined medieval past but also the conception of a "sentimentalized imagining of the paternalistic medieval [...] developed in popular culture from the Romantic comprehension of the past."[44]

The central role European Romanticism plays in the development of these ethnonationalist medievalisms signifies that even the purportedly anti-European thrust of much "creole medievalism" is itself indebted to European intellectual history – or, conversely, as Altschul puts it, "the paradox of searching for a nationalist-inflected medieval studies highlights the difficulties of placing non-European medievalist engagements within global European parameters."[45] Edgar Allan Poe's medievalisms speak par-

[41] Warren, *Creole Medievalism*, xii.
[42] Thomas Jefferson, *A Summary View*, 27. Emerson, *The Selected Lectures*, 186–202.
[43] Horsman, *Race and Manifest Destiny*, 177.
[44] Fay, *Romantic Medievalism*, 2.
[45] Altschul, *Geographies of Philological Knowledge*, 26.

ticularly clearly to this ambivalence in that they are integrated into his stories and poems as cultural artifacts, and his medievalisms often function as complex explorations of the cultural fantasy that American medievalisms construct. In the short story "The Fall of the House of Usher" (1839), for instance, immediately prior to the House of Usher's collapse, a chivalric romance titled *Mad Trist* is read aloud by the unnamed narrator.[46] Invented by Poe, this story is first described as "one of [Roderick's] favourite romances," and at the point when the chivalric romance is first referenced, the narrator has gone to Roderick's bedroom to weather a powerful storm.[47] After this initial introduction, the narrator reneges and amends his earlier assertion, admitting, "I had called [the romance] a favourite of Usher's more in sad jest than in earnest; for, in truth, there is little in its uncouth and unimaginative prolixity which could have had interest for the lofty and spiritual ideality of my friend."[48] The narrator's description of the book is no idealization of the chivalric romance (which is described as "uncouth" and "unimaginative") but renders the book as simply "the only book immediately at hand," a convenient choice.[49] The narration continues:

> I had arrived at that well-known portion of the story where Ethelred, the hero of the Trist, having sought in vain for peaceable admission into the dwelling of the hermit, proceeds to make good an entrance by force. Here, it will be remembered, the words of the narrative run thus: "And Ethelred, who was by nature of a doughty heart, and who was now mighty withal, on account of the powerfulness of the wine which he had drunken, waited no longer to hold parley with the hermit, who, in sooth, was of an obstinate and maliceful turn, but, feeling the rain upon his shoulders, and fearing the rising of the tempest, uplifted his mace outright, and, with blows, made quickly room in the plankings of the door for his gauntleted hand; and now pulling therewith sturdily, he so cracked, and ripped, and tore all asunder, that the noise of the dry and hollow-sounding wood alarummed and reverberated throughout the forest."[50]

The narrator assumes the reader is familiar with this text, stating that "the words of the narrative [...] will be remembered," and so skips over any background information regarding who Ethelred is, let alone why he is attempting to gain entrance to a hermit's dwelling. Sir Launcelot – the imagined author of this imagined text – says Ethelred has "a doughty

---

[46] Poe, *Collected Tales and Poems*, 231–44.
[47] Poe, *Collected Tales and Poems*, 242.
[48] Poe, *Collected Tales and Poems*, 242.
[49] Poe, *Collected Tales and Poems*, 242.
[50] Poe, *Collected Tales and Poems*, 242–3.

heart," and Sir Launcelot's speech is clearly antiquated, with phrases like "in sooth," "gauntleted," and "alarummed," allowing Poe to foreground not only the textuality of the book but also the medieval roots of the English language. Speaking through this antiquated language, Poe reminds his nineteenth-century readers of the medieval roots of English itself, and such antiquated English allows Poe to present *Mad Trist* in decidedly ambivalent terms, as both thoroughly familiar – a narrative everyone knows – and archaic and unfamiliar.[51]

This ambivalence is mirrored by the conflation of the events recounted in *Mad Trist* – which tells of Ethelred's forceful entry into the cave of a hermit – and the collapse of the House of Usher. Concluding his reading of *Mad Trist*, the narrator "started, and for a moment, paused; for it appeared to me (although I at once concluded that my excited fancy had deceived me) – it appeared to me that, from some very remote portion of the mansion, there came, indistinctly, to my ears, what might have been, in its exact similarity of character, the echo (but a stifled and dull one certainly) of the very cracking and ripping sound which Sir Launcelot had so particularly described."[52] The world in which the narrator finds himself merges with the chivalric romance itself; the sounds of the breaking door become the sounds of Usher's disintegrating home. This synchronism between text and world intensifies as the narrator reads the chivalric romance, until he finally "leap[s] to [his] feet" and "rush[es] to the chair in which [Usher] sits." Usher says: "Not hear it! – yes, I hear it, and have heard it long-long-long many minutes, many hours, many days […] many, many days ago."[53] Time itself is rent asunder; the narrator repeatedly emphasizes the synchronicity of the reading and of the cracking, collapsing sounds of the house, and, finally, Roderick's confession at the close of the story culminates with the "many minutes, many hours, many days" that he has endured these sounds, anticipating Madeline's appearance at the bedroom door.

The narrator of "The Fall of the House of Usher" does not offer an interpretation of the anachronistic merging of the chivalric romance and the events of the story. Throughout the story, Poe dislocates Usher's house, avoiding providing either identifiable geographical or historical markers. Instead, Poe incorporates medievalized terms, figures, and texts into the

---

[51] The manner in which Poe presents the imagined medieval romance as both familiar and unfamiliar, in this sense, mirrors how psychoanalyst Sigmund Freud describes the "uncanny" [*Unheimlich*] as "familiar and agreeable" and "concealed and kept out of sight" (Sigmund Freud, *The Uncanny*, trans. David McLintock (New York, NY: Penguin Books, 2003), 123).
[52] Poe, *Collected Tales and Poems*, 243.
[53] Poe, *Collected Tales and Poems*, 243.

text, using medievalisms not as prototypes for his characters or templates for his stories but as artifacts embedded in the story itself.[54] If the medievalisms of American Anglo-Saxonism present the Middle Ages as an antecedent of the modern United States, Poe's subversive medievalisms, at least as they appear in "Fall of the House of Usher," complicate that progressive historicism, emphasizing how the medieval and modern are uncannily entwined.[55]

This uncanniness of Poe's medievalisms, moreover, is paired with a Gothic aesthetic that associates the Middle Ages specifically with morbidity and death.[56] In his short story "The Gold-Bug" (1843), for instance, an early example of detective fiction and the most popular of Poe's publications during his lifetime, Poe includes a cryptogram that, once decoded, reads:

> A good glass in the bishop's hostel in the devil's seat
> twenty-one degrees and thirteen minutes northeast and by north
> main branch seventh limb east side
> shoot from the left eye of the death's-head
> a bee line from the tree through the shot feet out.[57]

The central interpretive hurdle for William Legrand, the protagonist attempting to make sense of this cryptogram, revolves around the phrase "the bishop's hostel," which both the unnamed narrator and Legrand struggle to interpret:

> "It left me [...] in the dark," replied Legrand, "for a few days; during which I made diligent inquiry, in the neighborhood of Sullivan's Island, for any building which went by the name of the 'Bishop's Hotel'; for, of course, I dropped the obsolete word 'hostel.' Gaining no information on the subject, I was on the point of extending my sphere of search, and proceeding in a more systematic manner, when, one morning, it entered into my head, quite suddenly, that this 'Bishop's Hostel' might have some reference to an old family, of the name of Bessop, which,

---

[54] Poe's concept of "totality," which argues that texts should be self-contained, sensible in and of themselves, is a useful means, perhaps, of thinking of how he embeds the medieval within the present of the text, rather than peripheralizing it to some distant past: Edgar Allan Poe, "The Philosophy of Composition," *Essays and Reviews* (New York, NY: Library of America, 1984), 15.

[55] On the uncanny, see Freud, *The Uncanny*, 123.

[56] For more on neo-Gothic and Gothic medievalisms, see Matthews, *Medievalism: A Critical History*, 51–67. For more on Poe's Gothic aesthetic, see Benjamin Franklin Fisher, "Poe and the Gothic Tradition," in *The Cambridge Companion to Edgar Allan Poe*, ed. Kevin J. Hayes (Cambridge: Cambridge University Press, 2002), 72–91.

[57] Poe, *Collected Tales and Poems*, 67.

time out of mind, had held possession of an ancient manor-house, about four miles to the northward of the Island. I accordingly went over to the plantation, and reinstituted my inquiries among the older negroes of the place. At length one of the most aged of the women said that she had heard of such a place as Bessop's Castle, and thought that she could guide me to it, but that it was not a castle, nor a tavern, but a high rock."[58]

"Hostel," which Legrand deems "obsolete," had been revived from Middle English in 1808, along with "hostelry," by Walter Scott himself, who had likely noticed the term in Chaucer's "The House of Fame" (c. 1385) or Langland's *Piers Plowman*.[59] The term, as an antiquated form of "hotel," is often associated by mid-nineteenth-century U.S. writers with the medieval, with Washington Irving using the term in his description of the Alhambra, the palace and fortress in Granada, Spain, built by the Moors in the thirteenth and fourteenth centuries, and with Melville using the term as the title for the opening canto in *Clarel* (1876), an epic poem about a theology student's loss of faith and his travels through the Holy Land.[60] Poe's use of the term, especially juxtaposed with "bishop's" and "devil's," bespeaks a medievalized world of religiosity and antiquated English, and such medievality is further implied when Legrand discovers that "Bishop's Hostel" refers to a place called "Bessop's Castle," connecting the locale with not only the obsolete term "hostel" but also "castle," with all of its European medieval associations. The process of finding the chest of gold in "The Gold-Bug" requires that Legrand first decipher this cryptogram, then travel to "Bessop's Castle," which turns out to be the site of an ancient manor – correlating the medieval castle, in prototypical Southern Romantic medievalism fashion, with the Southern plantation.[61] Legrand must

---

[58] Poe, *Collected Tales and Poems*, 67.

[59] Walter Scott, *The Poetical Works of Walter Scott*, Vol. II (Boston, MA: Little, Brown and Company, 1857), 139, 143, 165; Geoffrey Chaucer, *The House of Fame: In Three Books* (Oxford: Clarendon Press, 1893), 42; William Langland, *The Vision of William Concerning Piers Plowman* (London: Trübner & Co., 1867), 309. The term also appears in both *Sir Gawain and the Green Knight* and *Merlin*, but neither of these texts was widely circulated in the mid-nineteenth century U.S. (Jessie Laidlay Weston, ed., *Sir Gawain and the Green Knight* (Cambridge, MA: Harvard University Press, 1900), 29; Robert de Boron, *Merlin* (Paris: Librairie de Firmin-Didot, 1886), 17).

[60] Washington Irving, *The Alhambra* (Philadelphia, PA: J.B. Lippincott and Co., 1870), 137; Herman Melville, *Clarel: A Poem and Pilgrimage in the Holy Land*, Vol. I (London: Constable and Co., 1924), 3.

[61] On the South's tendency to portray plantations as medieval castles, see Moreland, *The Medievalist Impulse in American Literature*, 43, as well as Faulkner, *Faulkner in the University*, 135.

then look through a telescope using the bearing denoted by the cryptogram to spot "death's head" (a skull) hanging from a tree branch. Finally, by dropping a weight through the left eye of that skull, Legrand finds the location of the buried treasure – once again associating this religiously tinged, medievalized cryptogram with death.[62]

Of death instincts (*Todestriebe*) Sigmund Freud says that the pleasure principle is overridden by the "compulsion to repeat" a traumatic experience – this "urge in organic life to restore an earlier state of things" amounts to a "pressure towards death [...] whose function is to assure that the organism follows its own path to death."[63] The U.S. compulsion to rehash medieval narratives and figures speaks to something like an unconscious compulsion to repeat the trauma that severs modernity from the unmodern. While James Fenimore Cooper presents this connection between the death wish and the medieval obliquely – through, for instance, the resonances between *Leatherstocking Tales* and *Ivanhoe*, especially their shared thematic concern for genocide[64] – Poe stands apart in his foregrounding of this Gothic motif of American medievalism.[65] Poe's poem "Eldorado," for instance, which was published six months before his own death and inspired by the California Gold Rush, depicts a gallant knight on a futile quest for the mythical city of gold:

> Gaily bedight,
> A gallant knight,
> In sunshine and in shadow,
> Had journeyed long,
> Singing a song,
> In search of Eldorado.
> But he grew old –

---

[62] Poe, *Collected Tales and Poems*, 67.

[63] Sigmund Freud, "Beyond the Pleasure Principle," in *On Metapsychology: the Theory of Psychoanalysis*, trans. James Strachey (New York, NY: Penguin Books, 1991), 311.

[64] On genocide in *Ivanhoe*, see Michael Ragussis, *Figures of Conversion: "The Jewish Question" and English National Identity* (Durham, NC: Duke University Press, 1995), 94–106. On the theme of genocide in *Leatherstocking Tales*, see James Morgart, "Haunted Grounds of Healing: Horrors of Normativity and Genocide in the Gothic Midwest," in *The Haunted States of America: Gothic Regionalism in Post-war American Fiction* (Cardiff: University of Wales Press, 2022), 89–118.

[65] Ingrid Fernandez, "Necro-Transcendence/Necro-Naturalism: Philosophy of Life in the Works of Ralph Waldo Emerson," in *Death Representations in Literature: Forms and Theories*, ed. Adriana Teodorescu (Newcastle upon Tyne: Cambridge Scholars Publishing, 2015), 122. For the canonical analysis of Hawthorne's medievalisms, see Charles Fiedelson, Jr., *Symbolism and American literature* (Chicago, IL: University of Chicago Press, 1953), 88.

> This knight so bold –
> And o'er his heart a shadow –
> Fell as he found
> No spot of ground
> That looked like Eldorado.
> And, as his strength
> Failed him at length,
> He met a pilgrim shadow –
> "Shadow," said he,
> "Where can it be –
> This land of Eldorado?"
> "Over the Mountains
> Of the Moon,
> Down the Valley of the Shadow,
> Ride, boldly ride,"
> The shade replied, –
> "If you seek for Eldorado!"[66]

Poe is remarkably aware of the futility of the California Gold Rush and satirizes the "search of Eldorado" as the errantry of a "gallant knight" who, though he has "gr[own] old" and lost his strength, remains as "bold" as ever. Poe presents this knight as definitely optimistic about the prospects of discovering Eldorado; he is "gaily bedight" and "singing a song" but, when his strength fails him, meets a "pilgrim shadow," who suggests that Eldorado is a fantasy. Poe, satirically in this case, confronts Manifest Destiny's "pilgrim shadow"; like Legrand being instructed to drop the weight through death's head in "The Gold-Bug," the knight in "Eldorado" is instructed by this shadow to pass through "the Valley of the Shadow," and this figure casts a pall over the western expansionist ethos, connecting the western frontier less with opportunity and wealth than with fruitless action and death.[67]

Indeed, the death instinct explored in "The Fall of the House of Usher" itself suggests, following D.H. Lawrence's reading of Poe, a relationship between American Anglo-Saxonism and what Lawrence – thinking of Freudian psychology – terms "incest-desire," exemplified by the fraught relationship between Roderick and his sister, Madeline.[68] Lawrence's discussion of Poe comes on the heels of his discussion of James Fenimore

---

[66] Poe, *Collected Tales and Poems*, 970.
[67] Stephen Innes, "Introduction: Fulfilling John Smith's Vision: Work and Labor in Early America," in *Work and Labor in Early America*, ed. Stephen Innes (Chapel Hill, NC: University of North Carolina Press, 1988), 13.
[68] Lawrence, "Studies in Classic American Literature," 289.

Cooper, and Lawrence begins his chapter on Poe by linking Cooper, Poe, and the question of race in the United States: "It seems a long way from Fenimore Cooper to Poe," Lawrence admits, "[b]ut in fact it is only a step. Leatherstocking is the last instance of the integral, progressive soul of the white man in America," while Poe, for Lawrence, explores not simply the movement "towards" death, as Cooper does, but death itself, "the process of the decomposition of the body," as well as the "living disintegration" of the psyche: "Poe shows us the first vivid, seething reduction of the psyche, the first convulsive spasm that sets-in in the human soul, when the last impulse of creative love, creative conjunction, is finished."[69] Read in this light, "The Fall of the House of Usher" becomes "lurid and melodramatic" in that it explores "a symbolic truth of what happens in the last stages of [an] inordinate love, which can recognize none of the sacred mystery of *otherness*, but must unite into unspeakable identification, oneness in death."[70] For Lawrence, Roderick's rejection of otherness – exemplified by his attachment to his sister, Madeline – is connected to a fundamental human desire for "unspeakable identification" that "aris[es] inevitably when man, through insistence of his will in one passion or aspiration, breaks the polarity of himself," and such an identification based on sameness maps onto American Anglo-Saxonism, for which the "unspeakable identification" is Northern European ancestry, understood, as Poe describes the Ushers, as an "ancient and decayed race."[71] While Cooper hints at "the collapse of the white psyche," Poe places that collapse front and center, with the rending of the House of Usher, in particular, serving as a remarkably coherent exploration of the fragility of European and Euro-American ethnonationalism.[72]

To say that unconscious desires such as the death instinct and incestuous desire are latent within American Anglo-Saxonism is, then, simply to note that American Anglo-Saxonism, as well as U.S. western expansionism and New World colonization more generally, propose political identities based on sameness, on consensus and similarity – identities that have "broken the polarity" of themselves.[73] Recognizing that the term "Anglo-Saxon" is itself a hybrid of the Angles and Saxons can be useful for

[69] Lawrence, "Studies in Classic American Literature," 278.
[70] Lawrence, "Studies in Classic American Literature," 289. Italics his own.
[71] Lawrence, "Studies in Classic American Literature," 289.
[72] Lawrence, *Studies in Classic American Literature*, 91. Notably, Poe emphasizes that "the stem of the Usher race, all time-honoured as it was, had put forth, at no period, any enduring branch; in other words, that the entire family lay in the direct line of descent, and had always, with very trifling and very temporary variation, so lain" – suggesting, following Lawrence's reading, that the Usher "race" is homogeneous and inbred (Poe, *Collected Tales and Poems*, 172).
[73] Lawrence, "Studies in Classic American Literature," 289.

unsettling such a contestation, but if we observe the way that American ethnonationalist literature tends to deploy hybridic figures, such as Natty Bumppo, in the representation of American identity, we also can see the extent to which such hybridic figurations also exclude certain figures from the American cultural imaginary. Poe's construction of a world in which the medieval appears seemingly unbidden, destroying structures of filial identity and patronage, demonstrates how the medieval can be an integral site for dismantling such ethnonationalist contestations. This dismantling, however, requires that the medieval be foregrounded, read aloud, as it were, in the present of the text, rather than reside as an extratextual template upon which a story is based or a character patterned. Poe's medievalisms, from this vantage point, make the medieval not so much a historical antecedent to the United States as an abiding cultural fantasy that speaks to Euro-Americans' uncanny and "paradoxical status of belonging [to] and estrangement [from]" both Europe and the New World.[74]

---

[74] Altschul, *Geographies of Philological Knowledge*, 16.

4

The Time Machine in the Garden: Frontier Medievalisms, Owen Wister's *The Virginian*, and Mark Twain's Apophatic America

Like American Studies scholarship throughout the late nineteenth and early twentieth centuries, which focused largely on the Civil War rather than western expansionism – with Frederick Jackson Turner's "frontier thesis" serving as the noteworthy outlier – studies of U.S. medievalism have tended to focus fixedly upon the U.S. Civil War, with much scholarship, in particular, revolving around the South's fascination with *Ivanhoe* and its "infinite progeny."[1] The medievalisms of the western frontier, meanwhile, have generated only a few essays and book-length works, none of which connect these Western medievalisms to medievalism studies' analysis of periodization and sovereignty.[2] The first of these essays, titled "The Legacy of the Middle Ages in the American Wild West" (1965), written by the medievalist Lynn White, Jr., begins with

---

[1] Cervantes, *The Indigenous Hidalgo Don Quixote*, 53. After all, Twain's critique of *Ivanhoe* (see Twain, *Life on the Mississippi*, 314) bears a strong resemblance to Cervantes's critique of the various imitations of *Amadís de Gaula* (see Cervantes, *The Indigenous Hidalgo Don Quixote*, 51–4). For more on Southern medievalisms, see Pugh, *Queer Chivalry*; Pugh and Aronstein, *United States of Medievalism*; and Todd Hagstette, *Reading William Gilmore Simms: Essays or Introduction to the Author's Canon* (Columbia, SC: University of South Carolina Press, 2017). On the medievalisms of the U.S. North, see Lears, *No Place of Grace*, 141–82. For the canonical analysis of American Studies' preoccupation with the Civil War – as well as how Turner's "Frontier Thesis" disrupted that fixation – see Henry Nash Smith, *Virgin Land: American West as Myth and Symbol* (New York, NY: Vintage, 1950), 250.

[2] On Western medievalisms, see White, "The Legacy of the Middle Ages in the American Wild West," 191–202; Weckman, *The Medieval Heritage of Mexico*; Ulph, "The Legacy of the American Wild West in Medieval Scholarship," 50–2, 88–91; and Kearney and Medrano, *Medieval Culture and the Mexican American Borderlands*. On periodization and sovereignty, see Davis, *Periodization and Sovereignty*, 1–11.

a trenchant summary of the links between medieval Christian and British colonial religious thought:

> A blind spot in the study of the history of the United States is [the] failure to recognize our detailed and massive continuity with the European Middle Ages. One reason for this is our angle of vision. The very vocal New England school of historians naturally has emphasized Puritanism as the basic stratum in our national ideology. Unfortunately, however, we have accepted at face value the Puritan's self-image as a rebel against all that the Middle Ages had stood for. But if we change our stance and look at the Reformation not from the twentieth but from the eleventh century, it appears very different: Protestantism becomes the culmination – or the *reductio ad absurdum*, depending on one's presuppositions – of the most powerful religious tendencies of the later Middle Ages: an erosion of the distinction between the "religious" and the secular life; a reaction against the institutionalization of religion; a new individuation and inwardness of piety. St. Bernard, St. Francis, William of Ockham, and Gerhard Groote are direct ancestors of Cotton Mather and Jonathon Edwards.[3]

White's essay not only emphasizes the medievalisms latent within the cultural productions of the American West but also posits a different "angle of vision" that recognizes the "detailed and massive continuity" between the United States and the Middle Ages. In response to White's essay, which eventually ventures into dubious claims about the "essential equipment" of the western frontier and its links to the European Middle Ages,[4] Americanist Owen Ulph has emphasized – utilizing a unique Western American vernacular – that the strongest bond linking medieval Europe to the American West is not Christian theology but colonization writ large:

> If the European Middle Ages left a sign on the American West more noticeable than the cold track of a lizard's ghost across forty sections of salt flats, it is not to be found in the fact that some medieval gadgets were being used, with or without improvement, by somebody, someplace, sometime later on [...] To invoke a "down-to-earth" insight such as White professed to admire in the scholarship of Walter Prescott Webb, the most fundamental aspect of historical continuity linking the

---

[3] White, "The Legacy of the Middle Ages in the American Wild West," 191. For more on the links between medieval Christianity and Puritanism, see Lynn White, Jr., "The Significance of Medieval Christianity," in *The Vitality of the Christian Tradition*, ed. G.F. Thomas (New York, NY: Harper & Collins, 1944), 87–115.

[4] White, "The Legacy of the Middle Ages in the American Wild West," 195–202.

development of the West with the European Middle Ages is ceaseless expansion through colonization and land settlement.[5]

In the only book-length work on this relationship between the American West and the European Middle Ages, Milo Kearney and Manuel Medrano respond to both White and Ulph by tracing the "medieval influences" shared by Mexican and U.S. cultures, persuasively demonstrating how the European Middle Ages afford a salient point of contact between Mexico and the United States.[6] Kearney and Medrano's work, however, does not reflect upon the "pseudo-history" that portrays the medieval as a cohesive historiographical periodization upon which modern national identities base themselves.[7] If we see the medieval as itself a modern cultural construction, the Middle Ages become yet another spatiotemporal world constructed by the modern colonial imaginary. In turn, these "frontier mediaevalisms" – White's term for the references and allusions to the European Middle Ages in representations of the U.S's western frontier – serve not so much as connections between two modern nation-states as means of framing western North America as an undeveloped region in need of European civilization and the Euro-American frontiersman as the harbinger of that "Anglo-Saxon white Christian culture."[8]

The history of the figure of the cowboy is a complicated one. Its direct antecedent is in the figure of "the *vaquero* of the high plains of mediaeval Spain."[9] As in the Americas, cattle herders in medieval Spain had to traverse large swathes of land to feed their cattle and, therefore, took to horseback for easier commute; the tradition of horse-mounted herders born from this practice – itself deeply indebted to medieval Iberia's Moorish cattle traditions, which developed technologies such as stirrups, spurs, and

---

[5] Owen Ulph, "The Legacy of the American Wild West in Medieval Scholarship," 88.

[6] Kearney and Medrano, *Medieval Culture and the Mexican American Borderlands*, 42.

[7] Geary, *Myth of Nations*, 11.

[8] White, "The Legacy of the Middle Ages in the American Wild West," 199. Dan T. Carter, *Unmasking the Klansman: The Double Life of Asa and Forrest Carter* (Athens, GA: University of Georgia Press, 2023), 312. Carter's text discusses the "double life" of Asa Carter, a Klansman from Alabama who eventually moved to Abilene, Texas, and masqueraded as a Cherokee American novelist, authoring several Western novels. As Dan T. Carter points out, Asa/Forrest Carter's life succinctly demonstrated the strong link between American racism and the cooptation of Native American land and heritage by means of western expansionism and, especially, the Western novel.

[9] White, "The Legacy of the Middle Ages in the American Wild West," 201–2. For more on this history, see Lawrence Clayton, Jim Hoy, and Jerald Underwood, *Vaqueros, Cowboys, and Buckaroos* (Austin, TX: University of Texas Press, 2001).

the solid-treed saddle – was transported wholesale to the Americas in the sixteenth century as Spanish Conquistadors brought their cattle culture across the Atlantic.[10] Over the course of the nineteenth century, this figure of western North America was adopted within American Anglo-Saxonist and U.S. western expansionist rhetoric. Jefferson's and Emerson's renderings of the American Anglo-Saxon, discussed in the previous chapter, connect the medieval figure of the Anglo-Saxon with the western frontier – with Jefferson extolling the virtues of the Saxon farmer cultivating the U.S.'s pastoral landscapes and Emerson deploying the "wild, exuberant tone of society in California" to describe the "Anglo-American."[11] James Fenimore Cooper, meanwhile, associates American Anglo-Saxons, especially in his "Anglo-American Novels," with not only the western frontier but also the medieval knight-errant itself, with Natty Bumppo, for instance, "function[ing] very much like a knight-errant," and, by the end of the nineteenth century, Owen Wister, author of the first Western novel, *The Virginian* (1902), would declare that "[i]n personal daring and in skill as to the horse, the knight and the cowboy are nothing but the same Saxon of different environments," effectively erasing the Spanish and Moorish roots of this figure, not to mention Native American territorial claims to western North America.[12]

The Virginian, in fact, incorporates this understanding of the cowboy into its narrative, describing the Virginian as an "unrewarded knight," honorable and humble, and willing to risk his life for any would-be damsel in distress.[13] In the first description of the Virginian, the narrator of Wister's novel, presenting himself as a classic tenderfoot arriving by train in Medicine Bow, Wyoming, recounts watching several cowboys attempt in vain to rein in a disobedient horse "rapid of limb" with an "undistracted eye."[14] The image bears a resemblance to the opening chapters of Mark Twain's semi-autobiographical travel book, *Roughing It* (1872), in which the narrator begins his story by recounting his trip by stagecoach westward along the Overland Trail.[15] Twain's narrator, in those early chapters, portrays himself as a naive tenderfoot, unsure of the rules of the frontier and laden with an imagination full of childish dreams of "Indians, deserts

---

[10] See Charles Julian Bishko, "The Peninsular Background of Latin American Cattle Ranching," *The Hispanic American Historical Review* 32:4 (November 1952), 491–515.

[11] Emerson, *The Selected Lectures*, 202. Jefferson, *A Summary View of the Rights of British Americans*, 27.

[12] Verhoevan, *James Fenimore Cooper*, 84; Wister, "The Evolution of the Cow-Puncher," 606.

[13] Owen Wister, *The Virginian* (New York, NY: Macmillan Co., 1902), 119.

[14] Wister, *The Virginian*, 1.

[15] Mark Twain, *Roughing It* (New York, NY: Signet Classics, 2008).

and sand bars."[16] And *Roughing It*, like Wister's novel, follows the narrator's transformation from an innocent tyro to a veteran of the western frontier, familiar with its lingo and customs. Both texts, moreover, superimpose medieval Europe onto those western landscapes, with Twain's narrator comparing the walls of Echo Canyon to the turrets of "mediaeval castles," while Wister, by his own account, models the Virginian after a knight-errant.[17]

The narrator's description of the Virginian, moreover, sexualizes the cowboy, highlighting the undulations of his muscles and connecting him with the phallic images of both a snake and rope. After several cowboys attempt to rein in the disobedient horse, the narrator "notice[s] a man [...] on the high gate of the corral, looking on, [who] now climbed down with the undulations of a tiger, smooth and easy, as if his muscles flowed beneath his skin [...] I did not see his arm lift or move [...] but like a sudden snake I saw the noose go out its length and fall true; and the thing was done."[18] This eroticization continues in the second description: after the narrator, in prototypical tenderfoot fashion, loses his luggage and becomes enthralled with the local argot of Medicine Bow, he sees "[l]ounging there at ease against the wall [...] a slim young giant, more beautiful than pictures. His broad, soft hat was pushed back; a loose-knotted, dull-scarlet handkerchief sagged from his throat; and one casual thumb was hooked in the cartridge-belt that slanted across his hips."[19] The image resembles Walt Whitman's portrait, featured on the frontispiece of the first edition of *Leaves of Grass* (1855) – the soft-rimmed, tipped cap; leaning, loafing at his ease – but the Virginian keeps, in lieu of an enlarged, "lapped" phallus, a holstered pistol at his hip.[20] This initial depiction of the Virginian evinces, in other words, the homoerotic love that Leslie Fiedler has described, thinking especially of *Moby Dick* (1851) and *Huckleberry Finn* (1884), as a consistent theme of canonical U.S. novels.[21] For Fiedler, "the basic pattern of our classic American novels involves a homoerotic

---

[16] For more on this reading of *Roughing It*, see Henry Nash Smith, *The Development of a Writer* (New York, NY: Atheneum, 1967), 52–70.

[17] Twain, *Roughing It*, 48.

[18] Wister, *The Virginian*, 2.

[19] Wister, *The Virginian*, 4.

[20] Whitman "had the representation of his own lapped penis enlarged in successive versions of the frontispiece," according to Matt Miller, *College of Myself: Walt Whitman and the Making of Leaves of Grass* (Lincoln, NE: University of Nebraska, 2010), 75.

[21] Leslie Fiedler, "'Come Back to the Raft Ag'in, Huck Honey!'" *Partisan Review* 15:6 (June 1948): 664–71.

relationship between a white man (or boy) and a colored man."[22] In the case of *The Virginian*, it is the love between the mestizo figure of the *vaquero*-cowboy and the white tenderfoot narrator – a romance set not on the High Seas or the Mississippi River but the western frontier.[23]

Indeed, the connection between the chivalric knight and the Virginian adds another element to Fiedler's homoerotic American topos: the homoerotic love between men featured in much canonical U.S. literature is not only interracial but also transhistorical. With respect to the Ishmael-Queequeg relationship, for instance, in a chapter titled "Knights and Squires," set shortly after the Pequod has set sail, Ishmael explains how Starbuck "selected [Queequeg] for his squire," and overtly compares the act of harpooning to a medieval jousting match.[24] Jim, meanwhile, "becomes for Tom," by the conclusion of *Huckleberry Finn*, "'the hero of a historical romance, a peer of the Man in the Iron Mask or the Count of Monte Cristo,' complete with a coat of arms because 'all the nobility' has one."[25] The association between nonwhite persons and the European Middle Ages reveals the extent to which these homoerotic American figurations are grappling with not only the possibility of love across races and within genders – as well as of a multiracial, "non-patriarchal" national identity[26] – but also with the extent to which the United States exists as an unlikely amalgam of the modern and the medieval, associating nonwhite individuals specifically with the unmodern – yet another instance of how European historical periodizing schema are integrated within the "web of contradictions" endemic to both American Anglo-Saxonism and the modern European colonial world-system more generally.[27]

---

[22] The quote is from Charles B. Harris's introduction to Fiedler's *Love and Death in the American Novel* (Dublin: Dalkey Archive Press, 1960), vi. Herman Melville, *Moby Dick* (Boston, MA: St. Botolph Society, 1892); Mark Twain, *The Adventures of Huckleberry Finn* (New York, NY: Harber & Brothers Publishers, 1904).

[23] Fiedler, "'Come Back to the Raft Ag'in, Huck Honey!'" 664–71.

[24] *Moby Dick*, 115.

[25] Moreland, *The Medievalist Impulse in American Literature*, 68.

[26] Prem Kumari Srivastava, *Leslie Fiedler: Critic, Provocateur, Pop Culture Guru* (Jefferson, NC: McFarland & Co., Inc., 2014), 193. On the relationship between homoeroticism and "non-patriarchal family metaphors" in Fiedlerian discourse, see Srivastava, *Leslie Fiedler*, 171–94.

[27] Morgan, *The Challenge of the American Revolution*, 172. Amy Kaplan, in "Manifest Domesticity" (1998), argues that the sharp separation of spheres between men and women in nineteenth-century America is rhetorically constructed in U.S. cultural productions. She posits that this separation leaves intact the structural opposition of the domestic versus the foreign. Kaplan's analysis highlights how domesticity unites men and women in a national domain while generating notions of the foreign against which the nation is imagined as home (Kaplan, "Manifest Domesticity," *American Literature* 70:3 (1998), 581–2). Kaplan recalibrates the relationship between gender discourses and Manifest Destiny, showing how it

The association between the Anglo-American cowboy and the U.S. western frontier, after all, functions to eschew the multiculturalism of western North America. The United States that Frederick Jackson Turner saw developing in the final decade of the nineteenth century was distinguished not so much by a coherent social structure but by a "geographic sectionalism," characterized by its heterogeneity, and such a conception of U.S. culture has been more fully developed by scholars in the fields of Chicana/o Studies, African American Studies, Native American Studies and other interdisciplinary ethnic studies fields concerned with the central role that non-European and non-Anglophone cultural productions play in U.S. cultural history.[28] In *Borderlands/La Frontera: The New Mestiza* (1987), for instance, cultural theorist Gloria Anzaldúa focuses on the U.S.-Mexico borderlands as the site of a "border culture," and she sees this border culture as producing a "new mestiza consciousness" that interprets culture itself as always already a "crosspollenization" of ethnicities, languages, habitats, and cultural productions.[29] The *corrido*, a narrative song or poem particularly popular during the Mexican Civil War (1910–20), affords a poignant primary text for Anzaldúa, for U.S. western expansionism looks remarkably different from the perspective of a Mexican-American ranchero than it does to a Texas Ranger.[30] For our purposes, the *corrido* form is of interest, moreover, because it is modelled overtly after the medieval Iberian romance ballad: "the corrido is composed of a certain number of verses of octosyllabic lines," writes Luis Weckmann, "in other words, its

---

separates not only men from women but also Anglo-Saxon U.S. citizens from other races and ethnicities: "[Sarah Josepha] Hale's writing makes race central to woman's sphere by excluding nonwhites from domestic nationalism and seeing domesticity as an innate characteristic of the Anglo-Saxon race" (597). Kaplan's argument, in other words, explores the intersectionality of Manifest Destiny, gender, and race, demonstrating how racial categories distinguish between citizens and noncitizens, and overlaying a racialized citizen/foreigner distinction onto the gendered private/public spheres. Attention to American medievalisms reveals another function of this "manifest domesticity": the separation of the medieval from the modern. The frontier's association with Anglo-Saxons constructs a temporal divide, associating the United States with modernity and the foreign with medieval Europe. Hale's claim that "The Anglo-Saxon peoples [...] represent home-life" excludes nonwhites from domestic nationalism and reconstructs medieval history in light of modern gender and racial norms (Sarah Josepha Hale, *Manners: Happy Homes and Good Society All the Year Round* (Boston, MA: Lee and Shepard, 1889), 6). Manifest Destiny (and manifest domesticity), as a subset of European colonialist discourse, reifies these ideologies, consolidating them into narratives that justify western expansionism.

[28] Michael C. Steiner, "The Significance of Turner's Sectional Thesis," *Western Historical Quarterly* 10:4 (1979), 437–66.

[29] Anzaldúa, *Borderlands/La Frontera*, 3, 179.

[30] See Paredes, *"With His Pistol in His Hand"*, for more on the *corrido* tradition.

metric structure is identical to that of the Andalusian romance-corrido."[31] Indeed, as Weckmann goes on to say:

> [T]he corrido [...] is a direct descendant – both musically and in a literary sense – of the *romance*, or ballad, of the Iberian Peninsula. Its origins go back to the so-called Andalusian "romance-corrido," influenced by Arabic, which spread all over New Spain with the exception of Yucatán. It is a chiefly narrative lyrical form, which in musical phrases recounts events of general interest; its melodies recall its Andalusian origin and give it a profoundly expressive character, as the revolutionary corridos of the upper Nazas basin demonstrate.[32]

The *corrido*, which is generally set within the U.S.–Mexico borderlands, speaks not only to the ethnic and linguistic cross-pollenizations endemic to the borderlands region, but also to the historiographical cross-pollenization that such contact zones engender.[33] The *corrido* is simultaneously medieval and modern, American and Mexican, and such a rejection of colonialist monosemy is, as Anzaldúa argues, emblematic of "the consciousness of the Borderlands":

> We all of us find ourselves in the position of being simultaneously both insider and outsider. The Spanish word "nosotras" means "us." I see this word with a slash (rajadura) between "nos" (us) and "otras" (others), and use it to theorize my identity narrative of "nos/otras." La rajadura gives us a third point of view, a perspective from the cracks and a way to reconfigure ourselves as subjects outside binary oppositions, outside existing dominant relations. By disrupting binary oppositions that reinforce relations of subordination and dominance, nos/otras suggests a position of being simultaneously insider/outsider, internal/external exile.[34]

Even Anzaldúa's notion that the consciousness of the Borderlands is "a new mestiza consciousness," then, can be critiqued for its "deification of newness" endemic to discourses that reify the medieval/modern divide.[35] The consciousness of the borderlands complicates notions of insider/outsider and internal/external, as well as conceptions of new/old and modern/

---

[31] Weckmann, *The Medieval Heritage of Mexico*, 521.
[32] Weckmann, *The Medieval Heritage of Mexico*, 521–2.
[33] For more on the concept of the "contact zone," see Mary Louise Pratt, "Arts of the Contact Zone," *Profession* (1991), 33–40.
[34] Gloria Anzaldúa, *Light in the Dark/Luz en lo Oscuro: Rewriting Identity, Spirituality, Reality* (Raleigh, NC: Duke University Press, 2015), 52.
[35] On the "deification of newness," see Quijano and Wallerstein, "Americanity as a Concept," 551.

unmodern, and that a cultural production like the *corrido* is simultaneously a reimagining of the medieval ballad and an early version of the Western "cowboy ballad" bespeaks this complexity with particular clarity.[36]

The "new mestiza consciousness," in fact, especially with medieval Iberia in mind, is not all that "new."[37] The history of the *mestizo* has clear antecedents in European medieval societies, especially the Hispano-Roman and Teutonic cultures of sixth-century Iberia: "The historical, cultural and political origins of racism can be traced to the Teutonic tribes in the sixth century in Spain. It is these tribes that establish a cultural and social foundation of racism that will continue, through the centuries, not only in Spain, but throughout Europe. These tribes bring into the Latin territory the concept of Aryanism, a warrior spirit and a barbarous culture," and this medieval Iberian conception of racism was used, during the colonization of the New World, to portray non-Europeans, especially Native Americans and African Americans, as allied with Moors, Gypsies, and Africans.[38] Medieval Iberia, like the U.S. western frontier, was a complex territory: "Medieval Iberia was a fascinating tapestry of linguistic varieties, with contact among them performing an enriching function, while at the same time generating tensions in terms of prestige, demographic movement, and competing usage."[39] Basque, Old Castilian, Brittonic, Scythian, Romani, Vandalic, Old Occitan, Sephardi Hebrew, Andalusian Arabic – the sheer quantity of languages spoken throughout medieval Iberia illustrates the extent to which linguistic contact and change played a central role in the region. Moreover, one of the more significant shifts in this tapestry of languages was the contact between Latin and Romance languages like Old Catalan, and the notion that Romance languages originated with Latin presumes that Latin itself existed as a discrete language after the fall of the Roman Empire, when Latin was in large part "an invention of the Carolingian Renaissance":[40]

> Prior to the eighth century in France and the end of the eleventh century in Spain (when Roman liturgy replaced the Visigothic) [...] no conscious distinction was drawn between Latin and Romance. Latin was regarded as the written mode of the spoken vernacular of each

---

[36] Paredes, *"With His Pistol in His Hand"*, 16.

[37] Anzaldúa, *Light in the Dark*, 52.

[38] Arnoldo C. Vento, *Mestizo: The History, Culture, and Politics of the Mexican and the Chicano* (New York, NY: University Press, 1998), 43.

[39] Ivy A. Corfis and Ray Harris-Northall, "Introduction," in *Medieval Iberia*, eds. Ivy A. Corfis and Ray Harris-Northall (London: Tamesis, 2007), xv.

[40] Thomas D. Cravens, "Perils of Speaking of *Orígenes de la Lengua*," in *Medieval Iberia*, eds. Ivy A Corfis and Ray Harris-Northall (London: Tamesis, 2007), 157.

locale. Accordingly, the literate, when reading, gave each Latin word its vernacular pronunciation, much as English speakers today articulate *knight* as [nájt] or as Francophones reproduce *doigt* 'finger' as [dwá].[41]

Prior to the eleventh century, Latin did not even exist in Iberia as a discrete language – at least as we understand that term today – but as "the written mode of the spoken vernacular."[42] Instead, multilingualism in the Iberian Peninsula was so prevalent that "the problem of identifying separate languages [...] remains acute":

> We can be sure that by the fourteenth century there were several related, but thought to be distinct, Romance languages in the Peninsula; at least Portuguese, Galician, Castilian, Aragonese and Catalan, which were distinguished conceptually not only from each other but also from Medieval Latin, which continued to be used as a separate entity. A case could be made for others, although the identification of Leonese, Asturian, Andaluz and other candidates as medieval languages rather than dialects tends to have depended on the modern political axes [...] These fragmentation processes were as politically loaded in the thirteenth and fourteenth centuries as they are now.[43]

The territory of Iberia itself is incoherent until at least the conclusion of the *Reconquista*, and the shifting frontiers throughout the peninsula – from the Fall of Rome to the Moorish conquest and, eventually, the Fall of Granada – illustrate that we only in retrospect can think of medieval Iberia as a coherent spatiotemporal region.

Something similar could be said about the nineteenth-century American West. The closing of the frontier which Turner noticed is not only a spatial but also a temporal contestation; it proclaims not only the end of western expansionism but also the end of a historiography that depends upon colonial expansion.[44] With the closure of the frontier, the United States could no longer frame the western frontier as the proper site for "a quest, a pilgrimage, a crusade, or some other form of expedition" but became, as Turner noted, a medley of languages and histories, of competing and overlapping

---

[41] Roger Wright, *Late Latin and Early Romance in Spain and Carolingian France* (Leeds: Francis Cairns, 1982), 104.
[42] Wright, *Late Latin and Early Romance*, 104.
[43] Roger Wright, "Bilingualism and diglossia in Medieval Iberia (350–1350)," in *A Comparative History of Literatures in the Iberian Peninsula*, eds. Fernando Cabo Aseguinolaza et al. (Philadelphia, PA: John Benjamins Publishing, 2010), 335.
[44] Turner, "The Significance of the Frontier," 220–1.

regions, sometimes in accord, sometimes in conflict.[45] The medievalisms of the Mexican–American borderlands, in this sense, illustrate not only a shared medieval past yoking Mexican and U.S. cultures but also the coevality of frontiers and anachronous temporalities themselves. U.S. medievalisms puncture chronological conceptions of time just as they puncture fixed conceptions of space and can, therefore, be seen as responses to the colonial preoccupation both with historical narratives of progress and decay and with geographical representations – such as the colonialist conception of space undergirding the ideology of western expansionism – that prioritize political sovereignty. In the U.S. cultural imaginary, the literary figure of the time machine, which arose also in the late nineteenth century, offers an escape hatch from these univocal, chronological temporalities and fixed, monosemous conceptions of space.[46]

On the morning of July 27, 1844, Nathaniel Hawthorne jotted down some notes as he sat in the woods outside of Concord, Massachusetts, not far from where Henry David Thoreau, a year later, would take up residence on the banks of Walden Pond:

> There is the tinkling of a cow-bell, a noise how peevishly dissonant if close at hand, but even musical now. But, hark! There is the whistle of the locomotive, – the long shriek, harsh above all other harshness, for the space of a mile cannot mollify it into harmony. It tells a story of busy men, citizens, from the hot street, who have come to spend a day in a country village, – men of business, – in short, of all unquietness; and no wonder that it gives such a startling shriek, since it brings the noisy world into the midst of our slumbrous peace.[47]

American Studies scholar Leo Marx, in *Machine in the Garden* (1964), reflecting on this passage, declared the seemingly innocuous moment to be of world-transformative import:

> [T]he fact is that nothing quite like the event announced by the train in the woods had occurred before. A sense of history as an unpredictable, irreversible sequence of unique events makes itself felt even in Hawthorne's notes. In spite of the resemblance between the train and the

---

[45] Jennifer Robin Goodman, *Chivalry and Exploration, 1298–1603* (Woodbridge: Boydell, 1998), 54. Turner, "The Significance of the Frontier," 220–7.

[46] On western expansionism's conception of political sovereignty, as well as its relationship to the expansion of slavery into the West, see Michael A. Morrison, *Slavery and the American West: The Eclipse of Manifest Destiny* (Chapel Hill, NC: University of North Carolina Press, 1997), 33.

[47] Julian Hawthorne, *Nathanial Hawthorne and his Wife: A Biography*, Vol. I (London: Chatto and Windus, 1885), 503.

archetypal city of Western literature, the "little event" creates an unprecedented situation. For in the stock contrast between city and country each had been assumed to occupy a more or less fixed location in space: the country here, the city there. But in 1844 the sound of a train in the Concord woods implies a radical change in the conventional pattern. Now the great world is invading the land, transforming the sensory texture of rural life – the way it looks and sounds – and threatening, in fact, to impose a new and more complete dominion over it.[48]

Leo Marx's notion that these idyllic representations of the western frontier imply a necessity to modernize that landscape presumes not only a vehicle of geographic transport – for him, thinking of Hawthorne's journal entry, exemplified by the train – but also a machine that creates "a sense of history as an unpredictable, irreversible sequence of unique events," and it is not surprising that the historical romance burgeoned alongside the railroad – the vehicle of geographic transport affording the traveler with the leisure time to travel back in history and, eventually, with science fiction, forward into the future.[49]

It is of general knowledge that the proliferation of railways in the mid-nineteenth century accompanied both a rapid increase in literacy rates and the development of a standardized system of time, giving rise to Greenwich Mean Time; but an implication of these links between literacy, the homogenization of time and the railroad is that the presence of the train in the western frontier runs parallel to the development of both a "book culture" and "leisure time" (and its opposite, "labor time"), with the literary figure of the time machine concisely speaking to this interplay between industrialization and literacy.[50] Preceding both H.G. Wells's "The Chronic Argonauts" (1887) and *The Time Machine* (1895), "The

---

[48] Leo Marx, *The Machine in the Garden: Technology and the Pastoral Ideal in America* (Oxford: Oxford University Press, 1964/2000), 31–2.

[49] Marx, *The Machine in the Garden*, 31–2. For more on connections between reading and railroad travel, see Michael Freeman, *Railways and the Victorian Imagination* (New Haven, CT: Yale University Press, 1999), 86.

[50] On railroads and the creation of a universal system of time (as well as its relationship to gender), see Patricia Murphy, *Time is of the Essence: Temporality, Gender, and the New Woman* (Albany, NY: State University of New York Press, 2001), 13. On literacy and railroad travel, see Wolfgang Schivelbusch, *The Railway Journey: the Industrialization of Time and Space in the Nineteenth Century* (Berkeley, CA: University of California Press, 1977), 69; Ronald J. Zboray, "The Railroad, the Community, and the Book," *Southwestern Review* 71:4 (Autumn 1986): 474–87. On the nineteenth century's "book culture," see David Kergel, *Digital Learning in Motion: From Book Culture to the Digital Age* (New York, NY: Routledge, 2021). On "leisure time" and "labor time," see Juliet B. Schor, *The Overworked American: The Unexpected Decline of Leisure* (New York, NY: Basic Books, 1992), 5, 49.

Clock that Went Backward" (1881), a short story by the American editor and author Edward Page Mitchell, includes the first instance in European or Euro-American literature of a machine being used to literally travel through time.[51] As the title suggests, the short story's plot revolves around a clock that, when wound backwards, reverses time; and such a literary device speaks to the ways in which the invention of Greenwich Mean Time was transforming how time itself, like space, was being reconceived at the close of the nineteenth century. As postmodern philosopher Michel Foucault, in his now famous essay on "heterotopias," notes:

> The great obsession of the nineteenth century was, as we know, history: with its themes of development and of suspension, of crisis, and cycle, themes of the ever-accumulating past, with its great preponderance of dead men and the menacing glaciation of the world. The nineteenth century found its essential mythological resources in the second principle of thermodynamics [...] The present epoch will perhaps be above all the epoch of space. We are in the epoch of simultaneity: we are in the epoch of juxtaposition, the epoch of the near and far, of the side-by-side, of the dispersed. We are at a moment, I believe, when our experience of the world is less that of a long life developing through time than that of a network that connects points and intersects with its own skein.[52]

The nineteenth century's fixation upon time and the twentieth century's fixation upon space, however, are distinguishable only by degrees.[53] The nineteenth-century themes of "development and of suspension, of crisis, and cycle" and the twentieth-century themes of "juxtaposition," "of the near and far, of the side-by-side, of the dispersed" are both enthralled, somewhat counterintuitively, with the notion that certain translations of Foucault's *Des espaces autres* (1967) have relegated to the Middle Ages – namely, "emplacement":

> One could say, by way of retracing this history of space very roughly, that in the Middle Ages there was a hierarchic ensemble of places:

---

[51] H.G. Wells, "The Chronic Argonauts," *The Scientific Romances of H.G. Wells* (London: Gollancz, 1933), 1–31; H.G. Wells, *The Time Machine* (London: William Heinemann, 1895); Edward Page Mitchell, "The Clock that Went Backwards," *The New York Sun* (September 18, 1881). For more on this history, see M. Keith Booker and Anne-Marie Thomas, *The Science Fiction Handbook* (Oxford: Wiley-Blackwell, 2009), 15.

[52] Michel Foucault, "Of Other Spaces," trans. Jay Miskowiec, *Diacritics* 16:1 (1986), 22.

[53] For more on this reading of Foucault, see Sebastian Dorsch, "Space/Time Practices and the Production of Space and Time," *Historical Social Research* 38:3 (2013), 7–21.

sacred places and profane places, protected places and open, exposed places; urban places and rural places (all these concern the real life of men). In cosmological theory, there were the supercelestial places as opposed to the celestial, and the celestial place was in its turn opposed to the terrestrial place. There were places where things had been put because they had been violently displaced, and then on the contrary places where things found their natural ground and stability. It was this complete hierarchy, this opposition, this intersection of places that constituted what could very roughly be called medieval space: the space of emplacement.[54]

The term that Jay Miskowiec translates as "emplacement," however, is not the French *emplacement* but *localisation*. "Foucault's terms are 'localisation,' 'étendue,' and 'emplacement,' which Miskowiec translated, successively, as 'emplacement,' 'extension,' and 'site' and Robert Hurley gave as 'localization,' 'extension,' and 'emplacement.' Miskowiec's 'emplacement for *localisation*,' when *emplacement* is Foucault's third term, creates an obvious conundrum. His 'site,' however, for Foucault's *emplacement* is far superior to the use of the all too false-friendly 'emplacement.'"[55] As Tony McHugh surmises, "The term 'emplacement' (*l'emplacement*) in French has a certain plasticity that does not translate well into English. *L'emplacement* refers to site, but also a relational sense involving location and support. In other words, 'emplacement' has a sense of both space and place: 'space' being more abstract than 'place'; 'place' being more tangible than 'space.'"[56]

Notwithstanding this translational conundrum, Foucault's assertion that medieval space was one of "emplacement" ("*localisation*") can be made only from the context of modern notions of space, place, and time. Foucault's own historicity, replete with a modern, purportedly non-hierarchical conception of space and time, allows him to imagine medieval space as hierarchical – an assertion that would be tautological to one operating from within a (so-called) "hierarchic ensemble" of space and time.[57] The advent of Universal Time is also, after all, the advent of its antithesis – discrete, localized time – and it makes sense, then, that the advent of the concept of time travel in Western literature is synchronous with the closure of the U.S.'s western

---

[54] Michel Foucault, "Of Other Spaces," trans. Jay Miskowiec, *Diacritics* 16:1 (1986), 22.
[55] Robert Harvey, *Sharing Common Ground: A Space for Ethics* (New York, NY: Bloomsbury, 2017), 105.
[56] Tony McHugh, "Barceloneta as Heterotopic Mirror: A Place of Different Spaces," in *Intercultural Mirrors: Dynamic Reconstruction of Identity*, eds. Marie-Claire Patron and Julia Kraven (Boston, MA: Brill, 2019), 145.
[57] Foucault, "Of Other Spaces," 22.

frontier.[58] The construction and simultaneous erasure of an undeveloped, "virgin land" necessitates a recognition of the limitations of universalizing conceptions of space and time, and no work speaks to the conflation of time travel and the closure of the frontier more directly than does Mark Twain's *A Connecticut Yankee in King Arthur's Court* (1889), which not only includes, at the novel's epicenter, a modern man's arrival in the Middle Ages but also regularly alludes to knights-errant as "cow-boys" ("Don't forget the cowboys, Sandy." "Cow-boys?" "Yes; the knights, you know.").[59]

Often deemed the first work of science fiction, *Connecticut Yankee* overtly explores themes of geographic displacement and historical anachronism; the novel begins with a preamble by a narrator who has, while touring Warwick Castle, happened upon a "curious stranger" who asks the narrator, "as one might speak of the weather, [...] 'You know about transmigration of souls; do you know about transposition of epochs – and bodies?'"[60] This "curious stranger," after four "persuaders" of "hot Scotch whisky," recounts his story, beginning: "I am an American. I was born and reared in Hartford, in the state of Connecticut – anyway, just over the river, in the country."[61] The fact that Hank Morgan is from Connecticut is of special import, for it was this state that more than any other "fueled western expansion":

> the broader industrial activity seen in Connecticut at the end of the 19th century directly fueled western expansion. Connecticut supplied guns, of course. But it also provided products, funding, ideas, and its people to develop what Easterners viewed as a frontier. [...] Connecticut was involved in the exploration, economic growth, and settlement of the West in myriad ways. These include the story of Connecticut's Western Reserve, Catherine Beecher's training of teachers and Cornwall's training of missionaries to help 'civilize' the new lands, partici-

[58] Turner, "The Significance of the Frontier in American History," 199–227.

[59] Smith, *Virgin Land*, 250. Mark Twain, *Connecticut Yankee in King Arthur's Court* (New York, NY: Harper and Brothers, 1901), 109.

[60] Twain, *Connecticut Yankee*, 2. While Twain's novel is often deemed the first work of science fiction, recent research in medieval studies, taking up works such as the Voynich Manuscript (c. 1404–38) or the story of Eilmer, an eleventh-century monk who, inspired by the myth of Icarus, endeavored to construct a pair of wings and fly from the roof of Malmesbury Abbey, emphasizes how "the genre could actually be considered hundreds of years old" (Carl Kears, "Science Fiction was Around in Medieval Times – here's what it looked like," September 12, 2018. Accessed March 13, 2024, https://www.manchester.ac.uk/discover/news/science-fiction-medieval-times/). For more, see Carl Kears and James Paz, eds., *Medieval Science Fiction* (London: Centre for Late Antique and Medieval Studies/Boydell & Brewer, 2016).

[61] Twain, *Connecticut Yankee*, 5.

pation in the Gold Rush, the flooding of communities to secure urban water supplies, and even the management of public lands, specifically forest and parks.[62]

Particularly important in this regard was the Connecticut Western Reserve in northeastern Ohio, "a large area of settlement that attracted like-minded peoples. The reserve had its origins in the many land schemes of the 1790s, when the state of Connecticut sold its reservation in the West to the Connecticut Land Company. In 1796 a surveying party under Moses Cleveland laid out at the mouth of the Cuyahoga River a town that would bear his name."[63] By connecting Morgan to Connecticut, in other words, Twain connects his protagonist with a western expansionist ethos that is only strengthened when we realize that Twain was, by the late 1880s, almost synonymous in the U.S. cultural imaginary with the burgeoning American West.[64]

This connection to western expansionism is, moreover, supplemented by *Connecticut Yankee*'s focus on anachronism and the complexity of historical narration. The common observation that Twain's novels and short stories, including *Connecticut Yankee*, tend to end abruptly is not so much a shortcoming as illustrative of Twain's reluctance to participate in the "utopian conclusion" deployed in historical romances such as *Ivanhoe*: "The instability of this utopian conclusion [...] comports with the literary realists' resistance to happy endings. Though *A Connecticut Yankee* scarcely could be identified as 'realistic' in the colloquial sense of the word, it shares with literary realism the aim of satirizing the revival of romance narratives in American culture."[65] Once the narrator finishes reading the manuscript prepared by Hank Morgan, Morgan attempts to compose one more "effect" but dies before doing so; this truncated conclusion only

---

[62] Elizabeth Normen, "The Influence of Connecticut in the American West," *Connecticut Explored* (Winter 2016–17), 202.

[63] Normen, "The Influence of Connecticut," 203.

[64] For more on Twain's relationship with the American West, see Joseph L. Coulombe, *Twain and the American West* (Columbia, MO: University of Missouri Press, 2011).

[65] Victor Doyno, "Great Dark, The," in *The Mark Twain Encyclopedia*, eds. J.R. LeMaster and James D. Wilson (New York, NY: Routledge, 1993), 339. Jennifer L. Lieberman, "Mark Twain and the Technological Fallacy," in *Power Lines: Electricity in American Life and Letters, 1882–1952* (Cambridge, MA: MIT Press, 2017), 45. For more on Twain's tendency to conclude his novels and short stories abruptly, see James M. Cox, "The Uncomfortable Ending of Huckleberry Finn," in *Adventures of Huckleberry Finn*, eds. Sculley Bradley et al. (New York, NY: W.W. Norton & Co., 1977), 350–7; Susan Gillman, *Dark Twins: Imposture and Identity in Mark Twain's America* (Chicago, IL: University of Chicago Press, 1989), 167–70; and Peter Messent, *Mark Twain* (London: Macmillan Press, 1997), 136–9.

serves to hammer home the point that is made clear in those last chapters – the "transposition of epochs" considered in the preface defies logic, making of reason a farce and narrative cohesion an impossibility.[66]

Connecticut Yankee is by no means unique in Twain's oeuvre in critiquing the historical romance by ambivalently invoking the Middle Ages and resisting any "utopian conclusion." Set in fifteenth-century Austria, Twain's unfinished, original manuscript of *The Mysterious Stranger* – as opposed to the edition published by Albert Paine in 1916 – concludes, for instance, with Satan musing about reality itself as a "Dream":

> It is true, that which I have revealed to you: there is no God, no universe, no human race, no earthly life, no heaven, no hell. It is all a Dream; a grotesque and foolish dream. Nothing exists but You. And You are but a *Thought* – a vagrant Thought, a useless Thought, a homeless Thought, wandering forlorn among the empty eternities!"
>
> He vanished, and left me [August Feldner] appalled; for I knew, and realized, that all he had said was true.[67]

According to Satan, history, like literature, is a dream and identity, a thought. That Feldner, the novel's protagonist, "realize[s] that all [Satan] said was true" only affirms that we are not to read these parting words sarcastically but as an earnest appraisal of reality. That this confession is made in medieval Europe, moreover, speaks to how Twain's medievalisms are entwined with an understanding of reality itself as fragmented and lacking narrative cohesion. In "An Awful – Terrible Medieval Romance" (1870), a short story set in a Brandenburg castle in the thirteenth century, a lord, sonless, raises his daughter as a boy so she might one day reign as duke.[68] Ethnicity, historical periodization, class, gender, and age all play a part in the story: Conrad (as the daughter is called) is born in Klugenstein, a fictional town near Brandenburg, Germany; she is ethnically German, of an elite class, female by birth, male by right, and twenty-eight years old at the time of the main events of the story.[69] The story recounts how Conrad's nephew, Constance, unmarried and with child, declares Conrad the father of her child before the royal court. Unsure how to respond, Conrad swoons and falls from his/her ducal chair, at which point the narrator of the story interrupts the narration:

---

[66] Twain, *Connecticut Yankee*, 433.

[67] Mark Twain, *No. 44, the Mysterious Stranger* (Berkeley, CA: University of California Press, 1969), 188.

[68] Mark Twain, *The Complete Short Stories* (New York, NY: Everyman's Library, 2012), 61–3.

[69] Twain, *The Complete Short Stories*, 61–2.

[The remainder of this thrilling and eventful story will NOT be found in this or any other publication, either now or at any future time.]

The truth is, I have got my hero (or heroine) into such a particularly close place, that I do not see how I am ever going to get him (or her) out of it again – and therefore I will wash my hands of the whole business, and leave that person to get out the best way that offers – or else stay there. I thought it was going to be easy enough to straighten out that little difficulty, but it looks different now.[70]

So ends the story. The narrator admits that he simply cannot devise a suitable resolution, so leaves the story's plot unsettled; he cannot bring himself to compose the miracle required by the chivalric romance tradition and, by resisting this resolution, transforms the story into a parody. While he has laid the groundwork for an *Ivanhoe* imitation – a medieval European setting; questions of regal succession; a central, heroic figure in disguise – Twain does not devise a means for his hero/heroine to exhibit his/her heroic qualities; there is, in other words, no hero to this story at all, only an unsettling feint punctuated by a resolute declaration that the conclusion "will NOT be found."[71]

This resonance between Twain's medievalisms and his unexpected, often haphazard endings suggests something else about Twain's conception of historiography – namely, that the writing of history is similar to the writing of Realist fiction in that both bestow narrative order upon historical or proto-historical events, and it is telling, then, that the text in Twain's oeuvre that most clearly avoids such a sudden, inchoate conclusion is the book that Twain himself "like[d] [...] best of all [his] books," for, according to him, "it is the best; I know it perfectly well" – the novel often remembered by literary critics as Twain's "worst book."[72] The end of

---

[70] Twain, *The Complete Short Stories*, 63.
[71] Twain, *The Complete Short Stories*, 63. It is in the final chapters of *Huckleberry Finn*, meanwhile, that the duke and king, those imposters of feudal royalty, appear, and it is in these final chapters that Tom also insists Jim make himself a medievalesque escutcheon (Twain, *Huckleberry Finn*, 332–4). In the *Prince and the Pauper* (1882), it is the Great Seal of England, that symbol of monarchy and feudal rule, that proves Edward the true king, and, as David Vanderwerken has argued, the conclusion to *Pudd'nhead Wilson* amounts to "the triumph of medievalism" in that "[t]hrough the story of Wilson's rise from a pudd'nhead to a 'made man' Twain questions the very possibility of democracy in America" (Mark Twain, *The Prince and the Pauper: A Tale for Young People of All Ages* (New York, NY: Harper & Brothers, 1917), 264; Mark Twain, *Pudd'nhead Wilson* (New York, NY: Charles L. Webster & Co, 1894); David L. Vanderwerken, "The Triumph of Medievalism in 'Pudd'nhead Wilson,'" *Mark Twain Journal* 18:4 (1977), 7.
[72] David Foster, "On the Theme of Mark Twain's *Personal Recollections of Joan of Arc*," *The Mark Twain Annual* 13:1 (2015), 43.

Personal Recollections of Joan of Arc (1896), which recounts Joan of Arc's trial and death, is fraught with both wit and sarcasm; Joan is compelled during her trial to discuss the "Voices" that famously directed her actions: "The University decided that it was blasphemy for Joan to say that her saints spoke French and not English, and were on the French side in political sympathies."[73] Sieur Louis de Conte, the fictional translator of Joan of Arc's fictional "recollections," goes on:

> I think that the thing which troubled the doctors of theology was this: they had decided that the three Voices were Satan and two other devils; but they had also decided that these Voices were *not* on the French side – thereby tacitly asserting that they were on the English side; and if on the English side, then they must be angels and not devils [...] You see, the University being the wisest and deepest and most erudite body in the world, it would like to be logical if it could.[74]

Twain's dry humor, overpowered throughout much of the text by an oversweet admiration for Joan of Arc, pierces through the personas of the novel just as Joan stands trial and prepares for her death. It is in these final chapters that Twain comes into his own, incorporating a sarcastic, Cervantesesque tone and resisting both the utopian conclusion of the medieval romance tradition and the haphazard conclusions of many of his other works.

The conclusion to *Huckleberry Finn*, meanwhile, adds yet another layer to this discussion, suggesting that the connection Twain draws between the essential arbitrariness of historical narration and the Middle Ages functions to cast the United States itself in the mold of a medieval power. That *Huckleberry Finn* is indebted to *Don Quixote* has long been recognized among Twain scholars. As early as 1922, Olin Harris Moore published "Mark Twain and Don Quixote" in *PMLA*, citing the connections between Twain's novels, especially *Huckleberry Finn* and *Tom Sawyer*, and *Don Quixote*: "For the man Don Quixote Mark Twain substitutes the boy Tom Sawyer," Moore declares, going on to explain: "Tom is a romantic youth, who has read a great many exciting tales and desires to play the roles of his heroes [...] In attempting [these] roles [...] Sawyer falls into frequent altercations with Huck Finn, which resemble closely the arguments between Don Quixote and Sancho Panza."[75] To illustrate his point,

---

[73] Mark Twain, *Personal Recollections of Joan of Arc* (New York, NY: Harper, 1908), 419.

[74] Twain, *Personal Recollections of Joan of Arc*, 419.

[75] Olin Harris Moore, "Mark Twain and Don Quixote," *PMLA* 37:2 (1922), 337; Mark Twain, *The Adventures of Tom Sawyer* (Hartford, CT: American Publishing Company, 1876).

Moore cites the exchange, in chapter three of *Huckleberry Finn*, when Huck recounts how Tom convinces Huck and their gang to ambush what Tom declares to be an invading army of "Spaniards and A-rabs" mounted on the backs of elephants:

> When we got the word we rushed out of the woods and down the hill. But there warn't no Spaniards and A-rabs, and there warn't no camels nor no elephants. It warn't anything but a Sunday-school picnic and only a primer class at that. We busted it up, and chased the children up the hollow; but we never got anything but some doughnuts and jam [...] I didn't see no di'monds, and I told Tom Sawyer so. He said there was loads of them there, anyway; and he said there was Arabs there, too, and elephants and things. I said, why couldn't we see them, then? He said if I warn't so ignorant but had read a book called Don Quixote, I would know without asking. He said it was all done by enchantment. He said there was hundreds of soldiers there, and elephants and treasure, and so on, but we had enemies which he called magicians, and they turned the whole thing into an infant Sunday-school, just out of spite. I said, all right; then the thing for us to do was to go for the magicians. Tom Sawyer said I was a numskull.[76]

Twain's direct reference to *Don Quixote* serves to confirm what is already, without that reference, clear: the relationship between Huck Finn and Tom Sawyer is demonstrative of the relationship between Don Quixote and Sancho Panza. To further confirm his point, Moore cites Tom's repeated chastisements of Huck – "If I was as ignorant as you I'd keep still," or "How *you* talk, you better say; you don't know anything at all" – and compares these to Quixote's critiques of Sancho Panza – "How mistaken you are!" or "I have already told you, Sancho, [...] that you know next to nothing on the subject of adventures."[77]

---

[76] Twain, *Huckleberry Finn*, 31.

[77] Twain, *Huckleberry Finn*, 310–11; Cervantes, *The Indigenous Hidalgo Don Quixote*, 81, 67. Moore's essay speaks clearly to the extent to which *Don Quixote* has affected American literature writ large and especially Twain's *Tom Sawyer* and *Huckleberry Finn*, and Stanley Williams cites Moore's essay in *The Spanish Background of American Literature* (1955), which traces the various ways U.S. novelists have been influenced by Cervantes, while M.F. Heiser, in an essay titled "Cervantes in the United States" (1947), cites Moore in his discussion of the various ways Cervantes has been adapted, translated and reimagined in U.S. novels – see Stanley Williams, *The Spanish Background of American Literature* (New Haven, CT: Yale University Press, 1955); M.F. Heiser, "Cervantes in the United States," *Hispanic Review* 15:4 (1947), 409–35. More recently, the influence of Cervantes on Twain has been taken up to consider the controversial issue of the conclusion to *Huckleberry Finn*, with Pedro Javier Pardo García arguing that *Huckleberry*

These discussions of *Huckleberry Finn*'s indebtedness to *Don Quixote* ignore a crucial element of this reception history – namely, the medievalism activated by this connection. Twain's representation of the United States stands in stark contrast to American Anglo-Saxonism; Twain employs medievalisms not as a means of stratifying society along racial and gender lines but, rather, as a means of revealing the irony that an egalitarian democratic republic would enact such stratification systems. In *Pudd'nhead Wilson*, *Joan of Arc*, "An Awful – Terrible Medieval Romance," and *Huckleberry Finn*, Twain emphasizes how racial and gender categories limit one's opportunities and, in so doing, grapples with the limits of U.S. egalitarianism itself. Twain's conclusions, similarly, especially in his later works like *Connecticut Yankee*, *Joan of Arc*, *Mysterious Stranger*, and *Pudd'nhead Wilson*, are deeply pessimistic: as Satan's final monologue and Pudd'nhead Wilson's eventual reinstitution of Dawson's Landing's racial hierarchy suggest, Twain is skeptical of the United States's ability to integrate women and people of color into its national identity in a way that fully dismantles the deep-seated systems of racism and patriarchy.

Twain's reluctance to imagine, in positive terms, a truly egalitarian U.S. social structure mirrors, in fact, the reluctance exhibited by certain medieval theologians in discussing the divine, and this connection can supplement the "detailed and massive continuity" noted by Lynn White, Jr., that binds medieval Christian theology and U.S. Protestant theology.[78] Indeed, while U.S. Puritanism owes a good deal to Christian Scholastic theologians like William of Ockham, the subversive tradition of U.S. authors, including Poe and Twain, shares a good deal with medieval apophatic theology – that is, the Christian theological tradition, sometimes referred to as the *via negativa*, that looks to define the divine not by what it is, as Thomas Aquinas and other Scholastic theologians maintained, but negatively, by what it is not.[79] A student of the Neoplatonist Proclus (412–485), Pseudo-Dionysius, often deemed the father of apophaticism, argued that all things "reveal in themselves the hidden goodness and are angels because they proclaim the divine silence and, as it were, present

---

Finn intertwines the picaresque with the quixotic in order to establish Huck as an American Adamic figure, while Aaron DeRosa focuses on how the quixotism of *Huckleberry Finn* is fundamentally undermined by Twain's attention to the deeply fraught issues of racism and slavery – Pedro Javier Padro García, "'Huckleberry Finn' as a Crossroads of Myth: the Adamic, the quixotic, the picaresque, and the problem of ending," *Links & Letters* 8 (2001), 61–70. Aaron DeRosa, "Europe, Darwin and the Escape from *Huckleberry Finn*," *American Literary Realism* 44:2 (2012), 157–73.

[78] White, "The Legacy of the Middle Ages in the American Wild West," 191.
[79] Louth, "Apophatic and Cataphatic Theology," 140.

clear lights which interpret that which is in secret."[80] Pseudo-Dionysius's apophaticism contends that the only appropriate means of discussing the divine is through negation, for when purportedly divine names are negated, "divine silence, darkness and unknowing" ensue: "We worship with reverent silence the unutterable truths and, with the unfathomable and holy veneration of our mind, approach that mystery of godhead that exceeds all mind and body."[81] Pseudo-Dionysius's apophaticism sees all things as "reveal[ing] the hidden goodness"; as a Neoplatonist, he denies the reality of evil altogether and, in so doing, resists seeing the world as a dualistic battle between opposites.

Such an apophatic hermeneutic is useful for considering Twain's medievalisms, for while there may be a tendency, like Twain, to read American medievalisms as bifurcated into the "pernicious work" that follows Scott and the "good work" that follows Cervantes, engagement with those medievalisms reveals that such a binary is simply inadequate: American medievalisms, like "creole medievalisms," are always already interweaving these and other strands into their works, and Twain's medievalisms themselves illustrate this ambivalence by simultaneously lampooning and romanticizing the medieval past.[82] His mockery of Merlin's "magic of fol-de-rol," in *Connecticut Yankee*, over and against the "magic of science," frames medieval England as a world of foolishness and ignorance, all the while emphasizing how modern science has itself been deeply destructive, and in the apocalyptic ending, when Hank Morgan uses Gatling guns to massacre some thirty thousand knights, the novel mocks not only the "innocen[ce] and idioc[y]" of the medieval knight-errant but also the callousness and cruelty of modern warfare – yet another illustration of his penchant for terse, abrupt conclusions.[83]

This ambivalence is crucial to understanding American medievalism as an entire discourse apparatus: "The antimodern quest for authenticity wore a Janus face," writes Lears, reading the American "medieval unconscious" as both an idealization of the premodern and a fetishization of what Lears calls "real life" – that "ever-elusive" sense of authenticity that, according to a Romantic hermeneutic, modernity withholds: "Wearied by struggles with religious doubt, impatient with the vagueness of liberal optimism, Americans hailed the 'childlike faith' of the Middle Ages 'in the reality of the visions that peopled the heavens and the earth'"

---

[80] R. Baine Harris, *Neoplatonism and Contemporary Thought: Part Two* (New York, NY: State University of New York Press, 2001), 143.

[81] Lois Malcolm, ed., *God: The Sources of Christian Theology* (Louisville, KY: Westminster John Knox Press, 2012), 83–6.

[82] Twain, *Life on the Mississippi*, 314. Warren, *Creole Medievalism*, 1–10.

[83] Twain, *Connecticut Yankee*, 396, 85, 428–44.

– emphasizing, in particular, "the key word 'reality.'"[84] This focus on the Janus-faced quality of American medievalisms retains a latent dualism, however; it implies that there exist precisely and only two opposing movements, an implication that reifies the dualism endemic to modern European colonial ideologies.[85] If we think of the various purported binaries constructed by the rhetoric of European colonialism and its U.S. offspring, including American Anglo-Saxonism, in relation to the apophaticism of medieval theologians like Pseudo-Dionysius, these supposed contradictions, however, become an "overdetermined" concatenation of cultural constructs "tangled" together in a Gordian knot of supposed binaries.[86]

If we think of ethnonationalism, following the twentieth-century political philosopher Hannah Arendt, as the fundamental contradiction of liberal democracies, it is in the overdetermined network of apparent contradictions constructed by ethnonationalism's binary oppositions that a diverse body politic is born.[87] Comprised of a multiethnic, multilingual citizenry, itself composed of many genders, classes, religions, histories, and age groups, a liberal democracy like the United States can ground its identity in binary oppositions for only so long; sooner or later those oppositions transmute into polymorphic, kaleidoscopic networks of cultural elements that leave us, like Pseudo-Dionysius thinking of the divine, speechless. It is in this sense that the medieval apophatic tradition speaks directly to post-Civil War notions of U.S. national identity. Pseudo-Dionysius and Meister Eckhart remind us of the overdetermined nature of abstract concepts like identity. "[O]ne must never imagine or judge concerning the general terms [*terminis generalibus*] such as being, unity, truth, wisdom, goodness and such like, according to the mode and nature of accidents," writes Meister Eckhart, arguing that such *termini generales* are necessarily inexpressible

---

[84] Lears, *No Place of Grace*, 150.

[85] On colonialism's use of dualism, see Syed Farid Alatas, "Alatas, Fanon, and Coloniality," in *Frantz Fanon and Emancipatory Social Theory*, eds. Dustin J. Byrd and Syed Farid Alatas (Boston, MA: Brill, 2020), 28.

[86] Louis Althusser, *For Marx*, trans. Ben Brewster (New York, NY: Verso, 1969), 107. The postmodern philosopher Louis Althusser, in "Contradictions and Overdeterminations" (1962), famously deploys the Freudian notion of overdetermination to critique a Hegelian conception of history, which "is regulated by the dialectic of the internal principles of each society, that is, the dialectic of the moments of the idea" (107). Althusser's argument maintains that, while contradictions rely on dualistic, Hegelian dialectics, overdeterminations rely on complex nexuses of relations, "tangles" as he calls them (107).

[87] Hannah Arendt, *Eichmann in Jerusalem: A Report on the Banality of Evil* (New York, NY: Penguin Books, 2006), 3–7.

in "accidental" terms.[88] Abstract concepts – or "general terms" in Eckhart's discourse – cannot be imagined in terms of accidental properties such as quantity, relation, time, or location; to represent such concepts in accidental terms is to specify them and so negate their abstract, general nature. This is the central dilemma that Twain exposes at the close of *The Mysterious Stranger*: "You are but a *Thought*," Satan insists and so renders identity itself an abstraction, "vagrant" and "useless," "homeless [...] wandering forlorn among the empty eternities"; Twain's Realism requires that he represent reality in accidental terms, but such representations make of abstract concepts dogma, and his suggestion that the United States exists as a kind of feudal society, with race and gender as corollaries to the caste systems of medieval European societies, gestures toward a recognition that Realist portrayals of national identity, such as American Anglo-Saxonism, operate upon this fundamentally non-egalitarian, dogmatic conception of the nation-state.[89] Such patriarchal and racist contestations are dependent upon not only a monological spatiality but also a monological temporality.[90] The science fiction and fantasy genres, meanwhile, as well as their close counterpart, the historical romance, become by no means niche genres but overt responses to a dominant, world-historical moment – namely, the collapse of European colonialism.

---

[88] Meister Eckhart, "Prologus generalis in Opus tripartitum," in *Meister Eckhart: Die lateinischen Werke*, ed. Josef Quint, vol. I (Stuttgart: W. Kohlhammer Verlag, 1936), 152. For more on this discussion, see Jeremiah Hackett, *A Companion to Meister Eckhart* (Boston, MA: Brill, 2013), 193–4.

[89] For more on the resemblance between caste systems and U.S. racism, see Isabel Wilkerson, *Caste: The Origins of Our Discontent* (New York, NY: Random House, 2020). Twain, *No. 44, the Mysterious Stranger*, 188.

[90] Davis, *Periodization and Sovereignty*, 20–2.

5

The Persistent Medieval: T.S. Eliot's *The Waste Land*, Ezra Pound's *The Cantos*, and William Faulkner's Organic Medievalism

"THE MAJOR DEVIATIONS from orthodoxy" that the twentieth-century American poet Ezra Pound made in his "grotesque mistranslations" of Chinese poetry, literary critic Hugh Kenner argues in *The Pound Era* (1971), "represent deliberate decisions of a man who was inventing a new kind of English poem and picking up hints where he could find them."[1] Pound, T.S. Eliot and other Modernists interested in making poetry and art relevant within an increasingly industrial world turned not only to Chinese and non-Western literary and aesthetic traditions for these "hints" but also to medieval cultural productions.[2] Set largely in modern London, T.S. Eliot's *The Waste Land* (1922), for instance, begins with a dedication to Ezra Pound, described as *il miglior fabbro*, "the better craftsman," echoing Dante's tribute to the twelfth-century Provençal poet Arnaut Daniel in Canto 26 of the *Purgatorio* (c. 1307), and Pound himself, in *Cantos* – the title itself serving as an allusion to Dante's epic – consistently refers to both Asiatic schools of thought, especially Confucianism, and European medieval history, poetry, and art.[3] The "persistent east" that Kenner notices in Pound's poetry, then,

---

[1] Hugh Kenner, *The Pound Era* (Berkeley, CA: University of California Press, 1971), 219, 213. Ezra Pound and Ernest Fenollosa, *Instigations: Together with an Essay on the Chinese Written Character* (New York, NY: Boni and Liveright, 1920), 378.

[2] On Modernist literature more generally, see Julian Hanna, ed., *Key Concepts in Modernist Literature* (New York, NY: Palgrave Macmillan, 2009), 12–16. For more on his medieval sources, see Jonathon Ullyot, *Ezra Pound and His Classical Sources* (New York, NY: Bloomsbury Academic, 2022), 9–10.

[3] On Pound's East Asian sources, see Zhaoming Qing, *Orientalism and Modernism: The Legacy of China in Pound and Williams* (Durham, NC: Duke University Press, 1995), 7–110. On Pound's indebtedness to Dante, see Stephen Sicari, *Pound's Epic Ambition: Dante and the Modern World* (Albany, NY: State University of New York Press, 1991).

is supplemented by a "persistent medieval" that, like the persistent east, affords Modernists – Europeans and European Americans alike – with an "alien poetic" that could be "made new" by Modernism.[4]

The adaptation of Asian and medieval cultural productions within many modern U.S. cultural productions has been the subject of much recent scholarship in medievalism studies. John Ganim, for instance, in *Medievalism and Orientalism* (2016) traces the "twinned association of medievalism and Orientalism" developed by nineteenth-century Western authors, historians, and anthropologists, who imagined the Middle Ages as "the White Orient," a "foreign land" in which western thinkers were, paradoxically, "always at home."[5] Ganim sees "the idea of the Middle Ages" as symptomatic of "an identity crisis [regarding] what the West is and should be" and, by linking medievalism and Orientalism, illustrates how the modern colonial system constructs not only spatial but also temporal systems to justify colonialism.[6] As Kathleen Davis puts it, many contemporary medievalisms "paradoxically claim […] the Middle Ages as the immature stage from which modernity developed, and as an inert, temporal space incapable of change," and she illustrates how even "contemporary critical examination of Orientalism – led by [Edward] Said's groundbreaking *Orientalism* – reinforces rather than disrupts [this] Westernizing temporal logic."[7]

The Waste Land, in particular, leverages medieval European literature and Eastern religions alike in the presentation of modernity as devoid of meaning.[8] As Eliot acknowledges in the poem's footnotes, "Not only the title, but the plan and a good deal of the incidental symbolism of the poem was suggested by Miss Jessie L. Weston's book [*From Ritual to Romance* (1920)]," which examines the sources for the motif of the Holy Grail in medieval Arthurian literature and those sources' connection to medieval paganism and Christianity.[9] Of particular interest to Weston is the motif, present in Irish mythology and French Arthuriana, of a Waste Land – a desolate, arid land, the barrenness of which is tied to a curse that must be broken by a hero: "I believe," Weston writes, "that the 'Waste Land' is really the very heart of our problem; a rightful appreciation of its position and

---

[4] Kenner, *The Pound Era*, 195. For a more general overview of British and U.S. "Modernist medievalism," see Alexander, *Medievalism*, 188–220.
[5] Ganim, *Medievalism and Orientalism*, 3, 107.
[6] Ganim, *Medievalism and Orientalism*, 3.
[7] Kathleen Davis, "Time Behind the Veil: The Media, the Middle Ages, and Orientalism Now," in *The Postcolonial Middle Ages*, ed. Jeffrey Jerome Cohen (New York, NY: Palgrave Macmillan, 2000), 107.
[8] Eliot, *The Waste Land*.
[9] Jessie Laidlay Weston, *From Ritual to Romance* (Mineola, NY: Dover Publications, 1920/1997).

significance will place us in possession of the clue which will lead us safely through the most bewildering mazes of the fully developed tale."[10] The "Waste Land," according to Weston, is a "clue" that will "lead us," modern readers, to an understanding of the Holy Grail myth, and Eliot integrates that argument into his poem, presenting the motif of the waste land as the central "clue" to understanding modernity.

The story of the Grail revolves around the knight-errant Perceval's encounter with the Fisher King, whose wound, "located in the thighs or groin, [...] is connected with the destitution of the Waste Land" over which the Fisher King rules.[11] Weston's work connects this legend with the nature cults of Wales, the Alps, and the Vosges, among other localities – her argument being that the Grail myth has as its basis "a ritual performance celebrating the renewal of the seasons."[12] Eliot takes up this connection between the Grail myth and the ritual renewal of the seasons, famously beginning the poem with an allusion to the opening lines of Geoffrey Chaucer's medieval epic *The Canterbury Tales* (c. 1400):

> April is the cruelest month, breeding
> Lilacs out of the dead land, mixing
> Memory and desire, stirring
> Dull roots with spring rain.[13]

The title of the first section of Eliot's *The Waste Land*, "Burial of the Dead," connects the poem with a religious event – burial – just as the opening line, with its allusions to Chaucer, suggests the medieval religious practice of pilgrimage.[14] The central questions of Eliot's poem are clear from the opening lines: what are the rituals of the modern world, and how, if at all, are these rituals inscribed with meaning? Like D.H. Lawrence's discussion of James Fenimore Cooper and Edgar Allan Poe (see Chapter 3),[15] Eliot turns to the seasons in response to these questions of meaninglessness:

> Winter kept us warm, covering
> Earth in forgetful snow, feeding
> A little life with dried tubers.

---

[10] Weston, *From Ritual to Romance*, 60.
[11] Christopher W. Bruce, *The Arthurian Name Dictionary* (New York, NY: Garland Publishing, Inc., 1999), 233. For more, see Chrétien de Troyes, *Perceval: The Story of the Grail*, trans. Burton Raffel (New Haven, CT: Yale University Press, 1999).
[12] Weston, *From Ritual to Romance*, 60.
[13] Eliot, *The Waste Land*, 135.
[14] Geoffrey Chaucer, *The Riverside Chaucer*, 3rd edn (Oxford: Oxford University Press, 1987), 23. For more on Eliot's allusions to Chaucer, see John Spiers, *Chaucer the Maker* (London: Faber and Faber, 1951) 99–121.
[15] Lawrence, "Studies in Classic American Literature," 278.

> Summer surprised us, coming over the Starnbergersee
> With a shower of rain; we stopped in the colonnade,
> And went on in sunlight, into the Hofgarten,
> And drank coffee, and talked for an hour.
> Bin gar keine Russin, stamm' aus Litauen, echt deutsch.
> And when we were children, staying at the arch-duke's
> My cousin's, he took me out on a sled,
> And I was frightened. He said, Marie,
> Marie, hold on tight. And down we went.
> In the mountains, there you feel free.
> I read, much of the night, and go south in the winter.[16]

Winter and summer, in the modern world, entwine; the images of summer – the colonnade, the sunlit Hofgarten – merge with a winter sled-ride at the arch-duke's mountain chalet. The seasons no longer correspond with their appropriate activities; they converge just as Marie's monologue offers fragmented, muddled narratives.[17] The final declaration that Marie "read[s], much of the night, and go[es] south in the winter" amounts to a paradoxical admission that now her annual ritual is a refusal to participate in such rituals; the sublime, with its terror and beauty, is withheld from her now, existing only as a dull, fragmented memory of which the spring "cruelly" reminds her. Marie's ensuing declaration – "I am not Russian at all; I come from Lithuania, pure German" – suggests another of the poem's concerns: the slipperiness of ethnonationalist identity.[18] Marie is from Lithuania, yet considers herself "pure German"; as the cousin of the arch-duke, she is also of a regal heritage. The poem, in its grappling with modern ritual practices, comes up against questions of ethnonationalism and nostalgia for a bygone European aristocracy, and these concerns are overlaid onto a medieval narrative, the story of the Fisher King, which provides narrative cohesion to the poem.

Like the U.S. medievalisms of the nineteenth century, Eliot's Modernist medievalisms connect the anxiety regarding the social order in a democratic republic to the question of how such a nation can construct its national identity, and Eliot adds to these concerns a preoccupation with the rituals that bind modern society itself together: he is interested in

---

[16] Eliot, *The Waste Land*, 135.
[17] On the "fragmentary self" in *The Waste Land*, see Dennis Brown, *The Modernist Self in Twentieth-Century English Literature: A Study in Self-fragmentation* (London: Palgrave Macmillan, 1989), 92–4.
[18] On Eliot, ethnonationalism and postmodern conceptions of identity, see Bernard Sharratt, "Eliot: Modernism, Postmodernism, and After," in *The Cambridge Companion to T.S. Eliot*, ed. Anthony David Moody (Cambridge: Cambridge University Press, 1994), 223–35.

the rites that define modernity, and in the first stanza he searches futilely for these rites among an aging, indolent aristocracy; the seasons of the year; and a convoluted, muddled ethnonationalism that breeds war. The remainder of "The Burial of the Dead" moves among these topics, focusing on the nostalgia of the aristocracy in the second stanza ("You gave me hyacinths first a year ago; / They called me the hyacinth girl."), the superstitions that masquerade, albeit often convincingly, as modern rituals in the third stanza ("Madame Sosostris [...] with a wicked pack of [tarot] cards" – an allusion to the fraudulent fortuneteller Sesostris featured in Aldous Huxley's *Crome Yellow* (1921)), and the brutality of war in the final stanza, which imagines dead bodies as seeds to be planted ("That corpse you planted last year in your garden, / Has it begun to sprout?").[19] The opening section of the poem, in other words, recapitulates the three topics alluded to in the opening stanza, continuing to overlay those concerns onto the medieval European literary figure of the waste land.

In the second section of the poem, "A Game of Chess," the synthetic quality of the room, in which "[t]he Chair she sat in, like a burnished throne, / Glowed on the marble," portrays the world of modernity as artificial and vapid.[20] That this description rests upon the medieval narrative of the Fisher King again illustrates succinctly the way Eliot presents the medieval as the "spatiotemporal baseline" of modernity, the essential element that one must understand to fully comprehend modernity.[21] Just as the superficiality and baroque aesthetic of the room in "A Game of Chess" is inscribed upon a medieval literary narrative, modernity seems, for Eliot, to be inscribed upon the Middle Ages, understood as fundamental.

Ezra Pound's medievalisms are no less Romantic. As Daniel Swift, quoting Frank Kermode, has shown in his study of Pound's years living in St. Elizabeth's hospital after World War II, "the modernist poets – [...] Eliot, Pound and Yeats – 'seek a historical period possessing the qualities they postulate for the image.' They dream of a historical moment which has the hard unity and clean lines of a poetic image."[22] Modernism, foregrounding fragmentation, searches for a historical moment that possesses the unity and cohesion of the image, using the Middle Ages – as well as non-Western cultures – as storehouses for these coherent, totalizing

---

[19] Aldous Huxley, *Crome Yellow* (London: Chatto and Windus, 1925), 282–4; Eliot, *The Waste Land*, 135.
[20] Eliot, *The Waste Land*, 137.
[21] Davis and Altschul, *The Idea of "The Middle Ages" outside Europe*, 1.
[22] Daniel Swift, *The Bughouse: The Poetry, Politics and Madness of Ezra Pound* (New York, NY: Farrar, Straus and Giroux, 2017), 139.

images, albeit necessarily fragmented in a "fallen," modern world.[23] The implications of such posturing, though, suggest that the poem's speaker has knowledge of a gestalt that is necessarily withheld from those not privy to the medieval substrata of modernity. Pound's medievalisms in *The Cantos*, for instance, begin before any reference is made to the historical Middle Ages; "Canto 1," published in 1925, opens with a loose translation of Book 11 of Homer's *Odyssey* – Odysseus's descent into the underworld – in which Pound uses English of a firmly Anglo-Saxon bent:

> And then went down to the ship,
> Set keel to breakers, forth on the godly sea, and
> We set up mast and sail on that swart ship,
> bore sheep aboard her, and our bodies also
> Heavy with weeping, and winds from sternward
> Bore us out onward with bellying canvas,
> Circe's this craft, the trim-coiffed goddess.[24]

"Down," "ship," "keel," "breakers," "forth," "sea," "sheep," "weeping," "sternward," "bore," "bellying," "craft," "trim-coiffed" – Pound uses nouns and verbs of Anglo-Saxon etymology, and the consistent use of caesura, alliteration, and a four-beat, non-iambic line – not to mention the nautical theme – bears a strong resemblance to his translation of the Anglo-Saxon poem "The Seafarer" (1911), which significantly contributed to the twentieth-century fascination with Old English verse.[25] Moreover, an imaginative retelling of *The Odyssey*, especially one appearing in a text titled *The Cantos*, alludes not only to Homer's epic but also to Canto XXVI of Dante's *Inferno* (1308), in which Odysseus, dwelling in the eighth circle of hell, tells of how he fled Circe in order to explore the world, rather than return to Penelope.[26] In "Canto I," Circe becomes, for Pound, the very ship in which the poem's speaker and his crew sail ("Circe's this craft, the trim-coiffed goddess"); in Homer's telling, she gives Odysseus the ship, as well as the wind that "bell[ies]" its sails, but, in Pound's rendering, Circe

---

[23] On Pound's attempt to "recohere" a modern "fallen world," see Stephen Fender, "Usable History: High Modernism and the Documentary Form," in *Pound and Referentiality*, ed. Hélène Aji (Paris: Presses de l'Université de Paris-Sorbonne, 2003), 292.

[24] Pound, *The Cantos*, 3.

[25] For more on the burgeoning of interest in Anglo-Saxon literature in the early twentieth century, see Mark Atherton, "Priming the Poets: The Making of Henry Sweet's *Anglo-Saxon Reader*," in *Anglo-Saxon Culture and the Modern Imagination*, eds. David Clark and Nicholas Perkins (Cambridge: D.S. Brewer, 2010), 31–3.

[26] Dante Alighieri, *Dante's Inferno: The Indiana Critical Edition*, ed. Mark Musa (Bloomington, IN: Indiana University Press, 1995), 191.

becomes, according to Hugh Kenner's reading of "Canto I" at least, the *psyche* – the soul – of not only the ship but also the poem itself, the breath of the poem's speaker.[27]

Like *The Waste Land*, with its allusion to *The Canterbury Tales*, *The Cantos* begins with an allusion to medieval literature, as well as religious imagery that regards the sea as "godly" and Circe as "the trim-coiffed goddess," animating not only Odysseus's ship but also Pound's poem itself. Circe exists as the muse of "Canto I," Hugh Kenner famously contends – and, by extension, *The Cantos* more generally – and this concern with deities speaks yet again to the way medievality is associated in modern cultural productions with religiosity.[28] In his *Companion to the Cantos*, Carroll Franklin Terrell argues that *The Cantos* is, at core, "a great religious poem," but Pound's religious beliefs cohere around not a particular creed but an understanding of divinity – or, as Pound deems it, "intimate essence" – as "operat[ing] through the persona continuously as a state of mind," and that Pound turns to a medieval theologian like John Scotus Eriugena (c. 815–77) to develop this conception of divinity speaks clearly to the Neoplatonic vein running through *The Cantos*, as well as to the way the poem reifies the medieval-religious association so endemic to the medieval/modern divide.[29]

Eriugena affords Pound with "specific ideas," especially "on light as a kataphatic expression of divinity, on the celestial hierarchy [and] on the flame of civilization kept alive in the transmission of Greek in the Carolingian Age"; Pound's kataphaticism – that is, the definition in positive terms of the divine and, therefore, the opposite of apophaticism[30] – illustrates particularly well the imperialist ideology undergirding much of *The Cantos*, utilizing as it does a syncretism that melds Eastern religious traditions like Buddhism and Confucianism with paganism and medieval Christianity.[31] As John Ganim has argued, "Romanticism obviously equated the Middle Ages and the Orient, but it kept them by and large on parallel tracks [...] the Medieval is accorded a direct connection to modernity, explaining the origin of national and civil identity, while the Orient is a living museum of the past, bracketed off from modern development or even excluded from

---

[27] Hugh Kenner, "Blood for the Ghosts," in *New Approaches to Ezra Pound*, ed. Eva Hesse (Berkeley, CA: University of California Press, 1969), 332.

[28] For more on the connections between the medieval/modern divide and the religious/secular divide, see Margaret Kim, "'Atheism' in Late Medieval Travel Writing," in *Bridging the Medieval–Modern Divide: Medieval Themes in the World of the Reformation*, ed. James Muldoon (New York, NY: Routledge, 2016), 65–86, as well as Davis, *Periodization and Sovereignty*, 15, 97–8.

[29] Carroll Franklin Terrell, *A Companion to the Cantos of Ezra Pound*, vol. 2 (Berkeley, CA: University of California Press, 1984), 568n166.

[30] See Pound, *The Cantos*, 114–16.

[31] Mark Bryon, *Ezra Pound's Eriugena* (New York, NY: Bloomsbury, 2014), 30.

the potential for development."[32] By the early twentieth century, however, even this distinction had eroded, and the Middle Ages and Asia converge to the point that Eliot can conclude *The Waste Land* with the conclusion to the *Upanishads*, "shantih shantih shantih," and Pound can, in the *Pisan Cantos*, interlace ancient Egyptian symbolism, Scholastic theology, Tu Fu, and Chinese ideograms:

> the great scarab is bowed at the altar
> the green light gleams in his shell
> plowed in the sacred field and unwound the silk worms early
> in tensile [insert symbol here]
> in the light of light is the *virtù*
> "sunt lumina" said Erigena Scotus
> as of Shun on Mt Taishan
> and in the hall of the forebears
> as from the beginning of wonders
> the paraclete that was present in Yao, the precision
> in Shun the compassionate
> in Yu the guider of waters[33]

Ancient China and the European Middle Ages, for Pound, exist as origin points for modern Western national identity; they are not on "parallel tracks" but amalgamated.[34] This early twentieth-century fusion of the medieval and East Asian cultures, in other words, reflects a growing cosmopolitanism that rejects simplistic east–west binaries but also treats both East Asian and medieval cultures as both peripheral (or antecedental) to modernity and a respite from the artificiality of modernity.

Indeed, this association of the Middle Ages and authenticity is a common trope of nineteenth- and twentieth-century American literature more generally.[35] Literary critic Kim Ilene Moreland, for instance, has noted the way both F. Scott Fitzgerald and Ernest Hemingway turn to the medieval for "an alternative worldview, a set of standards against which [they] could compare [their] own day."[36] With respect to Fitzgerald, this fascination with the medieval is clear in his portrayal of the American academician Henry Adams (1838–1918) in *This Side of Paradise* (1920) as "the Honorable Thornton Hancock, of Boston, ex-minister to the Hague, author of an erudite history of the Middle Ages and

---

[32] Ganim, *Medievalism and Orientalism*, 87.
[33] Pound, *The Cantos*, 449.
[34] Ganim, *Medievalism and Orientalism*, 87.
[35] On American medievalism and authenticity, see Lears, *No Place of Grace*, xv–xvii.
[36] Moreland, *The Medievalist Impulse in American Literature*, 120.

the last of a distinguished, patriotic, and brilliant family."[37] The Middle Ages become for Fitzgerald a way to emphasize "the destructive aspects of twentieth-century life," while Hemingway, in an interview, described *The Sun Also Rises* (1926) as "a fishing expedition in the Pass of Roland" and, like Eliot, uses titles and "pseudomedieval epigraphs" to construct a "chivalric suggestiveness."[38] Indeed, F. Scott Fitzgerald, in his short story "Philippe, Count of Darkness" (1935), even casts Hemingway himself as the ninth-century French aristocrat whose "spirit … in the course of the coming century would draw the scattered fragments of civilization into the beginnings of a new order in which would be contained, like a portent, the pattern, the characteristic tensions and contradictions of Western Civilization itself."[39]

All five authors – Eliot, Weston, Hemingway, Pound, and Fitzgerald – use the Middle Ages to accentuate the sense of disorientation and dislocation modern life bestows, and in this sense their medievalisms function as pedagogical tools, framing the medieval as a space-time with which modern readers must be familiar if they are to fully comprehend modernity, and such a contestation resembles the kind of "traditional" pedagogy that the Italian Marxist theorist Anthony Gramsci (1891–1937) critiques in his *Prison Notebooks* (1947): "traditional intellectuals," Gramsci argues, "put themselves forward as autonomous and independent of the dominant social group" and so buttress an "imperial intellectual cosmopolitanism" that separates intellectuals from "non-intellectuals" – a group that, to Gramsci, does not even precisely exist.[40] American Modernists' penchant for what might be termed *pedagogical medievalisms* serves to separate Eliot, Hemingway, and Fitzgerald from modern society, presenting them as "autonomous and independent" by nature of their knowledge of medieval cultures, and, as Gramsci makes clear, such intellectualism serves to support imperial interests: "It is necessary to go back to the Roman Empire and to the first concentration of 'cosmopolitan' ('imperial') intellectuals it produced," Gramsci writes in a letter to his sister-in-law, thinking about how "a real program of study and work" that analyzed the long history of European intellectualism is simply impossible to render in any comprehensive manner: "[O]ne has to study the formation of the Christian-Papal organization of clerks which shaped the legacy of imperial intellectual cosmopolitanism into the form

---

[37] F. Scott Fitzgerald, *This Side of Paradise* (New York, NY: Scribner, 1920), 26.
[38] Fitzgerald, *This Side of Paradise*, 120, 176, 175.
[39] Moreland, *The Medievalist Impulse in American Literature*, 26; Kermit Moyer, "Fitzgerald's Two Unfinished Novels: The Count and the Tycoon in Spenglerian Perspective," *Contemporary Literature* 15 (1974), 243.
[40] Antonio Gramsci, *Selections from the Prison Notebooks*, trans. Q. Hoare and G.N. Smith (New York, NY: International Publishers, 1971), 3–23.

of a European caste, etc., etc.," he goes on, linking traditional intellectualism with, first of all, a pre-eighteenth-century "cosmopolitanism," which he equates with "imperialism" (his own periodizing schema is apparent here), and, second of all, an eighteenth- and nineteenth-century nationalism that treats the nation itself as a totality.[41] In both cases, Gramsci insists that traditional intellectualism buttresses these hegemonic enterprises by promoting an ideology that transforms ideology itself into the purview of an elite, separate caste.

The Modernists' pedagogical medievalism – understood as an instance of such traditional intellectualism – bears some interesting resemblances, in fact, to the imperialism that characterized the Christianization of Western Europe itself. The monopolization of medieval historiography by Christian historians has resulted in the framing of the Christianization of Europe as a sudden transformation rather than as a centuries-long, syncretic process, occurring unevenly across space and time.[42] The Christianization of Saxony, as medievalist Ingrid Rembold has argued, is particularly illustrative of this process, for "[i]n its progression from an undeveloped, pagan and hitherto disunified territory to a Christian region of the Carolingian polity, Saxony represents an important test case for the nature of Christianization and Christian reform in the early medieval world."[43] In particular, Rembold, who utilizes network theory to interpret this period of medieval European history, asserts that "the brutality of the Saxon wars did not preclude acceptance of Christianity and Carolingian rule"; instead, the Christianization of Saxony, a nebulous territoriality corresponding "roughly to the German federal state of Lower Saxony (Niedersachsen), [along] with significant portions of North Rhine-Westphalia (Nordrhein-Westfalen), Schleswig-Holstein and Saxony-Anhalt (Sachsen-Anhalt)," occurred haphazardly and intermittently, with "great emphasis" placed on the Christian baptism of the Saxons in the wars of 772–85 but little emphasis placed on Christian baptism in the wars of 792–804.[44]

The Christianization of the Saxons, in other words, was not synonymous with the conquest of Saxony by the Carolingian Empire; indeed, as Rembold points out, the notion that Christian baptism immediately and irrevocably transformed the Saxons into Christians is itself a construct of Christian historiography. Even the notion that Saxons were "pagan" is a

---

[41] Antonio Gramsci, *Letters from Prison*, vol. II, trans. Raymond Rosenthal (New York, NY: Columbia University Press, 1994), 52.
[42] For a discussion of medieval Christianization and syncretism, see Wim Blockmans and Peter Hoppenbrouwers, *Introduction to Medieval Europe, 300–1500* (New York, NY: Routledge, 2014), 76–9.
[43] Rembold, *Conquest and Christianization*, 3.
[44] Rembold, *Conquest and Christianization*, 5, 39.

Christian historiographical construct: "Paganism," Rembold summarizes, "is fundamentally a Christian construct, a polemical term used to group together non-adherents to Christianity."[45] In turn, Christianity itself, understood as a coherent, singular religion, can be understood to be born from this opposition to paganism: "the categories 'pagan' and 'Christian' were applied to a broad spectrum of belief and practice, without doing justice to the countless shades of grey," Rembold points out.[46] The Christianization of Saxony, in other words, illustrates the complexity of these cultural changes, as well as the complexity of the categories paganism and Christianity themselves.

Central to Rembold's argument is the *Stellinga*, those Saxon freedmen who rebelled against their lords in the mid-ninth century; while this movement is often interpreted as a "pagan movement," Rembold, summarizing recent research on the subject, concludes that "[t]he *Stellinga* were not attempting to revert to paganism, nor were they seeking to unravel the changes which had followed Carolingian conquest and incorporation [...] they were not even a class-based movement which rallied around the destruction of elite privilege. Rather, they are better understood as a guild or horizontal association, which – in addition to a myriad of other functions – participated in the dispensing of customary justice."[47] Something similar could be said of Modernist medievalisms. The pedagogical medievalisms of Eliot, Weston, Pound, Hemingway, and Fitzgerald are symptomatic of modernity's industrialization, not a rejection of it.[48] Cultural critic T.J. Jackson Lears recognizes this complexity when he presents "antimodernism" as a core motivating factor for the Modernists, and he relates this rejection of modern industrialization to the "yearning for authentic experience" that dominated much of the American cultural landscape in the early twentieth century.[49] At issue, though, is Lears's term

---

[45] Rembold, *Conquest and Christianization*, 191.
[46] Rembold, *Conquest and Christianization*, 191.
[47] Rembold, *Conquest and Christianization*, 116.
[48] Rembold, *Conquest and Christianization*, 116. The subject of industrialization suggests the connection between these pedagogical medievalisms and the twentieth century's "infantilized" presentations of the medieval, as theorized by David Matthews (Matthews, *Medievalism*, 138). After World War I, writers such as J.R.R. Tolkien, C.S. Lewis, and T.S. Eliot began presenting the Middle Ages in "residual" or "infantilized" forms, contrasting with earlier high-art versions; Tolkien's *The Hobbit* (1937) and Lewis's *The Chronicles of Narnia* (1950–1956) focus on children or "small people," linking childhood and the medieval, implying that the medieval is childish, unserious, and disconnected from the modern, industrial world (Matthews, *Medievalism*, 121). For more on residual medievalisms, see Richard Utz, "Residual Medievalisms: Historical Pageants in Eastern Bavaria," *The Year's Work in Medievalism* 31 (2016), 75–81.
[49] Lears, *No Place of Grace*, xxvii.

"antimodernism" itself, which suggests that U.S. medievalisms are definable by their antithetical relationship to modernity rather than by any constructive element of their cultural productions. Lears's conception of antimodernism, in other words, bears resemblance to the historiographers of the Saxon wars that Rembold critiques; just as those interpreters frame the Christianization of Saxony as a dualistic battle between paganism and Christianity, Lears frames U.S. medievalisms as entrenched within a battle that pits modernism against antimodernism.[50] Rembold's reinterpretation of the Christianization of Saxony argues for a pluralistic conception of this cultural transformation, portraying that process not as a unidirectional movement from paganism to Christianity but as an overdetermined, multi-vector shift with both pre-conquest Saxony and post-conquest Saxony "lack[ing] any unity as a region, either in terms of politics, religion, ethnicity or material culture."[51] Rembold's use of network theory, in other words, complicates Lears's notion of antimodernism, for if we understand concepts like modernization and industrialization as neither static nor singular, we also understand their antitheses to be polysemous and protean. In the same way that Rembold frames the *Stellinga* as primarily a "guild," we can read Modernist medievalisms as engaging with the modernization and industrialization of the United States in the terms upon which that modernization and industrialization rely, including the binary opposition of the medieval and the modern.[52]

If the Middle Ages undergird T.S. Eliot's *The Waste Land* and Ezra Pound's *The Cantos* as a world that one must understand in order to rightly interpret modernity, the medieval haunts the very psyches of William Faulkner's characters. Like many of Twain's works, as well as Cervantes's *Don Quixote*, Faulkner's novels reckon with medieval Europe less as pedagogical tools and more as templates for his characters' imaginations. Put another way, Faulkner grapples with the representation of the medieval as a totality itself, treating the Middle Ages as, at least in part, a figment of the modern American cultural imaginary. In a discussion at the University of Virginia in 1959, Faulkner claimed of Miss Sophonsiba, Hubert Beauchamp's unmarried sister in *Go Down, Moses* (1942), that she "lived on Walter Scott, probably, and she had nothing to do, and she would read the fine, flamboyant tales of chivalry where the maiden cast the veil to the knight in the tournament."[53] The medieval, in Faulkner's novels, appears

---

[50] Rembold, *Conquest and Christianization*, 81.
[51] Rembold, *Conquest and Christianization*, 2.
[52] On the connections between industrialization and the modern world-system, see Jorge Larrain, *Theories of Development: Capitalism, Colonialism and Dependency* (Cambridge: Polity Press, 1989).
[53] Faulkner, *Faulkner in the University*, 135.

as a kind of repressed psychic substructure for his characters, too intimate to even be discussed, perhaps even noticed. Faulkner's medievalisms exist tacitly, undergirding his characters' actions and thought processes, and in this sense his medievalisms present the medieval, like Poe, as a U.S. cultural fantasy, disclosing a much more startling *mise en abyme* than do those of other Modernist medievalisms.[54]

Faulkner's medievalisms, with this said, often vacillate between the pedagogical and the subversive. Describing a gate at Hubert Beauchamp's plantation in "Was" – the first story in *Go Down, Moses* (1942) – the narrator says, "this was what Miss Sophonsiba was still reminding people was named Warwick even when they had already known for a long time that's what she aimed to have it called, until when they wouldn't call it Warwick she wouldn't even seem to know what they were talking about and it would sound like she and Mr. Hubert owned two separate plantations covering the same area of ground, one on top of the other."[55] In naming the gate outside her brother's plantation "Warwick," Miss Sophonsiba reveals her tendency to interpret the antebellum South through her readings of Walter Scott, historicizing her family's station in a similarly Romantic light – the Beauchamp family had served as Earls of Warwick throughout the late Middle Ages, so Miss Sophonsiba's naming connects her family to those historical figures and allows her to revel in a fantasy

[54] On Faulkner's many links to Modernism, see Jay Watson, *William Faulkner and the Faces of Modernity* (Oxford: Oxford University Press, 2019), and Daniel Joseph Singal, *William Faulkner: The Making of a Modernist* (Chapel Hill, NC: University of North Carolina Press, 2000). Faulkner's medievalisms, in this sense, entwine well with recent research on fantasy in medieval British literature, especially the work of Aisling Byrne, who notices the way that the "otherworlds" described in medieval texts like *Sir Orfeo* (c. 1330) and *Visio Tnugdali* (c. 1149) offered, to a medieval European readership, "an experience analogous to fiction itself [...] an extra perspective from which to view reality" (Aisling Byrne, *Otherworlds: Fantasy and History in Medieval Literature* (Oxford: Oxford University Press, 2016), 23). While much recent scholarship on these "otherworlds" of medieval literature accentuates these worlds' "strangeness and alterity," Byrne's interpretation frames such attention to the strangeness and alterity of medieval otherworlds as itself "relative rather than absolute"; in other words, modern scholarship often oversimplifies medieval distinctions between fiction and nonfiction: "Th[e] relationship [between reader and text] might be expressed by borrowing and extending J.R.R. Tolkien's formulation where the reader's own world and the world of the fictional text are envisioned as 'primary' and 'secondary' worlds respectively. In this perspective, otherworld realms in narratives may be considered 'tertiary' worlds" (Byrne, *Otherworlds*, 18–19, 27).
[55] William Faulkner, *Go Down, Moses* (New York, NY: Vintage Books, 2011), 11.

of aristocratic belonging.[56] A similar rendering of the medieval is present in *The Sound and the Fury* (1929), which is organized largely around Holy Week – the first section occurring on Holy Saturday, the third section on Good Friday and the fourth section on Easter Sunday.[57] Faulkner is not immune to framing his narratives around medieval or medievalized titles (one of his later short stories, about the county attorney Gavin Stevens, is titled "Knight's Gambit," while *The Sound and the Fury* itself refers to Shakespeare's *Macbeth* (1623), itself a reimagining of medieval Britain – not to mention Faulkner's tendency to deploy religious diction in titles like *Go Down, Moses* and *Absalom, Absalom!* (1936)).[58] This pedagogical medievalism, though, is supplemented by what we might call, thinking of Gramsci's distinction between traditional and organic intellectuals – that is, "an intellectual or someone of professional standing [...] who rises to that level from within a social class that does not normally produce intellectuals, and remains connected to that class"[59] – an *organic medievalism* that, in *The Sound and the Fury*, appears throughout all four sections of the book, with each narrator disclosing the extent to which his or her own psyche is populated by medieval or medievalized images and tropes.

The first section of *The Sound and the Fury*, which is narrated by Benjamin Compson, the intellectually disabled and youngest son of Jason Compson III and Caroline Compson, begins with a description of a golf game that Benjy and Luster, an African American servant, are watching from behind a fence:

> Through the fence, between the curling flower spaces, I could see them hitting. They were coming toward where the flag was and I went along the fence. Luster was hunting in the grass by the flower tree. They took the flag out, and they were hitting. Then they put the flag back and they went to the table, and he hit and the other hit. Then they went on, and I went along the fence. Luster came away from the flower tree and we went along the fence and they stopped and we stopped and I looked through the fence while Luster was hunting in the grass.

---

[56] Marvin Klotz, "Procrustean Revision in *Go Down, Moses*," in *On Faulkner*, eds. Louis J. Budd and Edwin H. Cady (Durham, NC: Duke University Press, 1989), 33.

[57] William Faulkner, *The Sound and the Fury* (New York, NY: The Modern Library, 2012).

[58] William Faulkner, *Knight's Gambit: Six Stories* (London: Chatto & Windus, 1951). On Faulkner's use of religious diction, see Jessie McGuire Coffee, *Faulkner's Un-Christlike Christians: Biblical Allusions in the Novels* (Ann Arbor, MI: University of Michigan Research Press, 1983).

[59] Ian Buchanon, ed. *A Dictionary of Critical Theory*, 1st edn (Oxford: Oxford University Press, 2010), 253.

"Here Caddy." He hit. They went across the pasture. I held to the fence and watched them going away.[60]

The golf course Benjy is observing had been sold by the Compson family to finance his sister's wedding and Quentin's Harvard education; the fence separates Benjy from the game that he loves, as well as from "Caddy" – the name of his beloved, older sister now expelled from the family for her infidelity. This opening scene is one of longing for an imagined past – the pasture which the Compsons sold and where, now, the golf course resides was deemed "Benjy's pasture" because he loved it so dearly, and he still, in the above passage, tends to see it as "a pasture" not a golf course. A clear sense of nostalgia permeates these opening lines. Benjamin casts the game of golf – with its flags and repeated "hitting" – as a kind of jousting match from which he is cruelly withheld, entwining the South's "chivalry silliness," as Twain deemed it, with his own family's lost fortune.[61] After watching the golf match, Benjy follows Luster through a "broken place" in the fence, where he snags himself on a nail.[62] Immediately, chronological time is broken, and Benjy remembers how Caddy, years ago, "uncaught" him from that nail just as Luster does now.[63]

Marked by italics, these breaks from the primary temporality of the text are, for Benjy at least, marked with a clear religiosity, a sense of belonging and beauty; "Caddy uncaught me and we crawled through," Benjy writes in this first flashback, going on to describe how Caddy cared for him: "You dont want your hands froze on Christmas, do you," he recalls her asking.[64] Breaking through that fence becomes a key motif for Benjy's flashbacks, in fact, as it is repeated in three of the first five analepses; moreover, these breaks in temporality are coeval with breaks in territoriality, and these ruptures in space-time are populated with flowers, Caddy, being cared for, Christmas, pigs being slaughtered, fire, and weeping – primal, elemental figurations for Benjy.[65] These are moments of "authenticity," to use Lears's term, that, like the medieval in *The Cantos* and *The Waste Land*, suggest to Benjy a totality that is, in the primary temporality of the text, decidedly withheld from him.[66]

[60] Faulkner, *The Sound and the Fury*, 3.
[61] Twain, *Life on the Mississippi*, 314.
[62] Faulkner, *The Sound and the Fury*, 3.
[63] Faulkner, *The Sound and the Fury*, 3.
[64] 440Faulkner, *The Sound and the Fury*, 3. On primary, secondary, and tertiary worlds of texts, as well as their connections to medieval literature, see Byrne, *Otherworlds*, 23.
[65] Faulkner, *The Sound and the Fury*, 3–23.
[66] Lears, *No Place of Grace*, xxvi.

Another disclosure of Faulkner's organic medievalism is present in the section narrated by Quentin, who, as Lynn Gartrell Levins argues in an analysis of *Absalom, Absalom!*, "re-creates Judith, Bon, and Henry as protagonists of a contemporary medieval romance."[67] But while Levins focuses on the way "Faulkner's characters function within the framework of the chivalric romance," expostulating on Faulkner's own pedagogical medievalism, Faulkner more subtly inscribes his characters' thought processes with medievalisms.[68] In a study of Faulkner's preoccupation with innocence – a concept that, along with authenticity, Lears also connects with American medievalism[69] – Lawrence Bowling points out that Herbert Head, Quentin's brother-in-law, describes Quentin as a "half-baked Galahad," when Quentin refuses to take a newly minted fifty-dollar bill for fear of Herbert's "unidealistic practicality"; "in *The Sound and the Fury*," Bowling summarizes, "Quentin views himself as the one whose fate it is to retrieve the family honor," a self-identification that Herbert Head lampoons as "identifying Quentin with the noblest and purest knight of the Round Table whose fate it was to retrieve the Holy Grail."[70] Quentin's narration, in fact, begins with a meditation on temporality itself:

> When the shadow of the sash appeared on the curtains it was between seven and eight o'clock and then I was in time again, hearing the watch. It was Grandfather's and when Father gave it to me he said I give you the mausoleum of all hope and desire; it's rather excruciatingly apt that you will use it to gain the *reducto* [sic] *absurdum* of all human experience which can fit your individual needs no better than it fitted his or his father's. I give it to you not that you may remember time, but that you might forget it now and then for a moment and not spend all your breath trying to conquer it. Because no battle is ever won he said. They are not even fought. The field only reveals to man his own folly and despair, and victory is an illusion of philosophers and fools.[71]

As with the opening sentences of Benjy's narration, these lines construct a binary opposition; they meditate on the difference between living "in time" and "forget[ting] it." While Benjy divides reality into a longed-for past and a vacuous present, Quentin, remembering his father's ominous

---

[67] Lynn Gartrell Levins, *Faulkner's Heroic Design: The Yoknapatawpha Novels* (Athens, GA: University of Georgia Press, 1976/2008), 116.
[68] Levins, *Faulkner's Heroic Design*, 116. The quote is from the third chapter, titled "Faulkner's Use of the Chivalric Romance."
[69] Lears, *No Place of Grace*, 144–9.
[70] Lawrence E. Bowling, "Faulkner and the Theme of Innocence," *Kenyon Review* 20:3 (1958), 468–9.
[71] Faulkner, *The Sound and the Fury*, 82.

advice to "forget [time] now and then," divides reality by the presence and absence of temporality.

Thinking of the medieval/modern divide, we could say that Quentin distinguishes between secularity – i.e. the temporality of his father's watch – and religious time – i.e. atemporality, the "moments" when he, paradoxically, "forget[s]" time.[72] Quentin's memory of his father's advice connects this atemporality with battlefields, fools, and *reductio ad absurdum* (playfully "reducing" the term to *"reducto absurdum"*) – concepts that invoke, respectively, warfare, court jesters (an important theme throughout Faulkner's oeuvre, especially in *The Sound and the Fury*[73]), and medieval Scholastic theology.[74] Quentin continues: "You can be oblivious to the sound [of a clock] for a long while, then in a second of ticking it can create in the mind unbroken the long diminishing parade of time you didn't hear. Like Father said down the long and lonely light-rays you might see Jesus walking, like. And the good Saint Francis that said Little Sister Death, that never had a sister."[75] Faulkner associates, in this case, a medieval cultural figure – Saint Francis – with death and atemporality, and his mention of "a sister" remembers Caddy, with whom, later in the chapter, Quentin will claim to have committed incest.[76] Echoing D.H.

---

[72] For more, see Taylor, *A Secular Age*, 718–19.

[73] On Faulkner's interest in the "fool tradition," see, for instance, Joy Farmer Shaw, "The South in Motley: A Study of the Fool Tradition in Selected Works by Faulkner, McCullers, and O'Connor," PhD diss., University of Virginia, 1978. This might be the opportunity, also, to reference the magisterial work of Jan M. Ziolkowski's *The Juggler of Notre Dame and the Medievalizing of Modernity*, a six-volume work that analyzes the reception history, from the thirteenth to the twenty-first century, of the medieval French poem, "Jongleur de Notre Dame," which tells of a juggler who, after joining a monastery, develops a unique form of devotional practice – namely, juggling or "tumbling." The fifth volume, subtitled "Tumbling into the Twentieth Century," delves into the medievalisms of Henry Adams, Charlie Chaplin, Wallace Stevens, and U.S. children's literature more broadly, among numerous other texts, emphasizing in particular the extent to which the medieval has been and continues to be associated with the figure of the jester, ecstatic prayer, and an ecumenical Christianity (Jan M. Ziolkowski, *The Juggler and the Medievalizing of Modernity: Tumbling into the Twentieth Century* (Cambridge: Open Books Publishers, 2018)).

[74] On the early twentieth-century association of warfare and the Middle Ages, at least within the British cultural imaginary, see Mike Horswell, *The Rise and Fall of British Crusader Medievalism* (New York, NY: Routledge, 2018). On the connections between Latin phrases like *reductio ad absurdum* and the Middle Ages, see Mary Catherine Davidson, *Medievalism, Multilingualism, Chaucer* (New York, NY: Palgrave Macmillan, 2010), 45–50.

[75] Faulkner, *The Sound and the Fury*, 73.

[76] The incest motif in *The Sound and the Fury* is explored further in Constance Hill Hall, *Incest in Faulkner: A Metaphor for the Fall* (Ann Arbor, MI: UMI Research Press, 1986), 43–8.

Lawrence's reading of Roderick Usher "breaking the polarity of himself," John T. Irwin, discussing Quentin's narcissism and repressed incestual desire, points out that "the internal narrative of [Quentin's] last day, clearly the narrative of someone who has gone insane, is dominated by Quentin's obsessive attempts to escape from his shadow, to 'trick his shadow,' as he says."[77] While Pound and Eliot deploy the medieval as templates upon which their texts depend, Faulkner grapples with the effects of such a pedagogy – namely, the extent to which such pedagogical medievalism peripheralizes the present both spatially and temporally. Quentin – like Hank Morgan in *Connecticut Yankee* and Roderick Usher in "Fall of the House of Usher" – is circumscribed within a world within which time is non-chronological and space less a Cartesian coordinate plane than a mysterious network where his life in the South interweaves with his life in Cambridge, and Quentin's narration – again like *Connecticut Yankee* and "The Fall of the House of Usher" – recounts Quentin's gradual separation from the primary world of the text, the narration becoming increasingly nonsensical and unmoored from his present life in Cambridge. Like Hank Morgan's death and the collapse of the House of Usher, the decline of the Compson family brings into stark relief the extent to which these lives and institutions rely upon a decidedly irrational fixation upon medieval Europe – a fixation that, when grappled with in a sustained fashion, bespeaks the powerful and dangerous repressed cultural anxieties latent within this tradition of Euro-American male authorship.

If Quentin's narration exemplifies the medievalisms of the Northern bourgeoisie, connecting the medieval with antimodernism and industrial ennui, the third section of *The Sound and the Fury*, set on Good Friday and narrated by Quentin's younger brother, Jason, connects the medieval with the Southern aristocracy, sublimating the Southern white patriarchy and demeaning all else, especially African Americans, Jews, and women. While Benjy's and Quentin's narrations are riddled through, respectively, with vivid descriptions and interior monologues, Jason's narration exhibits a deep, residing resentment of Quentin, Caddy, and Miss Quentin. This resentment, legible from the very first sentence of the narration ("Once a bitch always a bitch, what I say"), becomes displaced onto all manner of individuals and groups.[78] Obsessed with wealth and women, Jason narrates in the voice of Realism; if Quentin, as Harold Bloom opines, mimics

---

[77] John T. Irwin, *Doubling and Incest/Repetition and Revenge: A Speculative Reading of Faulkner* (Baltimore, MD: Johns Hopkins University Press, 1975), 35.
[78] Faulkner, *The Sound and the Fury*, 180.

Stephen Dedalus, Jason mimics Huck Finn – but crueler, a resentful double of Twain's "American Adam."[79]

Jason's anti-Semitism, in fact, is the clearest example of how Jason's imagination has been populated by pedagogical medievalisms. "I give every man his due, regardless of religion or anything else," Jason condescends, speaking to a man outside the shop where he clerks. "I have nothing against jews [sic] as an individual [...] It's just the race. You'll admit that they produce nothing. They follow the pioneers into a new country and sell them clothes."[80] As medievalist Richard Utz has argued, "medievalists have an ethical obligation to investigate and historicize religion and theology," and, in a sense, this is precisely what Faulkner is doing, embedding within *The Sound and the Fury* a Southern, racist, sexist, and anti-Semitic ideology.[81] Modern anti-Semitism, after all, with all of its connections to modern ethnonationalism, has clear "continuities" and "discontinuities" with the anti-Semitism and anti-Islamism of medieval European Christianity: American anti-Semitism "consist[s] of echoes of medieval Europe in the form of imagery and associations that would resonate in American society and culture, at least in part through religion, and for quite different purposes."[82] In the case of Jason's anti-Semitic rhetoric, these echoes of medieval Europe are also connected with the western frontier. After Jason describes Jews as those who "follow the pioneers into a new country to sell them clothes," his interlocuter – presumably Jewish – declares himself "an American," to which Jason says, "So am I [...] Not many of us left. What I'm talking about is the fellows that sit up there in New York and trim the sucker gamblers."[83] Jason's overt resentment of Quentin and Caddy becomes entwined with Southern resentment writ large, which itself – at least since Twain – has been recognized as entwined with the Southern "chivalry silliness" of Lost Cause nostalgia.[84] That Jason adds to this over-

[79] On notions of the American Adam, see R.W.B. Lewis, *The American Adam: Innocence, Tragedy, and Tradition in the Nineteenth Century* (Chicago, IL: University of Chicago Press, 1955), 100.

[80] Faulkner, *The Sound and the Fury*, 184.

[81] Richard Utz, *Medievalism: A Manifesto* (Yorkshire: ARC Humanities Press, 2017).

[82] Richard E. Frankel "The Deeper the Roots, the Deadlier the Antisemitism? Comparing Images of Jewish Financial Control in Modern Germany and the United States," in *The Medieval Roots of Antisemitism: Continuities and Discontinuities from the Middle Ages to the Present Day*, eds. Jonathon Adams and Cordelia Heß (New York, NY: Routledge, 2018), 352–60.

[83] Faulkner, *The Sound and the Fury*, 220.

[84] Twain, *Life on the Mississippi*, 314. On "Lost Cause nostalgia" – that is, the penchant in the American South to romanticize the antebellum period – see Steve Longenecker, *Pulpits of the Lost Cause: The Faith and Politics of Confederate Chaplains during Reconstruction* (Tuscaloosa, AL: University of Alabama Press, 2023), 75.

determined network of cultural associations the "pioneers" of the western frontier only illustrates once again the extent to which the frontier, as an "undeveloped" territory, is embedded within the American cultural imaginary as a spatiotemporal world akin to medieval Europe and non-Western cultures – that is, worlds of "authenticity," where people and things are as they appear (unlike, say, Miss Quentin, whom Jason maligns for "gobbing paint on her face," or Quentin, whose Harvard education taught him only "how to go for a swim at night").[85]

The concluding section of *The Sound and the Fury*, set on Easter Sunday, is the only section not narrated by a first-person narrator. Focalized around Dilsey, the elderly, matriarchal figure among the Compsons' African American servants, this section sees Dilsey take Benjy to her Black church for Easter Sunday services, and this setting constructs an ethos of religious fervor – or, to use Lears's language, "sacred passion."[86] Dilsey weeps openly throughout the church service and, thinking of the Compsons, imagines that she has "seed de first en de last"; "I seed de beginnin, en now I sees de endin," she reiterates to a fellow parishioner.[87] Religious diction, African American community, the Jim Crow South, non-standard English, the demise of a Euro-American estate: while the medieval is not mentioned overtly, the characters grapple openly in this section with the effects of a society constructed upon an ideology that bifurcates the world into black/white, religious/secular, medieval/modern, South/North, developed/undeveloped – a society that, as D.H. Lawrence says of Roderick Usher, has "broken the polarity of itself."

The final paragraphs of this fourth section, which revolve around Dilsey, Luster, and Jason calming Benjy's bouts of hysteria, speaks to the heart of the matter: the arbitrariness endemic to any proposed social order – "The broken flower drooped over Ben's fist," the unnamed narrator says, describing the carriage passing a statue of a Confederate soldier outside the town's white cemetery, "and his eyes were empty and blue and serene again as cornice and façade flowed smoothly once more from left to right, post and tree, window and doorway and signboard each in its ordered place."[88] The "ordered place" ascribed to each thing is a matter of perspective. Luster, returning from the church, had taken the carriage to the left of the statue, upsetting the normal route Benjy usually takes to the cemetery, and Benjy simply cannot withstand such disorder. He throws a fit and only when Jason arrives to turn the carriage around and take the accustomed route

---

[85] Lears, *No Place of Grace*, 138.
[86] Lears, *No Place of Grace*, 136, 138.
[87] Faulkner, *The Sound and the Fury*, 297, 301.
[88] Faulkner, *The Sound and the Fury*, 309.

does Benjy become "serene again."[89] Dilsey, Luster, and Jason – although especially the former two – work to keep Benjy calm and serene, and such serenity depends for Benjy upon a constancy of perspective.

The organic medievalisms explored in *The Sound and the Fury* speak to the extent to which U.S. ethnonationalism and imperialism depend upon a reputedly constant, unchanging historiographical perspective that rends the modern from the unmodern: "America," as postmodern philosopher Gilles Deleuze observed, "is a land of perversion," "a land without fathers," and the persistent American turn to the European medieval amounts, at least in part, to a search for father figures – the quintessential task of Oedipus.[90] Deleuze begins his essay "On the Superiority of Anglo-American Literature" (1977): "To leave, to escape, is to trace a line of flight," alluding to D.H. Lawrence's discussion of *Moby Dick*; "it is always one's father or mother (or worse) that one finds again on the voyage," Deleuze contends, still thinking of Lawrence's reading of *Moby Dick*.[91] U.S. medievalisms exist as clear instances of such "line[s] of flight"; they are not merely symptomatic or even suggestive of loss but are productive figurations, creating from their desire for belonging hybridic, monstrous figures – transhistorical, multicultural, and transoceanic. While Modernists like Pound and Eliot, searching for a gestalt with which to revitalize a purportedly fallen world, weave the medieval and East Asian figures into their texts, treating those non-Western and unmodern worlds as the totality Western modernity has displaced, Faulkner weaves the medieval into the very psyches of his characters, not so much using medievalisms as lines of flight as having his characters enact such lines of flight *in situ*. In turn, *The Sound and the Fury* – as well as *Absalom, Absalom!*, whose organic medievalisms could just as well be explored – becomes a text concerned not with the historical Middle Ages so much as with the American construction of an imagined medieval past. That Faulkner, like Twain, was fascinated with *Don Quixote* (Faulkner claimed to reread the novel every year, arguing that Cervantes's attention to character, rather than plot, was essential to the advent of the novel) makes particular sense in this regard.[92] Rather than following Sir Walter Scott's tradition of "chivalry silliness," Faulkner utilizes Cervantes's "subversive discourse" that "distances [the author] from his chosen chronicler [...] spatially and temporally."[93] The deployment of organic medievalisms illustrates one way that

---

[89] Faulkner, *The Sound and the Fury*, 321.

[90] Gregg Lambert, *Who's Afraid of Deleuze and Guattari?* (New York, NY: Continuum, 2006), 97.

[91] Gilles Deleuze, *Dialogues II*, trans. Hugh Tomlinson and Barbara Habberjam (New York, NY: Columbia University Press, 1987), 36–9.

[92] Levins, *Faulkner's Heroic Design*, 115.

[93] Parr, *Don Quixote: An Anatomy of Subversive Discourse*, 79. Twain, *Life on the Mississippi*, 314.

Faulkner, like Cervantes, Poe, and Twain, constructs such a subversive discourse; the Middle Ages are inherited but not as a static, fixed essence – such as the name of "Usher" – but, as Deleuze and Guattari say of the "rhizome," "from the middle, through the middle, coming and going rather than starting and finishing."[94] Pedagogical medievalisms lose sight of the creativity and arbitrariness inherent in such inheritance, framing the medieval as a static totality; Faulkner, however, presents the medieval as an invention of his characters, a cultural fantasy that, to this day, buttresses imperial and ethnonationalist ideologies, including American Anglo-Saxonism, anti-Semitism, and patriarchy.

---

[94] Deleuze and Guattari, *A Thousand Plateaus*, 27–8.

6

The Spectacle of the Medieval: America's New Feudalism, HBO's *Game of Thrones*, and Ursula K. Le Guin's Hainish Novels

U.S. MEDIEVALISMS HAVE become, since the end of World War II, increasingly embedded within a multimedia landscape in which, as Guy Debord famously writes in *Society of the Spectacle* (1967), "images detach [...] from every aspect of life [and] merge into a common stream in which the unity of that life can no longer be recovered."[1] Walt Disney films like *Snow White* (1937), *Cinderella* (1950), and *The Sword in the Stone* (1963); television series like *Buffy the Vampire Slayer* (1997–2003), *Game of Thrones* (2011–19), and *Mists of Avalon* (2001), as well as massively multiplayer role-playing games like *World of Warcraft* (2004–) and *The Elder Scrolls* (1994–), rely consistently upon medievalisms to constitute their fantastical worlds, which are, in turn, leveraged within a capitalist system for which "fragmented views of reality regroup themselves into a new unity as a separate pseudo-world that can only be looked at."[2] "Understood in its totality," Debord summarizes, "the spectacle is both the result and the goal of the dominant mode of productions. It is not a mere decoration added to

---

[1] Guy Debord, *Society of the Spectacle*, 7.
[2] Debord, *Society of the Spectacle*, 7; *Snow White* (Walt Disney Productions, 1937); *Cinderella* (Walt Disney Productions, 1950); *The Sword in the Stone* (Walt Disney Productions, 1963); *Buffy the Vampire Slayer*, television series, created by Joss Whedon (1997–2003; Los Angeles, CA: 20th Century Fox Television); *The Mists of Avalon*, television series, directed by Uli Edel (2001; Los Angeles, CA: TNT); *World of Warcraft*, video game, developed by Blizzard Entertainment (2004–; Irvine, CA: Blizzard Entertainment); *The Elder Scrolls*, video game series, developed by Bethesda Game Studios (1994–; Rockville, MD: Bethesda Softworks). On Disney's use of the Middle Ages, see Pugh and Aronstein, *The Disney Middle Ages*. On medievalisms in contemporary television, film and video games, including *Buffy the Vampire Slayer*, *Game of Thrones*, and *World of Warcraft*, see Helen Young, *The Middle Ages in Popular Culture: Medievalism and Genre* (Amherst, NY: Cambria Press, 2015).

the real world. It is the very heart of this real society's unreality. In all of its particular manifestations – news, propaganda, advertising, entertainment – the spectacle represents the dominant model of life."[3]

The medieval exists in the late twentieth- and early twenty-first-century United States as a fragment of "this real society's unreality," alienating its citizens from history itself by making of history a pseudo-world of dragons, castles, magic, and enchantment and selling that pseudo-world to citizens as "spectacular commodities."[4] Scholarship on medieval spectacle, however, can deepen our understanding of these spectacular medievalisms, which function to create the semblance of unity for a disparate and diverse society. Lawrence M. Bryant, for instance, has argued that "royal spectacles," such as processions, religious and guild dramas, and popular festive practices during the Lancastrian ascendancy of the early fifteenth century, utilized a "political inventiveness" that "opened new spaces for political expression and thought at a time when the customary political vocabulary was in disarray and incapable of addressing the malaise and near anarchy of existential conditions."[5] These spectacles gave the appearance of unity during a period of upheaval when Henry VI reigned as both king of England and the disputed king of France during the latter half of the Hundred Years' War: "Rather than one grand spectacle of a mystical union," Bryant writes, "these urban/royal encounters consisted of a series of minispectacles, each of which was produced by miscellaneous groups from town prostitutes to the highest officials. The king alone, like the thread in a necklace of many stones, connected spectacles that had foundations in different traditions and social groups."[6] These spectacles allowed King Henry VI to bolster his reign over England and France by inscribing himself within various ceremonies, pageants, and festivals, French and English alike, and this Lancastrian political inventiveness, as Bryant argues, functioned as a kind of bricolage, "a 'game' that begins with the presumption of equality among participants."[7]

It is fitting, then, that HBO's *Game of Thrones*, the television series based on George R.R. Martin's *A Song of Ice and Fire* (1996–) that includes a good deal of Debordian spectacle, is a reimagining of the Wars of the Roses (1455–87), a war between the House of Lancaster and the House of York – represented, respectively, as the House of Lannister and the House

[3] Debord, *Society of the Spectacle*, 8.
[4] Debord, *Society of the Spectacle*, 18.
[5] Lawrence M. Bryant, "Configurations of the Community in late Medieval Spectacles: Paris and London during the Dual Monarchy," in *City and Spectacle in Medieval Europe*, eds. Barbara Hanawalt and Kathryn Reyerson (Minneapolis, MN: University of Minnesota Press, 1994), 3.
[6] Bryant, "Configurations," 4–5.
[7] Bryant, "Configurations," 5.

of Stark.[8] *Game of Thrones* recalls the Lancastrian political inventiveness of the fifteenth century, even presenting battles among royalty for power as a "game" (the same term Bryant uses to describe Lancastrian spectacle).[9] The show integrates these historical elements within modern visual culture into its hour-long episodes, using computer-generated grandeur and violence.[10] Indeed, *Game of Thrones* encapsulates the twin strands of Romantic and Enlightenment renderings of the Middle Ages. The opulence and pageantry portrayed in the show romanticize this pseudo-medieval world, while the extravagant violence presents it as a Dark Age of brutality and death. Bryant's notion that "minispectacles" afford a means of tying together loosely connected political territorialities becomes a useful lens for understanding the television show's complex and overdetermined representation of the Middle Ages. Like American Anglo-Saxonist rhetoric, *Game of Thrones*' depiction of the War of the Roses sublimates a single, overdetermined figure: the pseudo-medieval world itself. This world, much like Debord's "pseudo-world" of the spectacle, can only be gazed at, never lived.[11]

These spectacular medievalisms, moreover, speak to the extent to which the U.S. has been conceived, for at least a century, as itself a "feudal" power – a term that, while precise in its historical context, has come to be used as a sort of shorthand for describing various forms of hierarchical and decentralized power structures.[12] Umberto Eco, in particular, has discussed the "new feudalism" endemic to twentieth-century Western nation-states:

> [T]here is no special reason for amazement at an avalanche of pseudo-medieval pulp in paperbacks, midway between Nazi nostalgia and occultism. A country able to produce Dianetics can do a lot in terms of wash-and-wear sorcery and Holy Grail *frappé*. It would be small wonder if the next porn hit stars Marilyn Chambers as La Princesse Lointaine

---

[8] Brian A. Pavlac, *Game of Thrones versus History: Written in Blood* (New York, NY: Wiley-Blackwell, 2017), 20. On the connections between Debordian spectacle and *Game of Thrones*, see Dan Hassler-Forest, *Science Fiction, Fantasy, and Politics: Transmedia World-Building Beyond Capitalism* (New York, NY: Rowman & Littlefield, 2016), 19, 129.

[9] Bryant, "Configurations," 5.

[10] For a discussion of spectacle in *Game of Thrones*, especially with respect to gender studies, see: Valerie Estelle Frankel, *Women in* Game of Thrones: *Power, Conformity and Resistance* (Jefferson, NC: McFarland & Co., 2014), 5, 35.

[11] Debord, "Society of the Spectacle," 7

[12] For more on the use of "feudal" as a shorthand term, see Susan Reynolds, *Fiefs and Vassals: The Medieval Evidence Reinterpreted* (Oxford: Oxford University Press, 1994); and Elizabeth A.R. Brown, "The Tyranny of a Construct: Feudalism and Historians of Medieval Europe," *American Historical Review* 79:4 (1974), 1063–88.

(if Americans have succeeded in transforming Rostand's *Chanteclair* into the *Fantastiks*, why not imagine the Princess of Tripoli offering the keys of her chastity belt to a bearded Burt Reynolds?). Not to mention such postmodern neomedieval Manhattan new castles as the Citicorp Center and Trump Tower, curious instances of a new feudalism, with their courts open to peasants and merchants and the well-protected high-level apartments reserved for the lords.[13]

This new feudalism, epitomized for Eco by Trump Tower, utilizes "pseudo-medieval pulp" as spectacles to subtly separate labor from leisure and the elite from the masses – as well as modernity from the unmodern. Spectacular medievalisms populate contemporary cultural productions – films, television shows, pulp fiction, comic books, and video games – that, in turn, consume the leisure time of an increasingly socioeconomically unequal citizenry.[14] These medievalisms are not "antimodern" so much as ultramodern, serving to exploit and isolate viewers from ideology itself.[15] They present culture, ideology, and the arts as mere spectacles to be viewed rather than experienced through active participation. This alienation supports a neoconservative ideology, endorsed by Donald Trump himself – the namesake and owner of Trump Tower – that promotes the unchecked growth of corporate capitalism, seen as the direct descendant of the modern colonial world-system.[16]

This "new feudalism," though, as Eco terms it, is not altogether new. After all, Gilded Age figures like Andrew Carnegie often placed themselves in the role of feudal lord – a role that allowed them to transform even universities into monuments to corporate philanthropy; the so-called Collegiate Gothic architectural movement, exemplified by structures like Cobb Lecture Hall at the University of Chicago or Yale University's Farnham Hall – both named after wealthy magnates – presented philanthropists as benevolent, king-like figures, charitably providing society with beautiful cultural productions.[17] Indeed, Andrew Carnegie himself

---

[13] Umberto Eco, *Travels in Hyper Reality: Essays*, trans. William Weaver (New York, NY: Houghton Mifflin, 1990), 62.

[14] For a discussion of increasing inequality, see: Joseph Stiglitz, *The Price of Inequality: How Today's Divided Society Endangers Our Society* (New York, NY: Norton & Co., 2012).

[15] Lears, *No Place of Grace*, xvi.

[16] On the connections between corporate capitalism and the colonial world-system, see Immanuel Wallerstein, *The Capitalism World-System* (Cambridge: Cambridge University Press, 1979).

[17] Kathleen Davis, "Tycoon Medievalism, Corporate Philanthropy, and American Pedagogy," *American Literary History* 22:4 (2010), 781–800. The link between Donald Trump and medievalism also points, within the context of South America, to the "political neomedievalism" of contemporary Brazilian politics,

claimed that "surplus wealth should be considered as a sacred trust to be administered by those into whose hands it falls, during their lives, for the good of the community," presenting surplus wealth as akin to the divine right of kings.[18] Carnegie's "Gospel of Wealth," even as it recognizes the arbitrariness of the distribution of capital and the extent to which wealthy individuals gain their wealth by means of their communities, is predicated on an assumption that surplus wealth is possessed by specific individuals and garnered through hard work and "personal simplicity and restraint."[19] Such an assumption prompts him to see "the advantages of poverty," and especially how "wealth left to young men, as a rule, is disadvantageous," rephrasing Emerson's "Saxon individualism" for the Industrial Age.[20]

The late nineteenth-century Progressive Movement, meanwhile, was no less willing to interpret U.S. socioeconomic classes as akin to feudal estates. Thorstein Veblen's *The Theory of the Leisure Class* (1899), a cornerstone of Progressive Era intellectual thought, presents industrial capitalism as a covert form of feudalism, creating a leisure class that conspicuously consumes – a phrase Veblen himself coins in that text – and a middle class and labor class that produce the goods for that conspicuous

---

especially that of Jair Bolsonaro, which Luiz Felipe Anchieta Guerra has noted is "most likely influenced in no small part by the medieval imagery by Donald J. Trump's supporters" (Luiz Felipe Anchieta Guerra, "The Internet Crusade against Communism: Political Neomedievalism in Twenty-first Century Brazil," in *The Modern Memory of the Military-Religious Orders: Engaging the Crusades*, Vol. VII, ed. Rorry MacLellan (New York, NY: Routledge Press, 2022), 91–110). Brazil, more generally, affords a fascinating case study for New World medievalisms due to the transfer of the Portuguese court to Brazil in 1807, where it remained until 1821. For more on Brazil and medievalisms, see Nadia Altschul, "Medievalism and the Contemporaneity of the Medieval in Postcolonial Brazil," in *Studies in Medievalism XXIV: Medievalism on the Margins*, ed. Karl Fugelso (Cambridge: D.S. Brewer, 2015), 139–54, as well as Luiz Felipe Anchieta Guerra, "*Neomedievalismo político no Brasil contemporâneo*," in *Medievalismos: em olhares e construções narrativas*, Vol. I, eds. Maria Eugênia Bertarelli, Renan Marques Birro and João Batista da Silva (Ananindeua: Editora Itacaúnas, 2021), 47–64.

[18] Andrew Carnegie, *The Gospel of Wealth, and Other Timely Essays* (New York, NY: The Century Co., 1901), 54.

[19] Carnegie, *The Gospel of Wealth*, 65.

[20] Carnegie, *The Gospel of Wealth*, 55; Ralph Waldo Emerson, *The Journals and Miscellaneous Notebooks of Ralph Waldo Emerson*, Vol XIII, eds. Ralph H. Orth and Alfred R. Ferguson (Cambridge, MA: Belknap Press, 1977), 95. Wealthy American business magnates during the turn of the twentieth century also often constructed mansions that mimicked European medieval castles. Boldt Castle in New York's Thousand Islands region was built by hotel magnate George Boldt between 1900 and 1904, while Bannerman Castle, also in New York, was constructed in 1901 by Francis Bannerman VI, an owner of a large military surplus store in New York City that recently served as the setting for the school of magic in the television adaptation of Lev Grossman's *The Magicians* (New York, NY: Viking Press, 2009).

consumption.[21] Upton Sinclair's *The Jungle* (1906), meanwhile, describes Mike Scully, the owner of the Chicago brickyards, as "the political lord of the district, the boss of Chicago's mayor," while Sinclair Lewis, in *Babbitt* (1923), describes how "[i]n the city of Zenith, in the barbarous twentieth century, a family's motor indicated its social rank as precisely as the grades of the peerage determined the rank of an English family – indeed, more precisely, considering the opinion of old county families upon newly created brewery barons and woolen-mill viscounts."[22]

With this said, the notion that both the Gilded Age and the Progressive Era fragmented U.S. society into a highly stratified one akin to feudal Europe's presumes that "feudal Europe" itself exists as a coherent sociopolitical entity. Since at least Marc Bloch's *Feudal Society* (1939), medievalists have worked to illustrate how the conception of medieval European society as hierarchized into distinct estates – the clergy, the nobility, and the peasantry – speaks only to a relatively brief period in the history of medieval Europe and, even then, only to specific regions within Europe.[23] Susan Reynolds, for instance, contends that "in so far as [concepts such as vassalage and the fief] are definable and comprehensible they are not helpful" to understanding the Middle Ages because those concepts are "post-medieval constructs."[24] Like so many medievalisms, the figures of the vassal and the fief, as well as the concept of feudalism itself, are filtered through "a framework of interpretation that was devised in the sixteenth century and elaborated in the seventeenth and eighteenth," especially a socioeconomic theory developed by Adam Smith and, eventually, Karl Marx that divided history into discrete periods based on a given society's economic system.[25] Reynolds traces the ways in which European scholars from the sixteenth to the nineteenth century divided history into periods, associating the Middle Ages specifically with an agrarian society. Her project looks to disrupt such a periodizing schema by emphasizing how, as she puts it, "[t]oo many models of feudalism used for comparisons, even

---

[21] Thorstein Veblen, *The Theory of the Leisure Class* (New York, NY: The Macmillan Company, 1899). Veblen's historiography is, of course, deeply informed by Karl Marx's conceptions of feudalism – see Karl Marx, *Capital: A Critique of Political Economy*, Vol. 1, trans. Ben Fowkes (New York, NY: Penguin Books, 1976), 874–5. One might also look at Mark Twain's own conception of feudalism, discussed by Henry Nash Smith in *Mark Twain's Fable of Progress: Political and Economic Ideas in* A Connecticut Yankee (New Brunswick, NJ: Rutgers University Press, 1964), 57–90.

[22] Upton Sinclair, *The Jungle* (New York, NY: Penguin Books, 1986), 312. Sinclair Lewis, *Main Street and Babbitt* (New York, NY: Library of America, 1992), 554.

[23] Marc Bloch, *Feudal Society*, trans. L.A. Manon (New York, NY: Routledge, 1962).

[24] Reynolds, *Fiefs and Vassals*, 4.

[25] Reynolds, *Fiefs and Vassals*, 4.

by Marxists, are still either constructed on the sixteenth-century basis or incorporate what, in a Marxist view, must surely be superficial or irrelevant features from it [...] It is not just that all the phenomena and notions of feudo-vassalic institutions never existed together anywhere, but that they are too incoherent, too loosely related, and too imperfectly reflected in medieval evidence to be envisaged as anything like an ideal type."[26]

This historiography has not hampered, however, the transferal of the post-medieval construct of feudalism onto colonial contexts. As Reynolds summarizes: "the comparative use of feudalism in [the] study of non-European societies, although generally conducted in what is intended to be a Marxist sense, is gravely hindered by a tendency to bring fiefs and vassals into the discussion in 'the Cinderella's slipper strategy' of trying to fit one whole society into a conceptual model derived from a quite different other."[27] If we think of feudalism itself as heterogeneous, the U.S. representation of itself as a feudal state becomes simply another iteration of feudalism itself. "The United States is a hybrid and segmented society," write sociologists Vladimir Shlapentokh and Joshua Woods in *Feudal America: Elements of the Middle Ages in Contemporary Society* (2011), "one that comprises several universal social forms," and Shlapentokh and Woods contend that "we need multiple models, including liberal, authoritarian, criminal, religious, and others" to grapple with this complexity.[28] Their use of a "feudal model" to understand U.S. society does not insist that the United States can be solely comprehended by means of this model but instead demonstrates the persistence of "egotistical interests of the few [to] challenge democratic principles."[29] Even as Shlapentokh and Woods notice the polyvocality of the United States, they neglect the polyvocality of feudalism itself. They see the "feudal model" as one means of understanding U.S. society when we could also see America's "new feudalism" as an instance of feudalism, itself understood as a post-medieval construct – with race and gender in particular serving as markers of social class.[30]

---

[26] Reynolds, *Fiefs and Vassals*, 11.
[27] Reynolds, *Fiefs and Vassals*, 5.
[28] Vladimir Shlapentokh and Joshua Woods, *Feudal America: Elements of the Middle Ages in Contemporary Society* (University Park, PA: Pennsylvania State University Press, 2011), ix.
[29] Shlapentokh and Woods, *Feudal America*, ix. Also see Yanis Varoufakis, *Technofeudalism: What Killed Capitalism* (Brooklyn, NY: Melville House, 2024), which explores the feudalistic elements of contemporary technology companies.
[30] For more on how race and gender have been employed as markers of social class, as well as that class system's links to medieval Europe, see Robert Yusef Rabiee, *Medieval America: Feudalism and Liberalism in Nineteenth-Century U.S. Culture* (Athens, GA: University of Georgia Press, 2020), 1–24, as well as Wilkerson, *Caste*, 39–88.

U.S. medievalisms have been and continue to be leveraged within this regressive, patriarchal, and racially fraught political ideology that, like nineteenth-century American Anglo-Saxonism, presents the white, Christian man as the prototypical U.S. citizen. As Tom Henthorne has written, "it is no coincidence that the popularity of such films [*Star Wars* and *E.T.*] peaked during Ronald Reagan's first term as president; neomedievalism and neoconservatism were both reactions to the supposed excesses of the late sixties and early seventies, particularly those associated with the feminist and other liberation movements."[31] Henthorne sees *Star Wars* and *E.T.* as "neomedieval romance[s]" that "affirm the conservative call for a return to older, simpler times and traditional values," and it is not difficult to trace this medievalism in the discourse of contemporary American politicians such as Ronald Reagan, George W. Bush, and Donald Trump.[32] "The United States is proud of your democracy," Ronald Reagan proclaimed in a speech to the German Bundestag in 1982, "but we cannot take credit for it. Heinrich Heine, in speaking of those who built the awe-inspiring cathedrals of medieval times, said that 'In those days people had convictions. We moderns have only opinions.'"[33] The Middle Ages exist for Reagan as a time of wonder and beauty, of awe and conviction, whereas modernity is a time of "opinion," an almost paradigmatic instance of Romantic medievalism – the implication being that we ought to return to that earlier, idealized epoch, a sentiment reiterated by George W. Bush within a week of the September 11 attacks: "This crusade, this war on terrorism is going to take a while," Bush famously declared, framing the Afghanistan War as a Christian crusade against an Islamic foe.[34] Donald Trump, meanwhile, in the second debate of the 2016 presidential election, responded to a question about alleged sexual assault with a non sequitur denouncing the Islamic State of Iraq and the Levant (ISIS): "When we have a world where you have ISIS chopping off heads, where you have – and, frankly, drowning people in steel cages, where you have wars and horrible, horrible sights all over, where you have so many bad things happening, this is like medieval times. We haven't seen anything like

---

[31] Tom Henthorne, "Boys to Men: Medievalism and Masculinity in *Star Wars* and *E.T.: The Extra-Terrestrial*," in *The Medieval Hero on Screen: Representations from Beowulf to Buffy*, eds. Martha W. Driver and Sid Ray (Jefferson, NC: McFarland & Co., 2004), 74.

[32] Henthorne, "Boys to Men," 180, 79.

[33] Ronald Reagan, *Public Papers of the Presidents of the United States: Ronald Reagan, 1982* (Washington D.C.: Public Papers of the Presidents of the United States, 1982), 754.

[34] George W. Bush, *The George W. Bush Foreign Policy Reader: Presidential Speeches and Commentary*, ed. John W. Dietrich (Armonk, NY: M.E. Sharpe, 2005), 41.

this, the carnage all over the world."³⁵ The Middle Ages exist for these conservative politicians as an epoch associated with war, conviction, violence, the Crusades, and carnage – with beheadings, "awe-inspiring cathedrals," and the Fall of the Twin Towers – spectacles of both violence and splendor.³⁶ If, following Debord and Bryant, we see such medievalized spectacles as a means of unifying a disparate society, we can see the ways in which these conservative politicians deploy the medieval as a means of codifying support among a specific citizenry – namely, white, Christian men.³⁷ Like American Anglo-Saxonism more generally, contemporary neoconservative medievalisms limit the possibilities of U.S. national identity. They integrate the rhetoric of American Anglo-Saxonism with that of Samuel Huntington's "clash of civilizations," recapitulating the long-standing use of Christian–Islamic antagonism in the figuration of New World social relations.³⁸

The American predilection to interpret U.S. society by means of an imagined feudal order reflects a desire for historical continuity with

---

³⁵ Katherine Haenschen, Michael Horning, and Jim A. Kuypers, "Donald J. Trump's Use of Twitter in the 2016 Campaign," *The 2016 American Presidential Campaign and the News: Implications for American Democracy and the Republic*, ed. Jim A. Kuypers (Lanham, MD: Lexington Books, 2018), 69.

³⁶ In promoting a proposed border wall along the Mexico–U.S. border, meanwhile, President Trump spoke of the wall as "medieval," an almost paradigmatic instance of how medievalisms can be leveraged in support of a thinly veiled contemporary ethnonationalism with particular poignancy along the Mexico–U.S. border (see Medrano and Kearney, *Medieval Culture and the Mexican American*, 1–2). Matthew Gabriele, "Trump says medieval walls worked. They didn't," *Washington Post*, January 10, 2019.

³⁷ On U.S. conservative's reliance on support from White, Christian men, see Anthea Butler, *White Evangelical Racism: The Politics of Morality in America* (Chapel Hill, NC: University of North Carolina Press, 2021).

³⁸ Chiara Bottici and Benolt Challand, *The Myth of the Clash of Civilizations* (New York, NY: Routledge, 2010), 2–5. Complicating the tendency to present medieval Europe as a monoethnic society, contemporary global medieval studies has only recently begun to push back against the resurgent White Supremacist and ethnonationalist agenda of American medievalism. At the July 2017 International Medieval Congress at Leeds, entitled "The Mediterranean Other and the Other Mediterranean: Perspective of Alterity in the Middle Ages," attendees, including keynote lecturer Vincent W.J. van Gerven Oei, noted that an overwhelming majority of the panelists "discussing 'otherness' were white, European men" (J. Clara Chan, "Medievalists, Recoiling from White Supremacy, Try to Diversify the Field," *Chronicle of Higher Education*, July 16, 2017, accessed September 29, 2017, http://www.chronicle.com/article/Medievalists-Recoiling-From/240666). This recognition has spurred reflection regarding how medieval Europe has been increasingly deployed in White Supremacist circles throughout the United States in the first decades of the twenty-first century. A variety of alt-right websites use language and imagery from the Crusades, most consistently the *Deus vult* ("God wills it") meme, which features the famous battle cry of the First Crusade (1096) to promote violence and hate speech against nonwhite individuals. The White

medieval Europe and an integrated national identity, but it also illustrates how modernity and medievalism reflexively construct and are constructed by each other. Indeed, the medievalisms of *Game of Thrones* highlight the fragmented and evolving nature of the Middle Ages as a cohesive historical epoch. The show's fusion of Romantic and Enlightenment medievalisms functions to unify consumers of these stories while emphasizing the disunity inherent in a modern, diverse citizenry. It is understandable, then, why postmodern philosophers themselves have often turned to medieval Europe for figurations to portray their concepts. As historian Bruce Holsinger has demonstrated, postmodern philosophers such as Georges Bataille and Jacques Lacan draw on the Middle Ages for figures and narratives that bespeak the "crisis of representation" famously diagnosed by Jean-François Lyotard in *The Postmodern Condition* (1979).[39] These postmodern medievalisms, shared by neoconservatives and postmodernists alike, neither romanticize nor demonize the Middle Ages so much as present the medieval as a historical referent for making sense of a postmodern, postcolonial world. Postmodern philosophers, have, in their critiques of grand historical narratives, too often continued to rely upon the medieval/modern divide, itself a grand narrative, and such an aporia serves to sublimate uneven social relations, especially anti-Semitism.[40] "[Frederic] Jameson's famous dictum – 'always historicize,'" writes Kathleen Biddick, thinking about the extent to which twentieth-century philosophers "have regarded typological (also known as figural) thinking as one of the great achievements of late antique and medieval scriptural exegesis," "is based on and draws its power from a figural move. Medieval figural thinking becomes with Jameson the figure of promise that his historicism fulfills. Yet, the richness of figural thinking so advocated by Auerbach, de Lubac, White, and Jameson constitutes for other scholars its unsettling historical problem" – namely, that of Christian supersessionism, with all of its inherent anti-Semitism.[41] Even medievalism studies, when it presents the medieval as a "spatiotemporal baseline" of modernity, risks developing a pedagogical medievalism that sees the medieval as fundamental to modernity, and the antidote to such a tendency, as both Biddick and Holsinger demonstrate, is to think comparatively between modernity

---

Supremacist Jeremy Joseph Christian, for example, who killed two bus passengers in Portland, Oregon in May 2017, posted via Facebook "Hail Vinland!!! Hail Victory!!!" weeks before his attack. Also see, Majid, *We Are All Moors*, 178–9.

[39] See Holsinger, *The Premodern Condition*; Lyotard, *The Postmodern Condition*, vii.

[40] Holsinger, *The Premodern Condition*, 4–9.

[41] Kathleen Biddick, *The Typological Imaginary: Circumcision, Technology, History* (Philadelphia, PA: University of Pennsylvania Press, 2003), 5–6.

and the unmodern, understood as either pre- or postmodern.[42] Such an approach takes the unmodern not as a spatiotemporal baseline or figural trope of modernity so much as an interlocutor with modernity, neither identical to nor radically distinct from it.

In his discussion of Lancastrian spectacles, moreover, Bryant emphasizes how women such as Joan of Arc and Christine de Pizan were central to the French resistance to English rule.[43] Indeed, Joan of Arc's rise, according to Bryant, was itself an impetus for the spectacles of Lancastrian power: "Because the unexpected coronation and the role of the maiden warrior, Joan of Arc, threatened to undermine the dual monarchy, plans were made for Henry VI to travel to France in order to restore the aura of majesty and legitimacy to his French crown."[44] That a "maiden warrior" would lead the resistance to a political system founded, at least in part, upon spectacles that tie together disparate communities and cultures seems particularly fitting with respect to contemporary spectacular medievalisms, especially if we see, as Henthorne does, those medievalisms as responses to "the supposed excesses of the late sixties and early seventies, particularly those associated with the feminist and other liberation movements."[45] The French resistance to Lancastrian rule, Bryant argues, was aided by a notion that "the problems of bad times were placed at the Lancastrian door and contrasted with the imaginary virtues of former kings as put forth by such capable publicists as Christine de Pisan."[46]

While Bryant does not discuss the implications of this notion that Lancastrian rule was buffeted by women like Christine de Pizan and Joan of Arc, scholarship on Christine de Pizan's *The Book of the City of Ladies* (c. 1405) becomes particularly relevant in exploring this means of resisting a "fundamentally spectaclist" society.[47] De Pizan's text, which tells of how the narrator, reading a work by Matheolus Perusinus, begins to "wonder why on earth it was that so many men, both clerks and others, have said

[42] Davis and Altschul, *The Idea of "The Middle Ages" outside Europe*, 1.
[43] Bryant, "Configurations," 14.
[44] Bryant, "Configurations," 14.
[45] Henthorne, "Boys to Men," 74.
[46] Bryant, "Configurations," 15.
[47] Debord, *Society of the Spectacle*, 10; Christine de Pizan, *The City of Ladies*, trans. Rosalind Brown-Grant (New York, NY: Penguin Books, 1999). For feminist interpretations of Christine de Pizan, see Renate Blumenfeld-Kosinski, *The Selected Writings of Christine de Pizan* (New York, NY: W.W. Norton, 1997), 3–25, 75–102; Earl Jeffrey Richards, *Christine de Pizan and Medieval French Lyric* (Gainesville, FL: University Press of Florida, 1998), 50–78, 135–60; Charity Cannon Willard, *Christine de Pizan: Her Life and Works* (New York, NY: Persea Books, 1984), 45–67, 120–45; Rosalind Brown-Grant, *Christine de Pizan and the Moral Defence of Women: Reading Beyond Gender* (Cambridge: Cambridge University Press, 1999), 20–46, 98–125; Nadia Margolis, *An Introduction to Christine de Pizan*

and continue to say and write such awful, damning things about women and their ways," constructs a complex allegory in which the book itself exists as the revelation of a city of ladies, housing the lives of famous women throughout history.[48] The text, as Jane Chance has argued, acts as the material manifestation of the city of ladies itself:

> The discursive strategy de Pizan employs to defend her narrator is the allegory of the city of women, a fantasy citadel that combines the visual image of a moated, gated castle with the retrieval of women's history (actually, legend and hagiography) – which produces for her the inhabitants of the city – and the text of the *Book of the City of Ladies*. De Pizan's genre of fantasy (visionary allegory) allows her to create her own space, not that of the male scholar alone in his study.[49]

Fantasy literature interacts with feminism both metonymically and metaphorically; on the one hand, it constructs worlds that "anticipate alternative cultural and political possibilities" and, on the other hand, relates directly to the history of the patriarchy, offering overt feminist critiques in the process.[50] De Pizan's text is itself the manifestation of the fantasy depicted in it; the text creates a space where women are recognized and esteemed, and this visionary allegory does not so much relate the patriarchal world of late medieval France to an imaginary sphere where women are lauded as it relates that fantasy world where women are lauded to the text itself.[51] De Pizan, as Chance puts it, "inverts" allegorical interpretation by textually portraying the book as a world unto itself, and such an inversion is "subversive" not only with respect to its feminist reinterpretation of society but also with respect to its "fantasization," its willingness to explore other, possible realities.[52]

Chance's own text, *The Literary Subversions of Medieval Women* (2007), emphasizes how the advent of the printing press allowed women such as de Pizan, Marie de France, and Margery Kempe to articulate subversive, feminist perspectives, and this tradition of subversion resonates well with the American literary tradition of subversive medievalism, which is taken up in the second half of the twentieth century by Ursula K. Le Guin

---

(Gainesville, FL: University Press of Florida, 2011), 33–59, 100–28; and Maureen Quilligan, *The Allegory of Female Authority: Christine de Pizan's 'Cité des Dames'* (Ithaca, NY: Cornell University Press, 1991), 14–38, 85–110.

[48] de Pizan, *The City of Ladies*, 5–6.
[49] Chance, *The Literary Subversions of Medieval Women*, 15.
[50] Alison Lewis, *Subverting Patriarchy: Feminism and Fantasy in the Works of Irmtraud Morgner* (Washington D.C.: Berg Publishers, 1995), 212.
[51] Chance, *The Literary Subversions of Medieval Women*, 15.
[52] Chance, *The Literary Subversions of Medieval Women*, 10–11.

(1929–2018). Le Guin, like de Pizan, constructs in her fantasy and science fiction "extrapolations," as Le Guin calls them, alternative histories or visionary fantasies that reveal particular aspects of the present.[53] As she puts it in her introduction to *The Left Hand of Darkness* (1969), these works fundamentally grapple with "the imagination":

> All fiction is metaphor. Science fiction is metaphor. What sets it apart from older forms of fiction seems to be its use of new metaphors, drawn from certain great dominants of our contemporary life – science, all the sciences, and technology, and the relativistic and the historical outlook, among them. Space travel is one of these metaphors; so is an alternative society, an alternative biology; the future is another. The future, in fiction, is a metaphor. A metaphor for what? If I could have said it non-metaphorically, I would not have written all these words, this novel; and Genly Ai would never have sat down at my desk and used up my ink and typewriter ribbon in informing me, and you, rather solemnly, that the truth is a matter of the imagination.[54]

For Le Guin, fictional representations of the future are metaphors just as, we might extrapolate, fictional representations of the past are metaphors; "for what?" she wonders, and her answer is the "here-and-now," the same phrase, coincidently, often used to translate Walter Benjamin's neologism "*Jetztzeit*" in "Theses on the Philosophy of History" (1940).[55] Le Guin continues:

> This book is not about the future. Yes, it begins by announcing that it's set in the "Ekumenical Year 1490–97," but surely you don't *believe* that? Yes, indeed the people in it are androgynous, but that doesn't mean that I'm predicting that in a millennium or so we will all be androgynous, or announcing that I think we damned well ought to be androgynous. I'm merely observing, in the peculiar, devious, and thought-experimental manner proper to science fiction, that if you look at us at certain odd times of day in certain weathers, we already are. I am not predicting, or prescribing. I am describing.[56]

In her Hainish novels, Le Guin avoids figural thinking by interweaving medievalized concepts like feudalism, castles, quests, and kingdoms with the (purportedly) modern themes of feminism and technological

---

[53] Ursula K. Le Guin, *The Language of the Night: Essays on Fantasy and Science Fiction*, ed. Susan Wood (New York, NY: Putnam, 1979), 155–6.
[54] Ursula K. Le Guin, *The Left Hand of Darkness* (New York, NY: Penguin Books, 1969/2016), xxiii, xxvii.
[55] Le Guin, *The Left Hand of Darkness*, xiii; Benjamin, *Illuminations*, 261.
[56] Le Guin, *The Left Hand of Darkness*, xxvi.

innovation. Her science fiction, in turn, plays imaginatively with historiography itself, interweaving modern and unmodern elements, premodern and postmodern alike, into a single world. Such bricolage manages to unite the modern and the unmodern in a way that does not define either monolithically; indeed, the modern and the unmodern, in Le Guin's Hainish novels, are inseparable – and such a cohesive "worlding" of the medieval and modern serves to subvert colonialist and patriarchal contestations alike, including ethnonationalism.[57] The past and the future converge in Le Guin's fiction; the universe created in the Hainish novels is an extrapolation of Le Guin's here-and-now, just as de Pizan's *City of Ladies* is an extrapolation of de Pizan's own here-and-now – not so much anticipatory as revelatory.[58]

The universe described in "The Dowry of Angyar" (1964), for instance, the short story that precipitated Le Guin's Hainish novels, is depicted in clearly unmodern terms: "She [Semley, the protagonist of the story] was of an ancient family, a descendant of the first kings of the Angyar, and for all her poverty her hair shone with the pure, steadfast gold of her inheritance. The little people, the Fiia, bowed when she passed them, even when she was a barefoot child running in the fields, the light and fiery comet of her hair brightening the troubled winds of Kirien."[59] Like many science fiction and fantasy universes, the one depicted in the Hainish novels includes both futuristic technologies – the term "ansible," Le Guin's early imagining of an internet-like communication system, is coined in *Rocannon's World* (1966) – and medievalisms: princes, kings, castles, dwarves, swords, and bronzed armor.[60] Unmodern figurations – futuristic and medieval alike – blend with aircars, computers, spaceships, and gender-fluid societies situated alongside kingdoms, castles, and knights in gleaming armor. Indeed, "The Dowry of Angyar," often noted for its similarities to Washington Irving's "Rip Van Winkle" (1819), describes how Semley, like Rip Van Winkle, encounters a strange, dwarf-like people who help her to travel through space and time, but when she returns, what seemed to her "one long night" was in fact nine years; her husband has died and her daughter has grown up, just as Rip Van Winkle finds his quaint Dutch

---

[57] For more on the "worlding" of American Studies, see Gillman, Gruesz, and Wilson, "Worlding American Studies," 259–70; as well as Rob Sean Wilson, "Worlding as Future Tactic," *The Worlding Project: Doing Cultural Studies in the Era of Globalization*, eds. Rob Sean Wilson and Christopher Leigh Connery (Berkeley, CA: North Atlantic Books, 2007), 209–23.

[58] Chance, *The Literary Subversions of Medieval Women*, 10.

[59] Ursula K. Le Guin, *The Unreal and the Real: The Selected Short Stories of Ursula K. Le Guin* (New York, NY: Saga Press, 2012), 339.

[60] Ursula K. Le Guin, *Rocannon's World* (New York, NY: Ace, 1966).

village utterly transformed after his long sleep.[61] In *Rocannon's World*, the first of the Hainish novels and an expansion of "The Dowry of Angyar," Rocannon's exploration of that world – to which he is a foreigner – reveals the ruins of castles; deeply prejudiced, stratified societies; and knight-like warriors, while Genly Ai's exploration of Winter, in *The Left Hand of Darkness* (1969), reveals a similarly stratified, medievalized world of villages "like [...] ancient castle[s] of Earth," complete with kings and armored warriors.[62] Perhaps the clearest example of Le Guin's medievalism, though, occurs in *The Dispossessed* (1974), which imagines the journey of Shevek, a scientist from the planet Anarres, to the world of Urras.[63] At the outset of the novel, Anarres, a moon of Urras, has recently been colonized by the Odonians, a radical, egalitarian sect of anarcho-syndicalists that seek to develop a truly equitable society upon the desolate world of Anarres. Shevek travels to Urras, a world closely resembling Le Guin's own mid-twentieth-century world, complete with a Cold War-like political divide between a highly stratified, capitalist country and a totalitarian, socialist state. During Shevek's travels throughout Urras, he takes particular pleasure in traveling to various castles "from the times of the kings," a deep history that his own world of Anarres lacks.[64] Shevek is captivated by these medievalized spectacles, finding them more alluring than the spectacles of consumerism that predominate in modern A-Io, the capitalist country that closely resembles the mid-twentieth-century United States.[65]

As Faulkner embeds his organic medievalisms within the psyches of his characters, Le Guin embeds medievalisms within her extrapolated worlds as spectacles not so much for her readers as for her characters themselves. *Rocannon's World*, *The Left Hand of Darkness*, and *The Dispossessed* all revolve around an alien figure – Rocannon, Genly Ai, and Shevek, respectively – exploring worlds populated with clear allusions to medieval Europe. That distant past is made legible to her characters as spectacles – Semley's necklace; ruined castles; armored, chivalrous men – and these medievalisms enchant her protagonists, revealing the ways in which medievalisms become spectacles rather than presenting those spectacles for the consumption of her readership. Like de Pizan's *City of*

---

[61] Le Guin, *The Unreal and the Real*, 340. Irving's "Rip Van Winkle" similarly utilizes a subversive medievalism; at the close of the short story, Rip Van Winkle notes how the portrait of King George III had been mysteriously replaced with that of George Washington – suggesting that the shift from monarchy to republicanism was, at least in the first decades of the United States, largely a changing of the guard, the substitution of one from of oligarchy for another – see Irving, *The Sketch Book*, 37–57.
[62] Le Guin, *The Left Hand of Darkness*, 229.
[63] Le Guin, *The Dispossessed*.
[64] Le Guin, *The Dispossessed*, 252.
[65] Le Guin, *The Dispossessed*, 248–60.

Ladies, in other words, which inverts the male/female binary, Le Guin's Hainish novels invert the medieval/modern divide, embedding the medieval within her futuristic worlds.

Understood as "visionary allegories," moreover, Le Guin's Hainish novels point to a bricolage that connects medievalisms, technological innovation, and feminism.[66] While the late nineteenth century saw the publication of works like *The Boy's King Arthur* (1880), designed for the edification of boys, postwar medievalisms, especially in the United States, often focalize around women; whether it is Le Guin's "The Dowry of Angyar," the various Disney princesses, or Marion Zimmer Bradley's *The Mists of Avalon* (1982), which places Morgan le Fay and other female characters at the center of the Arthurian myths, these feminist medievalisms often situate women at the center of their narratives, albeit in contexts that often reify conventional gender norms.[67] The troubling of both gender and the medieval is evident, for instance, in *The Left Hand of Darkness*, which is set on a medievalized planet where gender identity is fluid. As the fourth novel published in the Hainish Series, *The Left Hand of Darkness* explores Le Guin's alternative history, in which human civilization evolved on a planet named Hain, eventually settling on a variety of nearby planets, including Terra (Earth). Genly Ai, the protagonist of the novel, has been charged with being the envoy to Gethen, a world where the inhabitants are androgynous, living as nonsexual beings for three out of every four weeks, before going into "kemmer," a period of sexual drive during which the individual might take on male or female characteristics.[68] This gender play is set within a world, moreover, that is unaware of other planets. Genly Ai is the first envoy to Winter, which he hopes to usher into the League of All Worlds, and it is the existence of his spaceship, circling Winter's sun, that eventually serves to convince Winter's inhabitants of the veracity of his claims. Gethen, meanwhile, is a planet imbued with medieval elements, featuring feudal social structures, chivalric values, and religious mysticism, where political intrigue and perilous quests echo the themes of medieval literature – while the planet's archaic language and technology further immerse the reader in a setting that feels both ancient and otherworldly.

---

[66] Chance, *The Literary Subversions of Medieval Women*, 15.
[67] Le Guin, *The Unreal and the Real*, 339; Marion Zimmer Bradley, *The Mists of Avalon* (New York, NY: Alfred A. Knopf, 1982); Sidney Lanier, *The Boy's King Arthur: Sir Thomas Malory's History of King Arthur and His Knights of the Round Table* (New York, NY: Charles Scribner's Sons, 1880). On the relationship between feminism and Disney films, see Robyn Muir, *The Disney Princess Phenomenon: A Feminist Analysis* (Bristol: Bristol University Press, 2023).
[68] Le Guin, *The Left Hand of Darkness*, 10.

Gender, technology, world-transformative moments, and medievalism cohere, and it is with this in mind that we can see how the subversive tradition in U.S. literature – from Poe to Le Guin – can be associated not only with Cervantes but also with that subversive tradition of medieval women writers highlighted by Chance. De Pizan, among others, subverts her patriarchal world by inverting it, just as writers like Poe, Twain, Faulkner, and Le Guin overturn the medieval/modern divide by illustrating the extent to which the purportedly modern nation-state of the United States often more closely resembles a nondemocratic society than an egalitarian one.

Central, though, to such an understanding of Le Guin is a recognition of the primacy she places on the textuality of books, the way, as with de Pizan, a book exists as a world unto itself. In one of Le Guin's lesser-read Hainish novels, *City of Illusions* (1967), a totalitarian civilization, the Shing, has invaded Terra, reducing Terra's indigenous population to a handful of nomadic tribes and rural communes.[69] As with other Hainish novels, the plot revolves around an alien – named, in this case, Falk – exploring an unknown planet – in this case Terra – and that exploration reveals the deep history of the planet. Terra's deep history, in particular, involves its takeover by the Shing, and Falk's expedition across the dystopic landscapes of North America leads eventually to his escape from the planet, which, in turn, leads to the planet's liberation from the Shing. The plot is remarkably similar to those of *Rocannon's World* and *The Left Hand of Darkness* – both of which revolve around an alien liberating a given world from some form of totalitarian control, but, in the case of *City of Illusions*, the main struggle is not a physical quest but Falk's overcoming of the erasure of his memory by the Shing.[70] The Shing hope to indoctrinate Falk with a historiography that frames their reign on Terra as benevolent, as if the Shing were kind overseers of a utopic paradise – a historiography that, the Shing hope, Falk will communicate to his own home world of Werel in order to bolster the Shing's claim to Terra.[71]

If we see this work as an "extrapolation" of Le Guin's own here-and-now, Le Guin's argument is clear: earth's liberation from totalitarianism revolves around the ability to resist believing in and perpetuating totalitarian historiographies, and such resistance is aided by material texts.[72] Throughout his travels, including his capture by the Shing, Falk keeps a book with him – the ancient Chinese classic *Tao Te Ching* – that reminds him that the Shing are, indeed, a totalitarian regime.[73] A translator and

[69] Ursula K. Le Guin, *City of Illusions* (New York, NY: Harper & Row, 1974).
[70] Le Guin, *City of Illusions*, 174–7.
[71] Le Guin, *City of Illusions*, 185.
[72] Le Guin, *The Left Hand of Darkness*, xxiii.
[73] Le Guin, *City of Illusions*, vii, 124.

long-time reader of the *Tao*, Le Guin embeds this fourth-century BCE Chinese text into *City of Illusions*, taking particular care to emphasize the way that this text discourages dualistic thinking:

> *The way* ... [Falk] looked from the book to his own hand that held it. Whose hand, darkened and scarred beneath an alien sun? Whose hand? *The way that can be gone is not the eternal Way. The name* ... He could not remember the name; he would not read it. In a dream he had read those words, in a long sleep, a death, a dream. *The name that can be named is not the eternal Name.* And with that the dream rose up overwhelming him like a wave rising, and broke. He was Falk, and he was Ramarren. He was the fool and the wise man: one man twice born.[74]

There is certainly some hint of pedagogical medievalism here – deploying an unmodern, Asian text as the bearer of truth – but, with Jane Chance's reading of de Pizan in mind, we can also see the way that the presence of the *Tao Te Ching* in *City of Illusions* foregrounds the materiality of texts more generally. It is the reading of an actual book that goads Falk to remember his forgotten identity, which, in turn, allows him to unite the opposed personalities – Falk and Ramarren – that have arisen as a result of his amnesia.

In an essay on the "alleged decline of reading" (2008), Le Guin writes, "one can perceive through the Middle Ages, a slow broadening of the light of the written word, which brightens into the Renaissance and shines out with Gutenberg. Then, before you know it, slaves are reading, and revolutions are written on paper called Declarations of this and that, and schoolmarms replace gunslingers all across the Wild West, and people are mobbing the steamer delivering the latest installment of a new novel."[75] Le Guin sees books themselves as especially powerful in a capitalist world-system because "contemporary, corporation-owned publishing compan[ies] [...] think they can sell books as commodities," when, in fact, "reading is active, an act of attention, of absorbed alertness [...] a book is a challenge: it can't lull you with surging music or deafen you with screeching laugh tracks or fire gunshots in your living room."[76] Books are "complex and extremely efficient," "reliable," "a thing, physically there, durable, indefinitely reusable," and they are, therefore, according to Le Guin, something of an enigma for corporate capitalism, which, she argues, only promotes book publishing with the hope that corporations

---

[74] Le Guin, *City of Illusions*, vii, 171.
[75] Ursula K. Le Guin, "Staying Awake: Notes on the alleged decline of reading," *Harper's Magazine* (February 2008), 34.
[76] Le Guin, "Staying Awake," 37–8.

might "control what's printed."[77] Thinking of the medieval/modern divide and Debord's society of the spectacle, we might add that printed books themselves, which have adroitly bridged the medieval/modern divide, are remarkably resilient in their promotion of subversive discourses, for they require the attention – "absorbed alertness" – that such discourses both engender and demand rather than the "news, propaganda, advertising [and] entertainment" endemic to the society of the spectacle.[78] Books, as cultural artifacts, simultaneously modern and unmodern, blur the line between leisure and labor, imagination and literality, fiction and reality, and such blurring demands a complex historiography that does not insist upon one particular spatiality or temporality but revels in anachronism, displacement, and ambivalence.[79] Le Guin's titular City of Illusions, named Es Toch, is defined by its fixation upon a single historiography that upholds Shing hegemony, while de Pizan's City of Ladies is imagined in response to the narrator's abhorrence of Matheolus's *Lamentations* with all of its misogynistic patriarchalism.[80] A complex historiography that sees the medieval as a repressed spatiotemporal modality of modernity constructs a world more akin to the City of Ladies, one that does not insist upon a single historiography or periodizing schema but revels in the possibilities open to us when we treat historiography as a visionary, creative task.

Indeed, the genres of science fiction and fantasy have long been thought of as intimately tied to feminism itself. Jenny Wolmark, summarizing these theoretical connections, says that "[t]he task of science fiction, which is also the task of theory, is to re-invent the real as fiction," and she goes on to discuss how, because "[t]he privileged realms of authenticity and high art are reserved for the masculine," feminism intersects with this "reinventing [of] the real as fiction."[81] Le Guin's novels, especially those set in the Hainish universe, bring together these vectors of late twentieth-century thought, suggesting that science fiction and fantasy can also subvert patriarchalism, imperialist geographies, and imperialist historiographies such as the medieval/modern divide. While cultural productions like HBO's *Game of Thrones* and the "new feudalism" of Trump Tower deploy the medieval as spectacular commodities for the modern consumer, Le Guin's Hainish novels invert such a contestation by presenting the medieval

---

[77] Le Guin, "Staying Awake," 37–8.
[78] Le Guin, "Staying Awake," 37–8; Debord, *Society of the Spectacle*, 3.
[79] For more on medievalisms' connections to anachronism, displacement, and ambivalence, see Nadia Altschul, "Transfer," in *Medievalism: Key Critical Terms*, eds. Elizabeth Emery and Richard Utz (Cambridge: D.S. Brewer, 2014), 239–45.
[80] Chance, *The Literary Subversions of Medieval Women*, 12.
[81] Jenny Wolmark, *Aliens and Others: Science Fiction, Feminism and Postmodernism* (Iowa City, IA: University of Iowa Press, 1994), 15–16.

as mundane, boring, even.[82] Le Guin merges past and future, male and female, utopia and dystopia, "the real and the unreal" (as she titles one of her short story collections, echoing the phrase Foucault himself uses to describe "heterotopias"[83]) and so reveals her preoccupation with demonstrating that supposed opposites are not so much opposed as coeval – the result being an understanding of her texts themselves, nonfiction and fiction alike, as material manifestations of a non-patriarchal, anarcho-syndicalist present, just as de Pizan, at least as Jane Chance reads her work, situates *The Book of the City of Ladies* as the embodied, emplaced worlding of a City of Ladies.

---

[82] Eco, *Travels in Hyper Reality*, 62.
[83] Foucault, "Of Other Spaces," 23–7.

Conclusion

Included in *American Literary History*'s 2010 issue titled "Medieval America," literary critics Kathy Lavezzo and Harilaos Stecopoulos's essay "Leslie Fiedler's Medieval America" begins with the various charges levied against the myth and symbol school of literary criticism connected with American Studies scholars such as Henry Nash Smith, Perry Miller, Leslie Fiedler, and Leo Marx: "Americanists have argued persuasively that the myth and symbol critics were perpetrators of 'consensus history or cold-war criticism' who sought a 'common ground, a unified vision, yet ignor[ed] fundamental conflicts and tensions in American culture.'"[1] Lavezzo and Stecopoulos, however, use Fiedler's training as a medievalist to demonstrate how his reading of the American literary canon as defined by the homoerotic and interracial love between men complicates this critique of the myth and symbol school:

> For Fiedler, the strange wonder of the American novelist emerges from an unsettling capacity to recall with a twist what might be the most disturbing legacy of the Middle Ages: the realization that no "manifestoes," "barricades," no revolts – no hallmarks of the revolutionary – can ever eliminate "the hidden world of nightward" that lurks within "human beings and human society." Long before Bruno Latour, that is, Fiedler understood that we have never been modern. This realization stands in stark contrast with contemporaneous representations of both premodernity and America. Such postwar social scientists as Walt Rostow and Edward Shils regularly deployed the word "feudal" as a pejorative that consigned certain underdeveloped nations or regions to a distant premodernity while claiming for the U.S. a privileged relationship to pro-

---

[1] Kathy Lavezzo and Harilaos Stecopoulos, "Leslie Fiedler's Medieval America," *American Literary History* 22:4 (Winter 2010), 867. The embedded quote is from Morris Dickstein, *Double Agent: The Critic and Society* (Oxford: Oxford University Press, 1983), 150.

gress. Alternately, such myth and symbol scholars as R.W.B. Lewis and Henry Nash Smith often claimed that the best U.S. writers attempted to elide history in their representation of American protagonists who, like the first man, Adam, were liberated from the burdens of ancestry and thus could independently encounter the virgin land. Yet in his work on the American novel, Fiedler adopted a very different stance with respect to his nation's historicity. For this maverick scholar, the American novelist makes evident that the U.S. is neither the instantiation of vanguard progress nor – the equally flawed view – the American Adam innocently roaming the garden. By recognizing in American literature socio-sexual dynamics that draw upon and reinflect a rebellious medieval love discourse, that of the Troubadours, Fiedler suggests that the U.S. is in fact neither outside or [sic] ahead of history, but rather profoundly connected to the past in surprising and disjunctive ways.[2]

Lavezzo and Stecopoulos are suggesting that the common and warranted critique of the myth and symbol school as employing either an Enlightenment historicism that treats "feudal" as a pejorative or a Romantic historicism that portrays the western frontier as an Edenic paradise are sublimated in Fiedler's appraisal of the nation as "never [...] modern." This is, in fact, what much medievalism studies scholarship achieves: it complicates the medieval/modern divide by emphasizing the extent to which so-called "modern" cultural productions are riddled through with medieval narratives, concepts, and figurations. With this said, Lavezzo and Stecopoulos depict Fiedler as resolving this dilemma using Western rhetoric's dialectic, and considering Kathleen Biddick's critique of Fredric Jameson (see Chapter 6), we should recognize how such dialectical thinking often is embedded with a latent trinitarianism, itself shaped by a supersessionist view of history where Judaism merely foreshadows Christianity rather than existing in parallel or in dialogue with it.[3]

The history of Christian trinitarianism is a muddled one. Its origin may well lie not in Christianity at all but in, as Daniel Boyarin has argued, "non-Christian Jewish accounts of the second and visible God, variously in Logos (*Memra*), Wisdom, or even perhaps Son of God."[4] In any case, the figure of the Trinity was fundamental to medieval Christian theology, utilized by such mainstays of systematic theology as Thomas Aquinas,

---

[2] Lavezzo and Stecopoulos, "Leslie Fiedler's Medieval America," 880–1.
[3] Biddick, *The Typological Imaginary*, 5–6. On supersessionism and its connections to anti-Semitism, cf. Timothy P. Jackson, *Mordecai Would Not Bow Down: Anti-Semitism, the Holocaust, and Christian Supersessionism* (Oxford: Oxford University Press, 2021).
[4] Daniel Boyarin, "The Gospel of the Memra: Jewish Binatarianism and the Prologue to John," *The Harvard Theological Review* 94:3 (July 2001), 249.

Abelard, and William of Ockham.[5] Deeply associated with the Aristotelian syllogism, Aquinas's trinitarianism was specifically connected with his Christology: "St. Thomas speaks of [the Trinity] as key to Christian life, a recipe for beatitude," but this "recipe" is intimately linked with often overt forms of anti-Semitism.[6] Augustine, in *On the Trinity*, for instance, mentions the Jews only as those who "did not see" Christ's divinity or who "will be punished for persisting in their wickedness,"[7] while Aquinas, in his discussion of Paul's letter to the Romans, writes:

> [Paul] wrote fourteen letters, nine of which instructed the church of the Gentiles; four, the prelates and princes of the church, i.e., *kings*; and one to the people of *Israel*, namely, the letter to the Hebrews. For this entire teaching is about Christ's grace, which can be considered in three ways: In one way, as it is in the Head, namely, Christ, and in this regard it is explained in the letter to the Hebrews. In another way, as it is found in the chief members of the Mystical Body, and this is explained in the letters to the prelates. In a third way, as it is found in the Mystical Body itself, that is, the Church, and this is explained in the letters sent to the Gentiles.[8]

Aquinas, in other words, connects the Pauline corpus to the Christian Trinity – with gentiles being associated with the Holy Spirit, the "prelates and princes of the church" to the Father, and the Jews to Christ, and while such a hermeneutic might seem to suggest that Aquinas "sustain[s] a positive theological view of the Jewish people," such a defense of Aquinas neglects the fact that, for Aquinas, "the incarnation's origin and cause is found in the eternal processions of the Son from the Father and of the Holy Spirit from the Father and the Son."[9] For Aquinas, Christ's role within the Trinity is associated overtly with the Jewish people, understood as the "origin and cause" of the Christian divinity – an almost paradigmatic instance of Christian supersessionist historicism.

Within the discourse of nineteenth- and twentieth-century philosophy, meanwhile, the dialectic has also been associated, albeit more covertly,

---

[5] On Systematic theologians' conception of the Trinity, cf. Kathryn Tanner, *Jesus, Humanity and the Trinity: A Brief Systematic Theology* (Philadelphia, PA: Fortress Press, 2001).

[6] Dominic Legge, O.P., *The Trinitarian Christology of St Thomas Aquinas* (Oxford: Oxford University Press, 2017), 1.

[7] Aurelius Augustine, *The Works of Aurelius Augustine*, trans. Marcus Dods (Berkeley, CA: University of California Press, 1873), 35.

[8] Matthew Levering and Michael Dauphinais, *Reading* Romans *with St. Thomas Aquinas* (Washington, DC: Catholic University of America, 2012), 60.

[9] Stephen Boguslawski, O.P., *Thomas Aquinas on the Jews: Insights into His Commentary on Romans 9–11* (New York, NY: Paulist Press, 1989), xvi. Legge, *The Trinitarian Christology of St. Thomas Aquinas*, 5.

with a trinitarian framework. Johann Gottlieb Fichte, while coining the terms "thesis" (*These*), "antithesis" (*Antithese*), and "synthesis" (*Synthese*), was responding to Gottlob Ernst Schulze's *Aenesidemus* (1792), which critiqued Karl Leonhard Reinhold's defense of Kant's *Critique of Pure Reason* (1781).[10] Fichte's use of dialectic terminology aimed to systematize and clarify Kant's philosophy, addressing its limitations without dismantling its core principles. Like Erich Auerbach's "vision of medieval figural thinking to champion new forms of historicism," Fichte's terms, informed by medieval Scholasticism, transpose a Christian trinitarianism onto the very foundations of thought, as if to Christianize human cognition itself.[11] Even Theodor Adorno, in his critique of the Fichtean dialectic in *Negative Dialectics* (1966), begins by declaring that "Philosophy, which once seemed obsolete, lives on because the moment to realize it was missed," and he bemoans the fact that "[p]hilosophy offers no place from which theory as such might be concretely convicted of the anachronisms it is suspected of."[12] Undergirding Adorno's assertion, in other words, is a historicism reminiscent of that of Romantic medievalism, according to which modernity is associated with the effete and superficial, and such a critique is not merely another illustration of how "[h]aving broken its pledge to be as one with reality or at the point of realization, philosophy is obliged ruthlessly to criticize itself."[13] The irony of Adorno's "negative dialectics," as Jürgen Habermas has demonstrated, is that "[t]he totalizing self-critique of reason gets caught in a performative contradiction since subject-centered reason can only be convicted of being authoritarian when having recourse to its own tools. The tools of thought, which […] are imbued with the 'metaphysics of presence' (Derrida), are nevertheless the only available means for uncovering their insufficiency."[14]

Such pessimism, however, is shortsighted, and Habermas's and Adorno's shared interest in Walter Benjamin affords a philosopher who does not so much resolve the dialectic between the Enlightenment and Romanticism so

---

[10] On Fichte's dialectic terminology, see Allen W. Wood, *Fichte's Ethical Thought* (Oxford: Oxford University Press, 2016), 296–319.

[11] Biddick, *The Typological Imaginary*, 5. On Heidegger's conception of Western metaphysics, see Iain Thomson, "Ontotheology," in *The Bloomsbury Companion to Heidegger*, eds. Eric S. Nelson and Francois Raffoul (New York, NY: Bloomsbury Publishing, 2013), 319–28. For more on Fichte's dialectics and their connections to Christian trinitarianism, see Cyril O'Regan, "Kant, Hegel and Schelling," in *The Oxford Handbook of the Trinity*, eds. Gilles Emery, O.P. and Matthew Levering (Oxford: Oxford University Press, 2011), 256.

[12] Theodor Adorno, *Negative Dialectics*, trans. E.B. Ashton (New York, NY: Continuum Press, 2007), 3.

[13] Adorno, *Negative Dialectics*, 3.

[14] Jürgen Habermas, *The Philosophical Discourse of Modernity*, trans. Frederick G. Lawrence (Boston, MA: MIT Press, 1990), 185.

much as propose a radically divergent historiography altogether – namely, that of historical materialism.[15] If, following Benjamin, we think of historiography not as the narrativizing of the historicist but as the reminiscences of the historical materialist, then Fichtean dialectics, as well as any other means of inscribing history with narrative or sequential structure, becomes erroneous; Frederic Jameson's admonition to "always historicize," in this sense, does not encourage us to narrativize history but to attend to one's "involuntary memory," as Benjamin puts it, the figures that "flash up," unbidden, merging two purportedly distinct space-times into a single, albeit heterogeneous and partial, vision.[16] Indeed, such historical materialism is, perhaps, the clearest difference between an ethnonationalist medievalism and a subversive medievalism. While the former focuses on continuities between or among ethnicities and nation-states, those who construct subversive medievalisms, such as Poe, Twain, Faulkner, and Le Guin, explore how the medieval "flashes up" within purportedly modern texts and contexts – or, as in Twain's *Connecticut Yankee*, how the modern itself "flashes up" in the Middle Ages.[17]

A more suitable system for considering American medievalisms, then, might not be that of the Enlightenment/Romanticism dialectic so much as a geographic system such as Fiedler himself offers in *The Return of the Vanishing American* (1976).[18] As Gilles Deleuze and Félix Guattari succinctly summarize it in *A Thousand Plateaus* (1980), Fiedler's fourfold *topoi* of American literature revolve around the four cardinal directions:

> In the East, there was the search for a specifically American code and for a recoding of Europe (Henry James, Eliot, Pound, etc.); in the South, there was the overcoding of the slave system, with its ruin and the ruin of the plantations during the Civil War (Faulkner, Caldwell); from the North came capitalist decoding (Dos Passos, Dreiser); the West, however, played the role of a line of flight combining travel, hallucination, madness, the Indians, perceptive and mental experimentation, the shifting of frontiers, the rhizome (Ken Kesey and his "fog machine," the beat generation, etc.). Every great American author creates a cartography, even in his or her style; in contrast to what is done in Europe, each

---

[15] Benjamin, *Illuminations*, 211.
[16] Frederic Jameson, *The Political Unconscious: Narrative as a Socially Symbolic Act* (Ithaca, NY: Cornell University Press, 1981/2014), 9; Benjamin, *Illuminations*, 211. For more on Jameson's admonition to "always historicize," especially with respect to anti-Semitism, see Biddick, *The Typological Imaginary*, 5–6.
[17] Twain, *Connecticut Yankee*, 2.
[18] Fiedler, *The Return of the Vanishing American*, 16.

makes a map that is directly connected to the real social movements crossing America.[19]

Fiedler's reading of American literature foregrounds the cartography created by U.S. authors, and when we think of the authors associated with these *topoi* in terms of their medievalisms, we see how the literatures of the American North and American South are connected by a shared concern for socioeconomic systems, while the literatures of the American East and the American West share a concern for transnational cultural exchanges.[20]

Fiedler's Northern and Southern *topoi*, the former exploring the "decoding" of capitalism and the latter the "overcoding" of the slave system, exist as two distinct means of interpreting U.S. socioeconomics, and their similar framing of the medieval as directly opposed to industrial capitalism demonstrates the extent to which the decoding of capitalism is necessarily entwined with the decoding of race and racism.[21] The American authors that Deleuze and Guattari connect with the Northern *topoi*, Theodore Dreiser (1871–1945) and John Dos Passos (1896–1970), for instance, engage with the medieval by framing advocates of workers' rights as chivalric knights, battling industrial capitalism. In *The 42nd Parallel* (1930), in a section focalized around J. Ward Moorehouse, a corrupt salesman from Delaware, Dos Passos describes the "feudal conditions" of the steel mills in Pittsburgh:

> [A] strike came on at Homestead and there were strikers killed by the mine guards and certain writers from New York and Chicago who were sentimentalists began to take a good deal of space in the press with articles flaying the steel industry and the feudal conditions in Pittsburgh as they called them, and the progressives in Congress were making a howl, and it was rumoured that people wanting to make politics out of it were calling for a congressional investigation.[22]

The Northern vector of American medievalism, we might say, is deeply indebted to Marx, but that Marxism is couched so as to distance the texts' protagonists from outright Marxist proselytizing.[23] It is the "sentimentalists," not Moorehouse himself, who describe the working conditions

---

[19] Deleuze and Guattari, *A Thousand Plateaus*, 571n18.
[20] Fiedler, *The Return of the Vanishing American*, 16.
[21] On racism and capitalism, see Carter A. Wilson, *Racism: From Slavery to Advanced Capitalism* (New York, NY: SAGE Publications, 1996).
[22] John Dos Passos, *The 42nd Parallel* (Boston, MA: Houghton Mifflin, 1930/2000), 200.
[23] On Dos Passos's attempt to "Americanize Marx," see Robert C. Rosen, *John Dos Passos, Politics and the Writer* (Lincoln: University of Nebraska Press, 1981), 77.

as "feudal," just as Theodore Dreiser, in *Sister Carrie* (1900), presents the Brooklyn street-car strikes, organized by the "Knights of Labour," in equivocal terms: "Hurstwood at first sympathized with the demands of these men," Dreiser writes of George Hurstwood, Sister Carrie's disgruntled lover.[24] "'They're foolish to strike in this sort of weather,' he thought to himself. 'Let 'em win if they can, though.' The next day there was even a larger notice of it. "Brooklynites Walk," said the 'World.' 'Knights of Labour Tie up the Trolley Lines Across the Bridge.'"[25]

The similarities between these two passages are striking: both are written from a third-person perspective and focalized around a disaffected, middle-class, white man; both portray late nineteenth-century U.S. labor strikes, and both utilize medievalisms in that portrayal, with Dos Passos alluding to the "feudal conditions" of the Pittsburgh steel mills and Dreiser quoting a newspaper headline that references the Knights of Labour, the labor organization (with its medievalized moniker) founded in 1869 by Uriah Stephens.[26] Dos Passos, meanwhile, couches Moorehouse's assertion that the working conditions in the steel mills are feudal as the discourse of "the progressives in Congress," implying that Moorehouse no longer views the conditions that way, just as Dreiser couches the reference to the Knights of Labour as a headline in the *New York World*, not Moorehouse's own view. Dos Passos and Dreiser, in other words, both suggest that a "knight of to-day" involves opposing industrial capitalism, but both authors do so in a markedly taciturn way; Dos Passos presents this idea through the eyes of a disgruntled marketing man, clearly skeptical of the progressives in Congress, while Dreiser presents this assertion through a newspaper headline read by a man who "at first sympathized" with the protestors but goes on to cross the picket line and serve as a strikebreaker.[27]

The Northern distinction between industrial capitalism and feudalism, moreover, is recapitulated in many Southern medievalisms, which, like Dos Passos's and Dreiser's, connect modernity with industrial capitalism but, instead of connecting the medieval with workers' rights movements, connect the Middle Ages with the antebellum South.[28] Faulkner's medievalisms, explored in Chapter 5, demonstrate the extent to which the South's "chivalry silliness," as Twain deemed it, was embedded within the very psyches of his characters, with Miss Sophonsiba, for example,

[24] Theodore Dreiser, *Sister Carrie* (New York, NY: Bantam Books, 1900), 323.
[25] Dreiser, *Sister Carrie*, 323.
[26] For more on the Knights of Labour, see Elisabeth Israels Perry and Karen Manners Smith, *The Gilded Age and Progressive Eva: A Student Companion* (Oxford: Oxford University Press, 2006), 185.
[27] Dreiser, *Sister Carrie*, 92, 323.
[28] For more on Southern medievalisms, see Pugh, *Queer Chivalry*.

connecting the Beauchamps' plantation with Warwick Castle.[29] Along with Faulkner, Deleuze and Guattari include Erskine Caldwell in their *topos* of the American South, and Caldwell's novels "shred […] any pretensions of white chivalry in the South."[30] Caldwell's *Tobacco Road* (1932), for one, begins with the Lester family stealing a neighbor's turnips, and much of the plot revolves around Jeeter Lester refusing to work in an Augusta cotton mill, even though his family is destitute, insisting that "It wasn't intended for a man with the smell of the land in him to live in a mill in Augusta."[31] Jeeter thinks it divinely ordained that he remain on his family's property, and he uses that religious fervor to justify his reluctance to participate in industrial capitalism. In this novel, written and set during the Depression era, the South's preoccupation with chivalry is directly connected with Northern antimodernism, too, with Jeeter connecting a nostalgia for plantation life with an antimodernism that sees life in a city like Augusta as opposed to God's will. The South's preoccupation with chivalry and the North's antimodernism, in other words, both romanticize a pre-industrial world. This romanticized vision of pre-industrial life is not so much opposed to industrial life, as Lears's discussion of antimodernism implies, but coeval with it; an unattainable idyllic world, produced and reproduced by cultural productions, offers an inaccessible space-time that industrial capitalism can invoke as a spatio-temporal fix for capitalism's contradictions.[32] The medievalisms of the American South and American North, we might summarize, exist as pressure valves for the anxieties of an increasingly alienated population, simultaneously buttressing and exposing the contradictions latent within industrial capitalism.

To shift from the American South and North to the American East and West is, as Frederick Jackson Turner's frontier thesis intimates, to grapple overtly with the U.S.'s imbrication within the European colonization of the New World.[33] The medievalisms of the American East and West are concerned with more transnational or transoceanic vectors than are those of the American North and South. In particular, the medievalisms of authors like Ezra Pound, Henry James, and Jack Kerouac connect the medieval with non-U.S. territories, including East Asia, Mexico, and the Ottoman Empire, an association that functions, reflexively, to present the

---

[29] Twain, *Life on the Mississippi*, 314; Faulkner, *Go Down, Moses*, 11.

[30] Andrew Leiter, "Sexual Degeneracy and the Anti-Lynching Tradition in Erskine Caldwell's *Trouble in July*," in *Reading Erskine Caldwell: New Essays*, ed. Robert McDonald (Jefferson, NC: McFarland & Co., 2006), 219.

[31] Erskine Caldwell, *Tobacco Road* (Levelland, TX: Laughing Dog Press, 1932/2017), 57.

[32] Lears, *No Place of Grace*, xvi.

[33] Here I am following Henry Nash Smith's reading of the Frontier Thesis: Smith, *Virgin Land*, 250.

United States as modern. "All sorts of explanations," Anouar Majid writes, thinking of Europe's and the United States's "mounting anxiety over coexisting with Muslims and the seemingly unstoppable waves of illegal and nonassimilable immigrants," "have been offered about the [...] twin elements fueling the global crisis [...] but no one seems to be reading the intense debate over immigration and minorities who resist assimilation as the continuation of a much older conflict, the one pitting Christendom against the world of Islam."[34] In turn, Majid demonstrates the extent to which Western European and U.S. cultures alike have developed discourses that cast non-European minorities as Moors and Europeans (and Euro-Americans) as akin to Christian knights, recapitulating a Christian crusader rhetoric – the irony being that "secular, liberal Western culture and Islam were never really parted, [...] they have been traveling together since (at least) 1492, despite all attempts to demarcate, first, zones of Christian purity and, later, national homogeneity."[35] Majid's understanding of Christian–Islamic relations as integral to not only medieval but also modern national histories reveals the extent to which the modern world, including the United States, has been framed in terms of those relations, and the medievalisms of writers like Pound, Henry James, and Jack Kerouac can be seen as grappling – sometimes subversively, sometimes with ethnonationalist rhetoric – with these associations.

As Gayatri Spivak reminds us, "crossing borders [...] is a problematic affair," and the medievalisms of writers like Pound, James, and Kerouac, in thinking about the medieval in transnational and transoceanic terms, certainly illustrate that point.[36] Pound, as discussed in Chapter 5, connects medieval Scholastic theology consistently with Confucianism and East Asian poetry and leverages each of those discourses in support of an idiosyncratic ethnonationalism. Jack Kerouac envisioned *On the Road* (1957) as "a quest novel like Cervantes's *Don Quixote* or John Bunyan's *Pilgrim's Progress*," framing Mexico in particular as an unmodern territory open to exploration by the likes of Sal Paradise and Dean Moriarty.[37] "My first impression of Dean," Paradise proclaims early on in *On the Road*, "was of a young Gene Autry – trim, thin-hipped, blue-eyed, with a real Oklahoma accent – a side-burned hero of the snowy West."[38] Like Wister's Virginian, Kerouac's Dean Moriarty is a cowboy-knight, albeit riding not

[34] Majid, *We Are All Moors*, 2–3.
[35] Majid, *We Are All Moors*, 3.
[36] Gayatri Spivak, *Death of a Discipline* (New York, NY: Columbia University Press, 2003), 16.
[37] Ann Charters, "Introduction," in Jack Kerouac's *On the Road* (New York, NY: Penguin Books, 1957/1991), xiv.
[38] Kerouac, *On the Road*, 2.

a wild stallion but a '49 Hudson Commodore (Gene Autry, the so-called "Singing Cowboy," began his career with the Western variety radio show *Melody Ranch*, which relies heavily on "the chivalric code of the American cowboy": "The cowboy-knight is so much a part of the American psyche that the announcer for Gene Autry's *Melody Ranch* commented that boys and girls had at one time probably imagined themselves as knights dressed 'in shining armor, astride a powerful charger, thundering through adventure and hardships, to a romantic rescue'").[39] Sal Paradise's description of Moriarty as a young Gene Autry, then, enacts an adaptation of an adaptation, resituating the cowboy – itself an adaptation of both the Spanish *vaquero* and the chivalric knight – as a "thin-hipped, blue-eyed" Oklahoman driving across the vast landscapes of the American West.[40]

Indeed, Moriarty's overdetermined character mirrors the diverse landscapes through which Paradise and Moriarty travel – Denver, San Francisco, New York, Wyoming, Texas, and, eventually, Mexico: "the finale of the novel [is] the trip to Mexico that the trajectory of Part One prefigures," Hassan Melehy writes: "The contact zone between the United States and Mexico, which includes parts of each country, presents the greatest challenge in *On the Road* to the ideology of complacent, sedentary culture. The broadness of the zone, beginning in San Antonio with such signs as houses and streets indicating a cultural shift, is underscored by the six pages that the narrative takes to traverse it [...] Dean presents the border crossing as the terminus of all that has become familiar to him and Sal."[41] The various land- and cityscapes through which Sal and Dean travel are as sundry as the typologies upon which the novel's characters rely, and the departure from the United States and "all that they know" amounts to a departure from such typological thinking itself: the first thing Sal says when they cross the border into Mexico is that it "looked exactly like Mexico."[42] Mexico is a place not of façades – like those Main Streets in rural Wyoming[43] – but of reality, where things are as they seem, and such authenticity is clearly imbued with a kind of religious fervor for Sal and Dean: "It was only Nuevo Laredo but it looked like Holy Lhasa to us."[44]

The medievalisms in *On the Road*, however, are not only formal; while the text, according to Ann Charters, reenacts the medieval quest narrative,

---

[39] Katherine Barnes Echols, *King Arthur and Robin Hood on the Radio: Adaptations for American Listeners* (Jefferson, NC: McFarland & Co., 2017), 137.

[40] Jerald Underwood, "Vaqueros," in Clayton, Hoy and Underwood, *Vaqueros, Cowboys, and Buckaroos*, 2–6.

[41] Hassan Melehy, *Kerouac: Language, Poetics, and Territory* (New York, NY: Bloomsbury, 2017), 74.

[42] Kerouac, *On the Road*, 274.

[43] Kerouac, *On the Road*, 25, 83.

[44] Kerouac, *On the Road*, 274.

Sal's description of Mexico is also rendered in clearly unmodern, Orientalizing terms: "Old men sat on chairs in the night and looked like Oriental junkies and oracles," Sal states as he and Dean walk through the streets of Laredo, and it is while driving through Gregoria that Paradise famously "learn[s] [himself] among the Fellahin Indians of the world":

> The boys were sleeping, and I was alone in my eternity at the wheel, and the road ran straight as an arrow. Not like driving across Carolina, or Texas, or Arizona, or Illinois; but like driving across the world and into the places where we would finally learn ourselves among the Fellahin Indians of the world, the essential strain of the basic primitive, wailing humanity that stretches in a belt around the equatorial belly of the world from Malaya (the long fingernail of China) to India the great subcontinent to Arabia to Morocco to the selfsame deserts and jungles of Mexico and over the waves to Polynesia to mystic Siam of the Yellow Robe and on around, on around, so that you hear the same mournful wail by the rotted walls of Cádiz, Spain, that you hear 12,000 miles around in the depths of Benares the Capital of the World.[45]

Sal's globe-trotting vision resembles Walt Whitman's description in "Passage to India" (1871) ("Passage to India! / Cooling airs from Caucasus far, soothing cradle of man / The river Euphrates flowing, the past lit up again"); both Whitman's narrator and Sal Paradise imagine transoceanic vectors of cultural exchange, and intrinsic to that imagining is historiographic play, especially an exploration of the medieval.[46] For Whitman, a journey around the world remembers Marco Polo, Batouta the Moor, and other "medieval navigators," just as, for Kerouac, that voyage remembers the "Fellahin Indians" – the term "Fellahin" referring to an agricultural laborer of East and North Africa during the Ottoman Empire.[47] Both visions are certainly fraught with colonialist contestations – the implication being that the entire world is open to white, globetrotting men – but those visions are also fraught with a sense of global, transnational camaraderie, portrayed in particular by the coalescing of Moors, Native Americans, and Euro-Americans. Kerouac's Fellahin Indian resembles Jefferson's "Saxon yeoman" in its medievalism and agrarianism, but Kerouac deploys, in lieu of a figure of medieval Europe, figures of the Native American and the Moor.[48] Such a subversion is important, for it reimagines a U.S. citizen as the purported foe of both medieval Christian

---

[45] Charters, "Introduction" to *On the Road*, xiv; Kerouac, *On the Road*, 275, 280.
[46] Walt Whitman, *Passage to India* (New York, NY: Smith & McDougal, 1870), 10.
[47] Mahmoud Yazbak, "'Left Naked on the Beach': The Villagers of Aylut in the Grip of the New Templers," in *Struggle and Survival in Palestine/Israel*, eds. Mark LeVine and Gershon Shafir (Berkeley, CA: University of California Press, 2012), 30.
[48] Horsman, *Race and Manifest Destiny*, 41.

Europe and U.S. western expansionism, just as the "recoding of Europe" by writers like Pound and James subvert the transatlantic voyage – making of it an eastward, rather than a westward, expedition.

Rather than resituate an archetypal figure like the chivalric knight into a Fellahin Indian, though, the medievalisms of Pound and Henry James involve a reimagining of Europe itself as a site not of chivalric quests but of the mundane, the quotidian. Discussing *The Golden Bowl* (1904), Jonathon Ullyot writes that "James was developing the ideas for and writing his own unique version of the Grail story, which would differ sharply from the Victorian moralizing of Tennyson's version or the decadent and dreamy medievalism reflected in the art of the Pre-Raphaelities."[49] Instead, Ullyot continues, "[t]he characters in *The Golden Bowl* are preoccupied with the interpretation of an object that appears to be solid gold but turns out to be crystal gilded by some 'beautiful old process' – a product of a 'lost art' reflecting a 'lost time.'"[50] Like Eliot's *The Waste Land*, James's *The Golden Bowl* is distinct from the Victorian's and Tennyson's adaptations of the Grail myth – not to mention the medieval versions – because, as Ullyot puts it, in James's retelling the "people no longer believe in sacred relics."[51]

James's *The American* (1877), *Daisy Miller* (1879), *Portrait of a Lady* (1881), and *The Ambassadors* (1903), meanwhile, amount, at least within this context, to explorations of how wealthy Americans never quite fit into Europe's social class systems, themselves ambiguously associated with Europe's imagined medieval past.[52] In *Daisy Miller*, Frederick Winterbourne begins his courtship of the eponymous American heroine by taking Miller to Chillon Castle on Lake Geneva, during which Winterbourne realizes that the young woman "cared very little for feudal antiquities, and that the dusky traditions of Chillon made but a slight impression upon her."[53] The novella serves as a kind of warning to those who, like Miller, would disobey the customs of European high society, albeit as they are understood by an American ex-pat, Winterbourne. Miller, as a wealthy American, cannot find her place within the social structures of Europe, and those social structures are themselves portrayed as incoherent and incomprehensible. The hotel Trois Couronnes in Vavay, where Winterbourne

---

[49] Jonathon Ullyot, *The Medieval Presence in Modernist Literature: The Quest to Fail* (Cambridge: Cambridge University Press, 2016), 19.
[50] Ullyot, *The Medieval Presence*, 19.
[51] Ullyot, *The Medieval Presence*, 20.
[52] Henry James, *The American* (Boston, MA: James R. Osgood and Co., 1877); Henry James, *Daisy Miller*, eds. Kristin Boudreau and Megan Stoner Morgan (Buffalo: Broadview editions, 2012); Henry James, *Portrait of a Lady* (New York, NY: Charles Scribner's Sons, 1908); Henry James, *The Ambassadors* (New York, NY: Harper & Brothers, 1903).
[53] James, *Daisy Miller*, 67.

first meets Miller, is described in the opening paragraphs of the novel as simply one hotel among many; it is populated largely by Americans with "neat German waiters, who look like secretaries of legation; Russian princesses sitting in the garden; little Polish boys walking about, held by the hand, with their governors; a view of the sunny crest of the Dent du Midi and the picturesque towers of the Castle of Chillon."[54] James goes on: "I hardly know whether it was the analogies or the differences that were uppermost in the mind of a young American."[55] The setting of *Daisy Miller*, in other words, is fraught with "analogies" and "differences": the American travelers who flock to the hotel, which is described as "famous, even classical," seem to be drawn by its "maturity" ("One of the hotels at Vevey [...] is famous, even classical, being distinguished from many of its upstart neighbors by an air both of luxury and of maturity"), but the presence of Americans at this hotel "evoke[s] a vision, an echo, of Newport and Saratoga."[56] Miller's eventual enthrallment with Mr. Giovanelli mimics the chaos of the Trois Couronnes; Giovanelli, the young, handsome Italian, "is not a gentleman," according to Winterbourne, "only a clever imitation of one," and Miller's enchantment with this young Italian bespeaks not only Miller's "innocence and crudity" but also the incoherence of European high society itself.[57]

In *Portrait of a Lady*, meanwhile, which also features a wealthy American woman shepherded through Europe by a detached maternal figure and courted by a steady retinue of gallant young men, Isabel Archer follows the advice of the "aristocratic" Madame Merle and marries Gilbert Osmond, a wealthy ex-pat, only to have her marriage slowly deteriorate.[58] Taken together, the figures of Daisy Miller and Isabelle Archer suggest that young Americans are fated to remain excluded from Europe's *ancien régime* – be it French, English, or Italian: "Why will [Archer] not marry Lord Warburton," literary critic Anthony Thorlby wonders in his reading of *The Portrait of a Lady*:

> The answer is plain enough: she does not want to become Lady Warburton. She cannot accept this place, this role, in English society. Her comical American companion [Ralph Touchett] agrees with her, so it would seem: Americans do not hold with lords and ladies; they believe in the classless society. But nothing could be clearer than the fact that this democratic conviction is not what [ultimately] inspires Isabel to say

[54] James, *Daisy Miller*, 44.
[55] James, *Daisy Miller*, 44.
[56] James, *Daisy Miller*, 43–4.
[57] James, *Daisy Miller*, 68.
[58] James, *Portrait of a Lady*, 271.

"No". She refuses because she has a Romantic imagination. She wants to live "to the limits of her imagination."[59]

Archer's penchant for egalitarianism, however, can be seen as part and parcel with the Romantic imagination that incites Archer to live "to the limits of her imagination."[60] James's novels explore, in other words, the overdetermined nature of this American preoccupation with medieval Europe, and central to that preoccupation is the ambiguity of the U.S.'s relationship with the social structures of the *ancien régime* – the implication being not only that hierarchical social systems are anathema to democracy but also that those hierarchical systems are, at least within a modern European context, inchoate, never quite comprehensible (or, as literary critic Esther Sánchez-Pardo succinctly puts it in her reading of *The Ambassadors*, "Through the narrator and those he observes, James represents the esteem of late-nineteenth-century bourgeois for aesthetic wholeness and historical continuity as a function of the bourgeois' own social lack, and consequent desire for an integral, continuous, and historical class identity, or 'family' structure.")[61]

Kerouac, Pound, and James, in other words, all connect the medieval directly to a non-U.S. territory (Pound, in his work of literary criticism *The Spirit of Romance* (1952), declares bluntly that "The Middle Ages are in Russia"[62]), accentuating the extent to which U.S. national identity is often defined reflexively as the antithesis to the medieval in the same way that Northern and Southern medievalisms accentuate the extent to which modern economics are often rendered in terms of their divergence from feudalism. Both interactions – the North/South and East/West – we might summarize, mourn the imagined loss of what Deleuze and Guattari call a "sedentary space," a structured, hierarchical, "striated" space regulated by established boundaries, norms, and institutions.[63] For the South, that sedentary space (or space-time) is the antebellum U.S., imagined as an agrarian, medievalized world, while for the North, that sedentary space

---

[59] Anthony Thorlby, "Self-consciousness and Social Consciousness in Literature," in *Aspects of History and Class Consciousness*, Vol. 30, ed. Istvan Meszaros (New York, NY: Routledge, 2016), 188.

[60] James, *Portrait of a Lady*, 212.

[61] Esther Sánchez-Pardo, "James's Sociology of Taste: *The Ambassadors*, Commodity Consumption and Cultural Critique," in *Henry James's Europe: Heritage and Transfer*, eds. Dennis Tredy, Annick Duperray and Adrian Harding (Cambridge: OpenBook, 2011), 44.

[62] Ezra Pound, *The Spirit of Romance* (New York, NY: New Directions, 1952/2005), 6.

[63] On sedentary and nomad spaces, see Deleuze and Guattari, *A Thousand Plateaus*, 458.

is the pre-industrial world of enchantment, passion, and agrarianism. For the East, that sedentary space is the medieval academy, the medieval church, or *ancien régime*, imagined as the refuge of the few, while for the West that sedentary space is the world of the "Fellahin Indians of the world," "that essential strain of the basic primitive, wailing humanity" – with all of its problematic primitivizing.[64] The polarity between ethnonationalist literatures and subversive literatures can, in turn, be rethought not as oppositional so much as a difference of imagination. The subversive medievalisms of Poe, Twain, Faulkner, and Le Guin imagine a conclusion to America's preoccupation with the (imagined) sedentary space of the Middle Ages; the fall of the House of Usher, the collapse of Hank Morgan's Camelot, the demise of the Compson family, and Winter's revelation that it is a world among numerous other worlds are intuitive reckonings with the longing for sedentary space – reckonings that involve both destruction and revelation, the collapse of fixed notions of identity and the birth of reimagined, polyvocal identities.[65] The medievalisms that buttress, rather than subvert, monolithic contestations, meanwhile, simply do not imagine the conclusion to such monolithic thinking – James Fenimore Cooper is, as D.H. Lawrence contends, indeed, "only a step" from Poe.[66]

---

[64] Kerouac, *On the Road*, 280.
[65] Poe, *Collected Tales and Poems*, 182; Twain, *Connecticut Yankee*, 428–44; Faulkner, *The Sound and the Fury*, 297–301; Le Guin, *The Left Hand of Darkness*, 276–86.
[66] Lawrence, *Studies in Classic American Literature*, 29.

Bibliography

Adams, Henry. *Education of Henry Adams*. Boston, MA: Massachusetts Historical Society, 1918.
Adams, Jonathon and Cordelia Heß, eds. *The Medieval Roots of Antisemitism: Continuities and Discontinuities from the Middle Ages to the Present Day*. New York, NY: Routledge, 2018.
Adorno, Theodor. *Negative Dialectics*. Translated by E.B. Ashton. New York, NY: Continuum Press, 2007.
Aji, Hélène, ed. *Pound and Referentiality*. Paris: Presses de l'Université de Paris-Sorbonne, 2003.
Aladro-Font, Jorge. "Don Quijote y Cristóbal Colón: O, La sinrazón de la realidad." *Lienzo* 15 (1994), 37–54.
Alatas, Syed Farid. "Alatas, Fanon, and Coloniality." In *Frantz Fanon and Emancipatory Social Theory*, eds. Dustin J. Byrd and Syed Farid Alatas, 27–46. Boston, MA: Brill, 2020.
Alexander, Michael. *Medievalism: The Middle Ages in Modern England*. New Haven, CT: Yale University Press, 2017.
Ali Shah, Zulfiqar. *St. Thomas Aquinas and Muslim Thought*. Milpitas, CA: Claritas Books, 2022.
Alighieri, Dante. *Dante's Inferno: The Indiana Critical Edition*, ed. Mark Musa. Bloomington, IN: Indiana University Press, 1995.
Allen, Theodore. *The Invention of the White Race*, Vol. 1. New York, NY: Verso, 1994.
Althusser, Louis. *For Marx*. Translated by Ben Brewster. New York, NY: Verso, 1969.
Altschul, Nadia. *Geographies of Philological Knowledge: Postcoloniality and the Transatlantic National Epic*. Chicago, IL: University of Chicago Press, 2012.
——. "Medievalism and the Contemporaneity of the Medieval in Postcolonial Brazil." In *Studies in Medievalism XXIV: Medievalism on the Margins*, ed. Karl Fugelso, 139–54. Cambridge: D.S. Brewer, 2015.
Anchieta Guerra, Luiz Felipe. "*Neomedievalismo político no Brasil contemporâneo*." In *Medievalismos: em olhares e construções narrativas*, Vol. I, eds. Maria Eugênia Bertarelli, Renan Marques Birro, and João Batista da Silva, 47–64. Ananindeua: Editora Itacaúnas, 2021.
Anzaldúa, Gloria. *Borderlands/La Frontera: The New Mestiza*. San Francisco: Aunt Lute, 1987.
——. *Light in the Dark/Luz en lo Oscuro: Rewriting Identity, Spirituality, Reality*. Raleigh, NC: Duke University Press, 2015.
Appiah, Kwame Anthony. "Race." In *Critical Terms for Literary Study*, 2nd edn, eds. Frank Lentricchia and Thomas McLaughlin, 274–87. Chicago, IL: University of Chicago Press, 1995.
Arendt, Hannah. *Eichmann in Jerusalem: A Report on the Banality of Evil*. New York, NY: Penguin Books, 2006.

Asbridge, Thomas. *The Crusades: The Authoritative History of the War for the Holy Land*. New York, NY: Ecco, 2010.

Ashcroft, Bill, Gareth Griffiths, and Helen Tiffin. *The Empire Writes Back: Theory and Practice in Post-Colonial Literatures*. New York, NY: Routledge, 1989.

Auerbach, Erich. *Mimesis: The Representation of Reality in Western Thought*. Princeton, NJ: Princeton University Press, 1953.

Augustine, Aurelius. *The Works of Aurelius Augustine*. Translated by Marcus Dods. Berkeley, CA: University of California Press, 1873.

Aurell, Martin, Florian Besson, Justine Breton, and Lucie Malbos, eds. *Les médiévistes face aux médiévalismes*. Rennes: Presses Universitaires de Rennes, 2023.

Barnyard, Joseph. *Plymouth and the Pilgrims*. Boston, MA: Gould and Lincoln, 1851.

Barthes, Roland. *The Rustle of Language*. Translated by Richard Howard. Berkeley, CA: University of California Press, 1989.

Bello, Andrés. *Obras Completas*, Vol. 2. Santiago: Impreso por Pedro G. Ramírez, 1881.

Benjamin, Walter. *Illuminations*. Translated by Harry Zohn. New York, NY: Shocken Books, 1968.

Biddick, Kathleen. *The Shock of Medievalism*. Durham, NC: Duke University Press, 1998.

———. *The Typological Imaginary: Circumcision, Technology, History*. Philadelphia, PA: University of Pennsylvania Press, 2003.

Bishko, Charles Julian. "The Peninsular Background of Latin American Cattle Ranching," *The Hispanic American Historical Review* 32:4 (Nov. 1952): 491–515.

Bloch, Marc. *Feudal Society*. Translated by L.A. Manon. New York, NY: Routledge, 1962.

Blockmans, Wim and Peter Hoppenbrouwers. *Introduction to Medieval Europe, 300–1500*. New York, NY: Routledge, 2014.

Blumenfeld-Kosinski, Renate, ed. *The Selected Writings of Christine de Pizan*. New York, NY: W.W. Norton, 1997.

Booker, M. Keith and Anne-Marie Thomas. *The Science Fiction Handbook*. Oxford: Wiley-Blackwell, 2009.

Boron, Robert de. *Merlin*. Paris: Librairie de Firmin-Didot, 1886.

Bottici, Chiara and Benolt Challand. *The Myth of the Clash of Civilizations*. New York, NY: Routledge, 2010.

Bowling, Lawrence E. "Faulkner and the Theme of Innocence," *Kenyon Review* 20:3 (1958), 466–87.

Boyarin, Daniel. "The Gospel of the Memra: Jewish Binatarianism and the Prologue to John," *The Harvard Theological Review* 94:3 (July 2001), 243–84.

Bradley, Marion Zimmer. *The Mists of Avalon*. New York, NY: Alfred A. Knopf, 1982.

Brault, Gerard J., ed. *The Song of Roland: Oxford Text and English Translation*. University Park, PA: Pennsylvania State University, 1978.

Brown, Dennis. *The Modernist Self in Twentieth-Century English Literature: A Study in Self-fragmentation*. London: Palgrave Macmillan, 1989.

Brown, Elizabeth A.R. "The Tyranny of a Construct: Feudalism and Historians of Medieval Europe," *American Historical Review* 79:4 (1974), 1063–88.

Brown, Norman O. *The Challenge of Islam: the Prophetic Traditions.* Berkeley, CA: North Atlantic Books, 2009.

Brown-Grant, Rosalind. *Christine de Pizan and the Moral Defence of Women: Reading beyond Gender.* Cambridge: Cambridge University Press, 1999.

Bruce, Christopher W. *The Arthurian Name Dictionary.* New York, NY: Garland Publishing, Inc., 1999.

Bryant, Lawrence M. "Configurations of the Community in late Medieval Spectacles: Paris and London during the Dual Monarchy." In *City and Spectacle in Medieval Europe*, eds. Barbara Hanawalt and Kathryn Reyerson, 3–33. Minneapolis, MN: University of Minnesota Press, 1994.

Bryon, Mark. *Ezra Pound's Eriugena.* New York, NY: Bloomsbury, 2014.

Buchanon, Ian, ed. *A Dictionary of Critical Theory*, 1st edn. Oxford: Oxford University Press, 2010.

Budd, Louis J. and Edwin H. Cady, eds. *On Faulkner.* Durham, NC: Duke University Press, 1989.

Buell, Lawrence. "American Literary Emergence as a Postcolonial Phenomenon," *American Literary History* 4:3 (1992), 411–42.

Buenviaje, Dino. *The Yanks Are Coming Over There: Anglo-Saxonism and American Involvement in the First World War.* Jefferson, NC: McFarland & Co., 2017.

Buffy the Vampire Slayer. Created by Joss Whedon. Los Angeles, CA: 20th Century Fox Television, 1997–2003.

Boguslawski, O.P., Stephen. *Thomas Aquinas on the Jews: Insights into His Commentary on Romans 9–11.* New York, NY: Paulist Press, 1989.

Bulfinch, Thomas. *The Age of Chivalry; Or Legends of King Arthur.* Boston, MA: Crosby, Nichols, and Company, 1858.

——. *The Age of Fable, or Stories of the Gods.* Boston, MA: Sanborn, Carter, Bazin and Company, 1855.

——. *Bulfinch's Mythology.* Edited by Edward Everett Hale. New York, NY: Review of Reviews Co., 1913.

——. *Legends of Charlemagne, or Romance of the Middle Ages.* Boston, MA: Crosby, Nichols, Lee and Company, 1862.

Burge, Amy. *Representing Difference in the Medieval and Modern Orientalist Romance.* New York, NY: Palgrave Macmillan, 2017.

Burgett, Bruce and Glenn Hendler, eds. *Keywords for American Cultural Studies*, 2nd edn. New York, NY: New York University Press, 2014.

Burns, S.J., Robert I., ed. *Las Siete Partidas*, Vol. III. Translated by Samuel Parsons Scott. Philadelphia, PA: University of Pennsylvania Press, 2001.

Bush, George W. *The George W. Bush Foreign Policy Reader: Presidential Speeches and Commentary.* Edited by John W. Dietrich. Armonk, NY: M.E. Sharpe, 2005.

Butler, Anthea. *White Evangelical Racism: The Politics of Morality in America.* Chapel Hill, NC: University of North Carolina Press, 2021.

Byrd, II, William. *History of the Dividing Line and Other Tracts*, Vol. I. Richmond, VA: 1866.

Byrne, Aisling. *Otherworlds: Fantasy and History in Medieval Literature*. Oxford: Oxford University Press, 2016.

Caldwell, Erskine. *Tobacco Road*. Levelland, TX: Laughing Dog Press, 1932/2017.

Carnegie, Andrew. *The Gospel of Wealth, and Other Timely Essays*. New York, NY: The Century Co., 1901.

Carter, Dan T. *Unmasking the Klansman: The Double Life of Asa and Forrest Carter*. Athens, GA: University of Georgia Press, 2023.

Casaliggi, Carmen and Porscha Fermanis. *Romanticism: A Literary and Cultural History*. New York, NY: Routledge, 2016.

Cervantes Saavedra, Miguel de. *Don Quixote*. Translated by James H. Montgomery. Indianapolis, IN: Hackett Publish Company, 2009.

——. *The Indigenous Hidalgo Don Quixote de la Mancha*. Translated by John Rutherford. New York, NY: Penguin Books, 2000.

Césaire, Aimé. *The Discourse of Colonialism*. Translated by Joan Pinkham. New York, NY: Monthly Review Press, 1972.

Chan, J. Clara. "Medievalists, Recoiling from White Supremacy, Try to Diversify the Field." *Chronicle of Higher Education*, July 16, 2017. Accessed September 29, 2017. http://www.chronicle.com/article/Medievalists-Recoiling-From/240666.

Chance, Jane. *The Literary Subversions of Medieval Women*. New York, NY: Palgrave, 2007.

Chapman, Charles E. *A History of California: The Spanish Period*. New York, NY: Macmillan, 1921.

Chaucer, Geoffrey. *The House of Fame: In Three Books*. Oxford: Clarendon Press, 1893.

——. *The Riverside Chaucer*, 3rd edn. Oxford: Oxford University Press, 1987.

Cheever, George Barrell. *The Pilgrim Fathers*. London: T.W. Collins, 1849.

Childers, William. "Reading Don Quixote in the Americas." In *Approaches to Teaching Cervantes's Don Quixote*, eds. James Parr and Lisa Vollendorf, 279–90. New York, NY: Modern Language Association of America, 2015.

——. *Transnational Cervantes*. Toronto: University of Toronto Press, 2006.

Chléirigh, Léan Ní. "Nova Peregrinatio: The First Crusade as a Pilgrimage in Contemporary Latin Narratives." In *Writing the Early Crusades*, eds. Marcus Bull and Damien Kempf, 63–74. Woodbridge: Boydell Press, 2014.

Cinderella. Directed by Clyde Geronimi, Hamilton Luske, and Wilfred Jackson. Walt Disney Productions, 1950.

Civantos, Christina. *The Afterlife of Al-Andalus: Muslim Iberia in Contemporary Arab and Hispanic Narratives*. Albany, NY: SUNY Press, 2017.

Clark, David and Nicholas Perkins, eds. *Anglo-Saxon Culture and the Modern Imagination*. Cambridge: D.S. Brewer, 2010.

Clayton, Lawrence, Jim Hoy, and Jerald Underwood. *Vaqueros, Cowboys, and Buckaroos*. Austin, TX: University of Texas Press, 2001.

Coffee, Jessie McGuire. *Faulkner's Un-Christlike Christians: Biblical Allusions in the Novels*. Ann Arbor, MI: University of Michigan Press, 1983.

Cohen, Jeffrey Jerome. *Hybridity, Identity and Monstrosity in Medieval Britain: On Difficult Middles*. New York, NY: Palgrave Macmillan, 2016.

——. *The Postcolonial Middle Ages*. New York, NY: Palgrave Macmillan, 2000.

Cohen, Jeffrey Jerome, ed. *Cultural Diversity in the British Middle Ages: Archipelago, Island, England.* New York, NY: Palgrave Macmillan, 2008.

Constable, Giles. *Crusaders and Crusading in the Twelfth Century.* New York, NY: Routledge, 2016.

Corfis, Ivy A. and Ray Harris-Northall, eds. *Medieval Iberia.* London: Tamesis, 2007.

Costea, Ionut. "Medievalism. Historiographic Markers," *Studia Universitatis Babeș-Bolyai Historia* 68:1 (June 2023): 131–60.

Coulombe, Joseph L. *Twain and the American West.* Columbia, MO: University of Missouri Press, 2011.

Cox, James M. "The Uncomfortable Ending of Huckleberry Finn." In *Adventures of Huckleberry Finn*, eds. Sculley Bradley et al., 350–7. New York, NY: W.W. Norton & Co., 1977.

Cutter, Donald. "Sources of the Name 'California,'" *Arizona and the West* 3:3 (1961), 233–40.

Dahl, Adam. *Empire of the People: Settler Colonialism and the Foundations of Modern Democratic Thought.* Lawrence, KS: University of Kansas Press, 2018.

Davidson, Mary Catherine. *Medievalism, Multilingualism, Chaucer.* New York, NY: Palgrave Macmillan, 2010.

Davis, Kathleen. *Periodization and Sovereignty: How Ideas of Feudalism and Secularization Govern the Politics of Time.* Philadelphia, PA: University of Pennsylvania Press, 2008.

———. "Time Behind the Veil: The Media, the Middle Ages, and Orientalism Now." In *The Postcolonial Middle Ages*, ed. Jeffrey Jerome Cohen, 105–22. New York, NY: Palgrave, 2000.

———. "Tycoon Medievalism, Corporate Philanthropy, and American Pedagogy," *American Literary History* 22:4 (2010), 781–800.

Davis, Kathleen and Nadia Altschul, eds. *Medievalisms in the Postcolonial World: The Idea of "The Middle Ages" outside Europe.* Baltimore, MD: Johns Hopkins University Press, 2009.

Debord, Guy. *Society of the Spectacle.* Translated by Ken Knabb. London: Rebel Press, 2002.

Decrane, Susanne M. *Aquinas, Feminism and the Common Good.* Washington D.C.: Georgetown University Press, 2004.

Dekker, George. *James Fenimore Cooper: The American Scott.* New York, NY: Barnes & Noble, 1967.

Deleuze, Gilles. *Dialogues II.* Translated by Hugh Tomlinson and Barbara Habberjam. New York, NY: Columbia University Press, 1987.

Deleuze, Gilles and Félix Guattari, *Anti-Oedipus: Capitalism and Schizophrenia.* Translated by Robert Hurley. New York, NY: Continuum, 2009.

———. *A Thousand Plateaus: Capitalism and Schizophrenia.* Translated by Brian Massumi. New York, NY: Continuum, 1987.

DeRosa, Aaron. "Europe, Darwin and the Escape from Huckleberry Finn," *American Literary Realism* 44:2 (2012), 157–73.

Dickinson, Jonathon. *Jonathan Dickinson's Journal, or God's Protecting Providence. Being the Narrative of a Journey from Port Royal in Jamaica to Philadelphia between August 23, 1696 and April 1, 1697*. Philadelphia, PA: 1699.
Dickstein, Morris. *Double Agent: The Critic and Society*. Oxford: Oxford University Press, 1983.
Dimock, Wai Chee. *Through Other Continents: American Literature across Deep Time*. Princeton, NJ: Princeton University Press, 2006.
Dorsch, Sebastian. "Space/Time Practices and the Production of Space and Time," *Historical Social Research* 38:3 (2013), 7–21.
Dos Passos, John. *The 42nd Parallel*. Boston, MA: Houghton Mifflin, 1930/2000.
Douglass, Frederick and Harriet Jacobs. *Narrative of the Life of Frederick Douglass and Incidents in the Life of a Slave Girl*. New York, NY: Random House, 2000.
Dreiser, Theodore. *Sister Carrie*. New York, NY: Bantam Books, 1900.
Driver, Martha W. and Sid Ray, eds. *The Medieval Hero on Screen: Representations from Beowulf to Buffy*. Jefferson, NC: McFarland & Co., 2004.
Earle, Rebecca. "Spaniards, Cannibals, and the Eucharist in the New World." In *To Feast on Us as Their Prey: Cannibalism and the Early Modern Atlantic*, ed. Rachel B. Herrmann, 81–96. Fayetteville, AR: University of Arkansas, 2019.
Echols, Katherine Barnes. *King Arthur and Robin Hood on the Radio: Adaptations for American Listeners*. Jefferson, NC: McFarland & Co., 2017.
Eckhart, Meister. "Prologus generalis in Opus tripartitum." In *Meister Eckhart: Die lateinischen Werke (Latin Works)*, Vol. I, ed. Josef Quint, 148–65. Stuttgart: W. Kohlhammer Verlag, 1936.
Eco, Umberto. *Travels in Hyper Reality: Essays*. Translated by William Weaver. New York, NY: Houghton Mifflin, 1990.
The Elder Scrolls. Developed by Bethesda Game Studios. Rockville, MD: Bethesda Softworks, 1994–.
Eliot, T.S. *The Waste Land: A Facsimile and Transcript of the Original Drafts, Including the Annotations of Ezra Pound*. New York, NY: Harvest Book, 1971.
Eltagouri, Marwa. "Jeff Sessions spoke of the 'Anglo-American heritage of law enforcement.' Here's what that means." *Washington Post*, February 12, 2018.
Emerson, Ralph Waldo. *Early Lectures*. Edited by Stephen E. Whicher and Robert E. Spiller. Cambridge, MA: Belknap Press, 1966.
———. *The Journals and Miscellaneous Notebooks of Ralph Waldo Emerson*, Vol XIII. Edited by Ralph H. Orth and Alfred R. Ferguson. Cambridge, MA: Belknap Press, 1977.
———. *The Later Lectures of Ralph Waldo Emerson, 1842–1871*, Vol. I. Edited by Ronald A. Bosco and Joel Myerson. Athens, GA: University of Georgia Press, 2001.
———. *The Selected Lectures of Ralph Waldo Emerson*. Edited by Ronald A. Bosco and Joel Myerson. Athens, GA: University of Georgia Press, 2005.
Emery, Elizabeth A. "Postcolonial Gothic: The Medievalism of America's 'National' Cathedrals." In *Medievalisms in the Postcolonial World: The Idea of "The Middle Ages" outside Europe*, eds. Nadia Altschul and Kathleen Davis, 237–64. Baltimore, MD: Johns Hopkins University Press, 2009.

Emery, Elizabeth and Richard Utz, eds. *Medievalism: Key Critical Terms*. Cambridge: D.S. Brewer, 2014.

Equiano, Olaudah. *The Interesting Narrative of the Life of Olaudah Equiano*. Boston, MA: The Floating Press, 2009.

Eysteinsson, Astradur. *The Concept of Modernism*. Ithaca, NY: Cornell University Press, 1990.

Faulkner, William. *Faulkner in the University*. Charlottesville, VA: University of Virginia Press, 1959/1995.

——. *Go Down, Moses*. New York, NY: Vintage Books, 2011.

——. *Knight's Gambit: Six Stories*. London: Chatto & Windus, 1951.

——. *The Sound and the Fury*. New York, NY: The Modern Library, 2012.

Fay, Elizabeth. *Romantic Medievalism: History and the Romantic Literary Ideal*. New York, NY: Palgrave, 2002.

Fernandez, Ingrid. "Necro-Transcendence/Necro-Naturalism: Philosophy of Life in the Works of Ralph Waldo Emerson." In *Death Representations in Literature: Forms and Theories*, ed. Adriana Teodorescu, 117–37. Newcastle upon Tyne: Cambridge Scholars Publishing, 2015.

Fernandez-Armesto, Felipe. *1492: The Year the World Began*. New York, NY: Bloomsbury Publishing, 2011.

Fiedelson, Jr., Charles. *Symbolism and American literature*. Chicago, IL: University of Chicago Press, 1953.

Fiedler, Leslie. "'Come Back to the Raft Ag'in, Huck Honey!'" *Partisan Review* 156 (June 1948): 664–71.

——. *The Return of the Vanishing American*. New York, NY: Stein and Day, 1976.

Fisher, Benjamin Franklin. "Poe and the Gothic Tradition." In *The Cambridge Companion to Edgar Allan Poe*, ed. Kevin J. Hayes, 72–91. Cambridge: Cambridge University Press, 2002.

Fitzgerald, F. Scott. *This Side of Paradise*. New York, NY: Scribner, 1920.

Fluck, Winfred, Donald Pease, and John Carlos Rowe, eds. *Reframing the Transnational Turn in American Studies*. Lebanon, NH: Dartmouth College Press, 2011.

Foster, David. "On the Theme of Mark Twain's Personal Recollections of Joan of Arc," *The Mark Twain Annual* 13:1 (2015), 43–62.

Foucault, Michel. "Of Other Spaces," *Architecture/Mouvement/Continuité*. Translated by Jay Miskowiec, *Diacritics* 16:1 (1986), 22–7.

France, John. *Mercenaries and Paid Men: The Mercenary Identity in the Middle Ages*. Boston, MA: Brill, 2008.

Frankel, Valerie Estelle. *Women in Game of Thrones: Power, Conformity and Resistance*. Jefferson, NC: McFarland & Co., 2014.

Frederickson, George. *Racism: A Short History*. Princeton, NJ: Princeton University Press, 2002.

Freeman, Michael. *Railways and the Victorian Imagination*. New Haven, CT: Yale University Press, 1999.

Freud, Sigmund. *On Metapsychology: The Theory of Psychoanalysis*. Translated by James Strachey. New York, NY: Penguin Books, 1991.

Bibliography

———. *The Uncanny*. Translated by David McLintock. New York, NY: Penguin Books, 2003.
Fried, Johannes. *The Middle Ages*. Translated by Peter Lewis. Cambridge, MA: Belknap Press, 2015.
Fugelso, Karl, ed. *Studies in Medievalism XVII: Defining Medievalism(s)*. Cambridge: D.S. Brewer, 2009.
Gabriele, Matthew. "Trump says medieval walls worked. They didn't." *Washington Post*, January 10, 2019.
Game of Thrones. Created by David Benioff and D.B. Weiss. Los Angeles, CA: HBO, 2011–19.
Ganim, John. *Medievalism and Orientalism*. New York, NY: Palgrave Macmillan, 2005.
Garcia, Pedro Javier Padro. "'Huckleberry Finn' as a Crossroads of Myth: the Adamic, the quixotic, the picaresque, and the problem of ending," *Links & Letters* 8 (2001), 61–70.
Geary, Patrick. *The Myth of Nations: The Medieval Origins of Europe*. Princeton, NJ: Princeton University Press, 2003.
Getz, Trevor R. *The Long Nineteenth Century, 1750–1914: Crucible of Modernity*. New York, NY: Bloomsbury Publishing, 2018.
Giles, Paul. *The Global Remapping of American Literature*. Princeton, NJ: Princeton University Press, 2011.
Gillman, Susan. *Dark Twins: Imposture and Identity in Mark Twain's America*. Chicago, IL: University of Chicago Press, 1989.
Gillman, Susan, Kirsten Silva Gruesz, and Rob Wilson. "Worlding American Studies," *Comparative American Studies: An International Journal* 2:3 (2004), 259–70.
Goodman, Jennifer Robin. *Chivalry and Exploration, 1298–1603*. Woodbridge: Boydell, 1998.
Graf, Eric Clifford. *Cervantes and Modernity*. Lewisburg, PA: Bucknell University Press, 2007.
Gramsci, Antonio. *Letters from Prison*, vol. II. Translated by Raymond Rosenthal. New York, NY: Columbia University Press, 1994.
———. *Selections from the Prison Notebooks*. Translated by Q. Hoare and G.N. Smith. New York, NY: International Publishers, 1971.
Greenlee, John Wyatt and Anna Fore Waymack. "Thinking Globally: Mandeville, Memory and Mappaemundi," *The Medieval Globe* (2018), 69–106.
Grossman, Lev. *The Magicians*. New York, NY: Viking Press, 2009.
Häberlein, Mark. *The Fuggers of Augsburg: Pursuing Wealth and Honor in Renaissance Germany*. Charlottesville, VA: University of Virginia Press, 2012.
Habermas, Jürgen. *The Philosophical Discourse of Modernity*. Translated by Frederick G. Lawrence. Boston, MA: MIT Press, 1990.
Hackett, Jeremiah. *A Companion to Meister Eckhart*. Boston, MA: Brill, 2013.
Hagstette, Todd. *Reading William Gilmore Simms: Essays or Introduction to the Author's Canon*. Columbia, SC: University of South Carolina Press, 2017.
Hale, Edward Everett. *His Level Best, and Other Stories*. Boston, MA: Roberts Brothers, 1872.

——. "The Queen of California," *The Atlantic* 13:77 (March 1864): 265–80.
Hale, Sarah Josepha. *Manners: Happy Homes and Good Society All the Year Round.* Boston, MA: Lee and Shepard, 1889.
Hall, Constance Hill. *Incest in Faulkner: A Metaphor for the Fall.* Ann Arbor, NY: UMI Research Press, 1986.
Hämäläinen, Pekka. *Indigenous Continent: The Epic Contest for North America.* New York, NY: Liveright Publishing, 2022.
Hanna, Julian, ed. *Key Concepts in Modernist Literature.* New York, NY: Palgrave Macmillan, 2009.
Harris, R. Baine. *Neoplatonism and Contemporary Thought: Part Two.* New York, NY: State University of New York Press, 2001.
Harvey, David. *The New Imperialism.* Oxford: Oxford University Press, 2005.
Harvey, Robert. *Sharing Common Ground: A Space for Ethics.* New York, NY: Bloomsbury, 2017.
Hassler-Forest, Dan. *Science Fiction, Fantasy, and Politics: Transmedia World-Building Beyond Capitalism.* New York, NY: Rowman & Littlefield, 2016.
Hawthorne, Julian. *Nathanial Hawthorne and His Wife: A Biography*, Vol. I. London: Chatto and Windus, 1885.
Hazell, Robert and James Melton, eds. *Magna Carta and its Modern Legacy.* Cambridge: Cambridge University Press, 2015.
Heiser, M.F. "Cervantes in the United States," *Hispanic Review* 15:4 (1947), 409–35.
Heng, Geraldine. *Empire of Magic: Medieval Romance and the Politics of Cultural Fantasy.* New York, NY: Columbia University Press, 2003.
Henthorne, Tom. "Boys to Men: Medievalism and Masculinity in Star Wars and E.T.: The Extra-Terrestrial." In *The Medieval Hero on Screen: Representations from Beowulf to Buffy*, eds. Martha W. Driver and Sid Ray, 73–90. Jefferson, NC: McFarland & Co., 2004.
Herman, Luc. *Concepts of Realism.* Columbia, SC: Camden House, 1996.
Herrmann, Rachel B. "The Black People Were Not Good to Eat." In *To Feast on Us as Their Prey: Cannibalism and the Early Modern Atlantic*, ed. Rachel B. Herrmann, 195–214. Fayetteville, AR: University of Arkansas, 2019.
——. "Introduction." In *To Feast on Us as Their Prey: Cannibalism and the Early Modern Atlantic*, ed. Rachel B. Herrmann, 1–17. Fayetteville, AR: University of Arkansas, 2019.
Hesse, Eva, ed. *New Approaches to Ezra Pound.* Berkeley, CA: UC Press, 1969.
Holman, David Marion. *A Certain Slant of Light: Regionalism and the Form of Southern and Midwestern Fiction.* Baton Rouge, LA: Louisiana State University Press, 1995.
Holsinger, Bruce. *The Premodern Condition: Medievalism and the Making of Theory.* Chicago, IL: University of Chicago Press, 2005.
Hood, John Y.B. *Aquinas and the Jews.* Philadelphia, PA: University of Pennsylvania Press, 1995.
Hooker, Juliet. *Theorizing Race in the Americas: Booker, Sarmiento, Du Bois, and Vasconcelos.* Oxford: Oxford University Press, 2017.
Horsman, Reginald. *Race and Manifest Destiny.* Cambridge, MA: Harvard University Press, 1981.

Horswell, Mike. *The Rise and Fall of British Crusader Medievalism*. New York, NY: Routledge, 2018.
Hurlock, Kathryn and Paul Oldfield, eds. *Crusading and Pilgrimage in the Norman World*. Woodbridge: Boydell Press, 2015.
Hutner, Gordon, ed. *American Literary History: Medieval America*, 22:4 (2010).
Huxley, Aldous. *Crome Yellow*. London: Chatto and Windus, 1925.
Innes, Stephen. "Introduction: Fulfilling John Smith's Vision: Work and Labor in Early America." In *Work and Labor in Early America*, ed. Stephen Innes, 3–48. Chapel Hill, NC: University of North Carolina Press, 1988.
Irving, Washington. *The Alhambra*. Philadelphia, PA: J.B. Lippincott and Co., 1870.
——. *The Sketch Book of Geoffry Crayon, Gent*. New York, NY: Longmans, Green, and Co., 1906.
Irwin, John T. *Doubling and Incest/Repetition and Revenge: A Speculative Reading of Faulkner*. Baltimore, MD: Johns Hopkins University Press, 1975.
Jackson, Shona N. *Creole Indigeneity: Between Myth and Nation in the Caribbean*. Minneapolis, MN: University of Minnesota Press, 2012.
Jackson, Timothy P. *Mordecai Would Not Bow Down: Anti-Semitism, the Holocaust, and Christian Supersessionism*. Oxford: Oxford University Press, 2021.
Jakobson, Roman. *Language in Literature*. Edited by Krystyna Pomorska and Stephen Rudy. Cambridge, MA: Belknap Press, 1987.
James, Henry. *The Ambassadors*. New York, NY: Harper & Brothers, 1903.
——. *The American*. Boston, MA: James R. Osgood and Co., 1877.
——. *The American Scene*. New York, NY: Harper Brothers, 1907.
——. *Daisy Miller*. Edited by Kristin Boudreau and Megan Stoner Morgan. Buffalo, NY: Broadview editions, 2012.
——. *Portrait of a Lady*. New York, NY: Charles Scribner's Sons, 1908.
Jameson, Frederic. *The Political Unconscious: Narrative as a Socially Symbolic Act*. Ithaca, NY: Cornell University Press, 1981/2014.
Jefferson, Thomas. *A Summary View of the Rights of British Americans*. Brooklyn, NY: Historical Printing Club, 1892.
Journal of the Proceedings of the Senate of the United States of America. Philadelphia, PA: William and Thomas Bradford: 1789. Accessed April 1, 2024. https://archive.org/details/journalof proceed00unit.
Kaltmeier, Olaf. "Politics of Indigeneity in the Andean Highlands: Indigenous Social Movements and the State in Ecuador, Bolivia, and Peru (1940–2015)." In *Indigeneity on the Move: Varying Manifestations of a Contested Concept*, eds. Eva Gerharz, Nasir Uddin and Pradeep Chakkarath, 172–98. New York, NY: Berghahn Books, 2018.
Kaplan, Amy. "Manifest Domesticity," *American Literature* 70:3 (1998), 581–606.
Kaplan, Amy and Donald Pease. *Cultures of U.S. Imperialism*. Durham, NC: Duke University, 1993.
Kearney, Milo and Manuel Medrano. *Medieval Culture and the Mexican American Borderlands*. College Station, TX: Texas A&M University Press, 2001.
Kears, Carl. "Science Fiction was Around in Medieval Times – here's what it looked like," September 12, 2018. Accessed March 13, 2024. https://www.manchester.ac.uk/ discover/news/science-fiction-medieval-times/.

Kears, Carl and James Paz, eds. *Medieval Science Fiction*. London: Centre for Late Antique and Medieval Studies/Boydell & Brewer, 2016.
Kemp, Roger L., ed. *Documents of American Democracy: A Collection of Essential Writings*. New York, NY: McFarland & Co., 2010.
Kennedy, Hugh. *Caliphate: The History of an Idea*. New York, NY: Basic Books, 2016.
Kenner, Hugh. *The Pound Era*. Berkeley, CA: University of California Press, 1971.
Kerouac, Jack. *On the Road*. New York, NY: Penguin Books, 1957/1991.
Kinoshita, Sharon. "Deprovincializing the Middle Ages." In *The Worlding Project: Doing Cultural Studies in the Era of Globalization*, eds. Rob Wilson and Chris Connery, 61–76. Berkeley, CA: North Atlantic, 2007.
——. "Medieval Mediterranean Literature," *PMLA* 124:2 (2009), 600–8.
Kjærulff, Berit. "Medievalism and the Post-medieval Middle Ages: A Review of Anglophone Medievalism Studies," *Orbis Litterarum* 73 (2018), 458–70.
Krauthammer, Anna. *The Representation of the Savage in James Fenimore Cooper and Herman Melville*. New York, NY: Peter Lang, 2008.
Kergel, David. *Digital Learning in Motion: From Book Culture to the Digital Age*. New York, NY: Routledge, 2021.
Krey, August C. *The First Crusade: The Accounts of Eyewitnesses and Participants*. Princeton, NJ: Princeton University Press, 1921.
Kuypers, Jim A., ed. *The 2016 American Presidential Campaign and the News: Implications for American Democracy and the Republic*. Lanham, MD: Lexington Books, 2018.
Lambert, Gregg. *Who's Afraid of Deleuze and Guattari?* New York, NY: Continuum, 2006.
Langland, William. *The Vision of William Concerning Piers Plowman*. London: Trübner & Co., 1867.
Lanier, Sidney. *The Boy's King Arthur: Sir Thomas Malory's History of King Arthur and His Knights of the Round Table*. New York, NY: Charles Scribner's Sons, 1880.
Larrain, Jorge. *Theories of Development: Capitalism, Colonialism and Dependency*. Cambridge: Polity Press, 1989.
Lavezzo, Kathy, ed. *Imagining a Medieval English Nation*. Minneapolis, MN: University of Minnesota, 2004.
Lavezzo, Kathy and Harilaos Stecopoulos. "Leslie Fiedler's Medieval America," *American Literary History* 22:4 (Winter 2010), 867–87.
Lawrence, D.H. "Studies in Classic American Literature," *The English Review* 28 (1919), 5, 88, 204, 278, 404, 477.
——. *Studies in Classic American Literature*. New York, NY: Thomas Seltzer, 1923.
——. *Studies in Classic American Literature*, Vol. 2. Edited by Ezra Greenspan, Lindeth Vasey and John Worthen. Cambridge: Cambridge University Press, 2003.
Le Guin, Ursula K. *City of Illusions*. New York, NY: Harper & Row, 1974.
——. *The Dispossessed*. New York, NY: Harper & Row, 1974.
——. *The Language of the Night: Essays on Fantasy and Science Fiction*. Edited by Susan Wood. New York, NY: Putnam, 1979.

———. *The Left Hand of Darkness*. New York, NY: Penguin Books, 1969/2016.
———. *Rocannon's World*. New York, NY: Ace, 1966.
———. "Staying Awake: Notes on the alleged decline of reading," *Harper's Magazine* (February 2008), 33–8.
———. *The Unreal and the Real: The Selected Short Stories of Ursula K. Le Guin*. New York, NY: Saga Press, 2012.
Lears, T.J. Jackson. *No Place of Grace: Antimodernism and the Transformation of American Culture, 1880–1920*. Chicago, IL: University of Chicago Press, 1981.
Legge, O.P., Dominic. *The Trinitarian Christology of St Thomas Aquinas*. Oxford: Oxford University Press, 2017.
LeMaster, J.R. and James D. Wilson, eds. *The Mark Twain Encyclopedia*. New York, NY: Routledge, 1993.
Leonard, Irving A. *Books of the Brave: Being an Account of Books and of Men in the Spanish Conquest and Settlement of the Sixteenth-century New World*. Berkeley, CA: University of California Press, 1992.
Levering, Matthew and Michael Dauphinais. *Reading Romans with St. Thomas Aquinas*. Washington, DC: Catholic University of America, 2012.
Levine, Mark and Gershon Shafir, eds. *Struggle and Survival in Palestine/Israel*. Berkeley, CA: University of California Press, 2012.
Levins, Lynn Gartrell. *Faulkner's Heroic Design: The Yoknapatawpha Novels*. Athens, GA: University of Georgia Press, 1976/2008.
Lewis, Alison. *Subverting Patriarchy: Feminism and Fantasy in the Works of Irmtraud Morgner*. Washington D.C.: Berg Publishers, 1995.
Lewis, C.S. *The Chronicles of Narnia*. London: Geoffrey Bles, 1950–1956.
Lewis, R.W.B. *The American Adam: Innocence, Tragedy, and Tradition in the Nineteenth Century*. Chicago, IL: University of Chicago Press, 1955.
Lewis, Sinclair. *Main Street & Babbitt*. New York, NY: Library of America, 1992.
Lieberman, Jennifer L. "Mark Twain and the Technological Fallacy." In *Power Lines: Electricity in American Life and Letters, 1882–1952*, 17–50. Cambridge, MA: MIT Press, 2017.
Liu, Tessie. "Race." In *A Companion to American Thought*, eds. Richard Fox and James Kloppenberg. Cambridge, MA: Blackwell Publishers, 1995.
———. "Teaching the Differences among Women from a Historical Perspective: Rethinking Race and Gender as Social Categories." In *Unequal Sisters: An Inclusive reading in U.S. Women's History*, eds. Vicki Ruiz and Ellen Carol DuBois, 29–40. New York, NY: Routledge, 2008.
Lohse, Stephanie Kristin. *Charlemagne, Roland, and the Islamic Other: Vicarious Reading and Virtual Identity*, Minneapolis, MN: University of Minnesota Press, 2007.
Longenecker, Steve. *Pulpits of the Lost Cause: The Faith and Politics of Confederate Chaplains during Reconstruction*. Tuscaloosa, AL: University of Alabama Press, 2023.
López, Ligia López. *The Making of Indigeneity, Curriculum History, and the Limits of Diversity*. New York, NY: Routledge, 2018.

Louth, Andrew. "Apophatic and Cataphatic Theology." In *The Cambridge Companion to Christian Mysticism*, eds. Amy Hollywood and Patricia Z. Beckman, 137–46. Cambridge: Cambridge University Press, 2012.

Lyotard, Jean-Francois. *The Postmodern Condition: A Report on Knowledge*. Translated by Geoff Bennington and Brian Massumi. Minneapolis, MN: University of Minnesota, 1979.

MacLellan, Rorry, ed. *The Modern Memory of the Military-Religious Orders: Engaging the Crusades*, Vol. VII. New York, NY: Routledge Press, 2022.

Maiolo, Francesco. *Medieval Sovereignty: Marsilius of Padua and Bartolus of Saxoferrato*. Delft: Eburon Academic Publishers, 2007.

Majid, Anouar. *We Are All Moors: Ending Centuries of Crusades Against Muslims and Other Minorities*. Minneapolis, MN: University of Minnesota Press, 2009.

Malcolm, Lois, ed. *God: The Sources of Christian Theology*. Louisville, KY: Westminster John Knox Press, 2012.

Mancing, Howard. "Bendito sea Alá: A New Edition of Belianís de Grecia," *Bulletin of the Cervantes Society of America*, Vol. XXI, Issue II (2001), 111–15.

Margolis, Nadia. *An Introduction to Christine de Pizan*. Gainesville, FL: University Press of Florida, 2011.

Marsden, Richard. "Medievalism: New discipline or scholarly no-man's land?" History Compass 16:2 (2018): https://onlinelibrary.wiley.com/doi/10.1111/hic3.12439.

Martin, George R.R. *A Game of Thrones*. New York, NY: Bantam Spectra, 1996.

——. *A Clash of Kings*. New York, NY: Bantam Spectra, 1998.

——. *A Storm of Swords*. New York, NY: Bantam Spectra, 2000.

——. *A Feast of Crows*. New York, NY: Bantam Spectra, 2005.

——. *A Dance with Dragons*. New York, NY: Bantam Spectra, 2011.

Marx, Karl. *Capital: A Critique of Political Economy*, Vol. I. Translated by Ben Fowkes. New York, NY: Penguin Books, 1976.

Marx, Leo. *The Machine in the Garden: Technology and the Pastoral Ideal in America*. Oxford: Oxford University Press, 1964/2000.

Mather, Cotton. *Magnalia Christi Americana*. London: Thomas Parkhurst, 1702.

Matthews, David. *Medievalism: A Critical History*. Cambridge: D.S. Brewer, 2015.

Mays, Kyle T. *An Afro-Indigenous History of the United States*. Boston, MA: Beacon Press, 2021.

McDonald, Robert, ed. *Reading Erskine Caldwell: New Essays*. Jefferson, NC: McFarland & Co., 2006.

McHugh, Tony. "Barceloneta as Heterotopic Mirror: A Place of Different Spaces." In *Intercultural Mirrors: Dynamic Reconstruction of Identity*, eds. Marie-Claire Patron and Julia Kraven, 127–46. Boston, MA: Brill, 2019.

Melehy, Hassan. *Kerouac: Language, Poetics, and Territory*. New York, NY: Bloomsbury, 2017.

Melville, Herman. *Clarel: A Poem and Pilgrimage in the Holy Land*, Vol. I. London: Constable and Co., 1924.

——. *Moby Dick*. Boston, MA: St. Botolph Society, 1892.

Merrim, Stephanie. *The Spectacular City, Mexico, and Colonial Hispanic Literary Culture*. Austin, TX: University of Texas Press, 2012.

Messent, Peter. *Mark Twain*. London: Macmillan Press, 1997.
Metcalfe, Alex. *Muslims in Medieval Italy*. Edinburgh: Edinburgh University Press, 2009.
Miller, Perry. *Errand into the Wilderness*. Cambridge, MA: Belknap Press, 1956.
The Mists of Avalon. Directed by Uli Edel. Los Angeles, CA: TNT, 2001.
Mitchell, Edward Page. "The Clock that Went Backwards," *The New York Sun* (September 18, 1881).
Mitchell, Jerome. *Scott, Chaucer, and Medieval Romance: A Study in Sir Walter Scott's Indebtedness to Medieval Literature*. Lexington, KY: University of Kentucky Press, 2021.
Montalvo, Garcí Rodriguez de. *Las sergas de Esplandián*. 1526.
Montoya, Alicia. *Medievalist Enlightenment: From Charles Perrault to Jean-Jacques Rousseau*. Cambridge: D.S. Brewer, 2013.
Moody, Anthony David, ed. *The Cambridge Companion to T.S. Eliot*. Cambridge: Cambridge University Press, 1994.
Moore, Olin Harris. "Mark Twain and Don Quixote," PMLA 37:2 (1922), 324–46.
Moreland, Kim Ileen. *The Medievalist Impulse in American Literature: Twain, Adams, Fitzgerald, and Hemingway*. Charlottesville, VA: University Press of Virginia, 1996.
Morgan, Edmund S. *The Challenge of the American Revolution*. New York, NY: W.W. Norton Co., 1978.
Morgart, James. *The Haunted States of America: Gothic Regionalism in Post-war American Fiction*. Cardiff: University of Wales Press, 2022.
Morrison, Michael A. *Slavery and the American West: The Eclipse of Manifest Destiny*. Chapel Hill, NC: University of North Carolina Press, 1997.
Moyer, Kermit. "Fitzgerald's Two Unfinished Novels: The Count and the Tycoon in Spenglerian Perspective," *Contemporary Literature* 15 (1974), 238–56.
Muir, Robyn. *The Disney Princess Phenomenon: A Feminist Analysis*. Bristol: Bristol University Press, 2023.
Muldoon, James, ed. *Bridging the Medieval-Modern Divide: Medieval Themes in the World of the Reformation*. New York, NY: Routledge, 2016.
Murphy, Patricia. *Time is of the Essence: Temporality, Gender, and the New Woman*. Albany, NY: State University of New York Press, 2001.
Murphy, Paul. "Disparate Medievalisms in Early Modern Spanish Music Theory." In *Studies in Medievalism XIII: Postmodern Medievalisms*, eds. Richard Utz and Jesse G. Swan, 17–26. Cambridge: D.S. Brewer, 2004.
Musson, Anthony. *Medieval Law in Context: The Growth of Legal Consciousness from Magna Carta to the Peasants' Revolt*. Manchester: Manchester University Press, 2001.
Normen, Elizabeth. "The Influence of Connecticut in the American West," *Connecticut Explored* (Winter 2016–17), 202–3.
O'Callaghan, Joseph F. *Reconquest and Crusade in Medieval Spain*. Philadelphia, PA: University of Pennsylvania Press, 2003.
O'Gorman, Edmundo. *The Invention of America: an inquiry into the historical nature of the New World and the meaning of its history*. Westport, CT: Greenwood Press, 1972.

O'Malley, Maria and Denys Van Renen, eds. *Beyond 1776: Globalizing the Cultures of the American Revolution*. Charlottesville, VA: University of Virginia Press, 2018.

O'Regan, Cyril. "Kant, Hegel and Schelling." In *The Oxford Handbook of the Trinity*, eds. Gilles Emery, O.P. and Matthew Levering, 254–66. Oxford: Oxford University Press, 2011.

Owens, Louis. *Mixedblood Messages: Literature, Film, Family, Place*. Norman, OK: University of Oklahoma Press, 2001.

Painter, Nell Irvin. *The History of White People*. New York, NY: W.W. Norton, 2010.

Paredes, Américo. *"With His Pistol in His Hand": A Border Ballad and its Hero*. Austin, TX: University of Texas Press, 2004.

Parr, James. *Don Quixote: An Anatomy of Subversive Discourse*. Newark, DE: Juan de la Cuesta, 1988.

Pavlac, Brian A. *Game of Thrones versus History: Written in Blood*. New York, NY: Wiley/Blackwell, 2017.

Perry, Elisabeth Israels and Karen Manners Smith. *The Gilded Age and Progressive Eva: A Student Companion*. Oxford: Oxford University Press, 2006.

Pinet, Simone. *Archipelagoes: Insular Fictions from Chivalric Romances to the Novel*. Minneapolis, MN: University of Minnesota Press, 2011.

Pizan, Christine de. *The City of Ladies*. Translated by Rosalind Brown-Grant. New York, NY: Penguin Books, 1999.

Poe, Edgar Allan. *The Collected Tales and Poems*. New York, NY: Modern Library, 1992.

——. *Essays and Reviews*. New York, NY: Library of America, 1984.

Polk, Dora. *The Island of California: A History of the Myth*. Lincoln, NE: University of Nebraska Press, 1995.

Pound, Ezra. *The Cantos*. New York, NY: New Directions, 1996.

——. *The Spirit of Romance*. New York, NY: New Directions, 1952/2005.

Pound, Ezra and Ernest Fenollosa. *Instigations: Together with an Essay on the Chinese Written Character*. New York, NY: Boni and Liveright, 1920.

Pratt, Mary Louise. "Arts of the Contact Zone," *Profession* (1991), 33–40.

Pugh, Tison. *Medievalisms: Making the Past in the Present*. New York, NY: Routledge, 2013.

——. *Queer Chivalry: Medievalism and the Myth of White Masculinity in Southern Literature*. Baton Rouge, LA: Louisiana State University Press, 2013.

Pugh, Tison and Susan Aronstein, eds. *The Disney Middle Ages: A Fairy-Tale and Fantasy Past*. New York, NY: Palgrave Macmillan, 2012.

Pugh, Tison, and Susan Aronstein, eds. *The United States of Medievalism*. Toronto: University of Toronto Press, 2021.

Pugh, Tison and Angela Jane Weisl. *Medievalisms: Making the Past in the Present*. New York, NY: Routledge, 2013.

Putnam, Ruth. *California: The Name*. Berkeley, CA: University of California Press, 1917.

Qing, Zhaoming. *Orientalism and Modernism: The Legacy of China in Pound and Williams*. Durham, NC: Duke University Press, 1995.

Quijano, Aníbal and Immanuel Wallerstein. "Americanity as a Concept, or the Americas in the Modern World-System." *International Social Science Journal* 44:4 (1992), 549–57.

Quilligan, Maureen. *The Allegory of Female Authority: Christine de Pizan's "Cité des Dames"*. Ithaca, NY: Cornell University Press, 1991.

Rabiee, Robert Yusef. *Medieval America: Feudalism and Liberalism in Nineteenth-Century U.S. Culture*. Athens, GA: University of Georgia Press, 2020.

Ragussis, Michael. *Figures of Conversion: "The Jewish Question" and English National Identity*. Durham, NC: Duke University Press, 1995.

Ramey, Lynn T. *Black Legacies: Race and the European Middle Ages*. Gainesville, FL: University Press of Florida, 2014.

Reagan, Ronald. *Public Papers of the Presidents of the United States: Ronald Reagan, 1982*. Washington D.C.: Public Papers of the Presidents of the United States, 1982.

Rembold, Ingrid. *Conquest and Christianization: Saxony and the Carolingian World, 772–888*. Cambridge: Cambridge University Press, 2018.

Reynolds, Susan. *Fiefs and Vassals: The Medieval Evidence Reinterpreted*. Oxford: Oxford University Press, 1994.

Richards, Earl Jeffrey. *Christine de Pizan and Medieval French Lyric*. Gainesville, FL: University Press of Florida, 1998.

Richards, Jason. *Imitation Nation: Red, White, and Blackface in Early and Antebellum Literature*. Charlottesville, VA: University of Virginia Press, 2017.

Richardson, Michael S. *Medievalism and Nationalism in German Opera*. New York, NY: Routledge, 2021.

Rigney, Ann. *The Afterlives of Walter Scott: Memory on the Move*. Oxford: Oxford University Press, 2012.

Riley, Scott Corbet. "Anachronous Antipodes: The Island of California, the Medieval Mediterranean and the Modern Pacific," *The Medieval Globe* 4:2 (2018), 107–28.

Riley-Smith, Jonathan. *The Crusades: A History*. New Haven, NJ: Yale University Press, 2005.

Robertson, Fiona, ed. *The Edinburgh Companion to Sir Walter Scott*. Edinburgh: Edinburgh University Press, 2012.

Rosen, Robert C. *John Dos Passos, Politics and the Writer*. Lincoln, NE: University of Nebraska Press, 1981.

Rosenthal, Bernard and Paul E. Szarmach, eds. *Medievalism in American Culture*. Binghamton, NY: Center for Medieval and Early Renaissance Studies, 1989.

Rowlandson, Mary. "Narrative of the Captivity and Restoration." In *Racism: A Global Reader*, eds. Kevin Reilly et al., 94–103. London: M.E. Sharpe, 2003.

Rushdie, Salman. *The Moor's Last Sigh*. New York, NY: Random House, 1995.

Sabatos, Charles. "The Ottoman Captivity Narrative as Transnational Genre in Central European Literature," *Archiv Orientální* 83:2 (2015), 233–54.

Said, Edward. *Orientalism*. New York, NY: Pantheon Books, 1978.

Sánchez-Pardo, Esther. "James's Sociology of Taste: The Ambassadors, Commodity Consumption and Cultural Critique." In *Henry James's Europe: Heritage and*

Transfer, eds. Dennis Tredy, Annick Duperray and Adrian Harding, 39–50. Cambridge: OpenBook, 2011.

Sardar, Ziauddin. "Development and the Location of Eurocentrism." In *Critical Development Theory: Contributions to a New Paradigm*, eds. Ronaldo Munck and Denis O'Hearn, 44–62. London: Zed Books, 1999.

Schiltberger, Johann. *The Bondage and Travels of Johann Schiltberger, a Native of Bavaria, in Europe, Asia, and Africa, 1396–1427*. Translated by Karl Friedrich Neumann. London: Hakluyt Society, 1879.

Schivelbusch, Wolfgang. *The Railway Journey: the Industrialization of Time and Space in the Nineteenth Century*. Berkeley, CA: University of California Press, 1977.

Schor, Juliet B. *The Overworked American: The Unexpected Decline of Leisure*. New York, NY: Basic Books, 1992.

Scott, Walter. *Ivanhoe*. New York, NY: E.P. Dutton 7 Co., 1942.

——. *The Poetical Works of Walter Scott*, Vol. II. Boston, MA: Little, Brown and Company, 1857.

Shaw, Joy Farmer. "The South in Motley: A Study of the Fool Tradition in Selected Works by Faulkner, McCullers, and O'Connor." Ph.D. dissertation. University of Virginia, 1978.

Shlapentokh, Vladimir and Joshua Woods. *Feudal America: Elements of the Middle Ages in Contemporary Society*. University Park, PA: Pennsylvania State University Press, 2011.

Shohat, Ella. "The Sephardi-Moorish Atlantic." In *Sajjilu Arab American: A reader in SWANA Studies*, eds. Louise Cainkar, Pauline Homsi Vinson, and Amira Jarmakani, 86–92. Syracuse, NY: Syracuse University Press, 2022.

Sicari, Stephen. *Pound's Epic Ambition: Dante and the Modern World*. Albany, NY: State University of New York Press, 1991.

Simmons, Clare A. *Medievalism and the Quest for the Real Middle Ages*. London: Frank Cass, 2001.

Sinclair, Upton. *The Jungle*. New York, NY: Penguin Books, 1986.

Singal, Daniel Joseph. *William Faulkner: The Making of a Modernist*. Chapel Hill, NC: University of North Carolina Press, 2000.

Singh, Amritjit and Peter Schmidt, eds. *Postcolonial Theory and the United States: Race, Ethnicity, and Literature*. Jackson, MS: University Press of Mississippi, 2000.

Sklar, Martin J. *The United States as a Developing Country: Studies in U.S. History in the Progressive Era and the 1920s*. Cambridge: Cambridge University Press, 1992.

Slack, Corliss Konwiser. *Crusader Charters 1138–1270*. Tempe, AZ: Arizona Center for Medieval and Renaissance Studies, 2001.

Slater, Candace. *Entangled Edens: Visions of the Amazon*. Berkeley, CA: University of California Press, 2010.

Smith, Henry Nash. *The Development of a Writer*. New York, NY: Atheneum, 1967.

——. *Mark Twain's Fable of Progress: Political and Economic Ideas in A Connecticut Yankee*. New Brunswick, NJ: Rutgers University Press, 1964.

———. *Virgin Land: American West as Myth and Symbol*. New York, NY: Vintage Books, 1950.

Smith, Neil. *Uneven Development: Nature, Capital, and the Production of Space*. Athens, GA: University of Georgia Press, 1984.

Snow White. Directed by David Hand. Walt Disney Productions, 1937.

Soja, Edward. *Postmodern Geographies: The Reassertion of Space in Critical Social Theory*. New York, NY: Verso Books, 1989.

Sokol, A.E. "California: A Possible Derivation of the Name," *California Historical Society Quarterly* 28:1 (1949), 23–30.

Spiers, John. *Chaucer the Maker*. London: Faber and Faber, 1951.

Spivak, Gayatri. *Death of a Discipline*. New York, NY: Columbia University Press, 2003.

Srivastava, Prem Kumari. *Leslie Fiedler: Critic, Provocateur, Pop Culture Guru*. Jefferson, NC: McFarland & Co., Inc., 2014.

Starkey, David. *Magna Carta: The True Story Behind the Charter*. London: Hodder and Stoughton, 2015.

Steiner, Michael C. "The Significance of Turner's Sectional Thesis," *Western Historical Quarterly* 10:4 (1979), 437–66.

Stiglitz, Joseph. *The Price of Inequality: How Today's Divided Society Endangers Our Society*. New York, NY: Norton & Co., 2012.

Stowell, William Hendry. *A History of the Puritans and the Pilgrim Fathers*. New York, NY: R. Carter and Bros., 1849.

Subirats, Eduardo. *El continente vacío: la conquista del Nuevo Mundo y la conciencia moderna*. México D.F.: Siglo XXI, 1994.

Swift, Daniel. *The Bughouse: The Poetry, Politics and Madness of Ezra Pound*. New York, NY: Farrar, Straus and Giroux, 2017.

The Sword in the Stone. Directed by Wolfgang Reitherman. Walt Disney Productions, 1963.

Symes, Carol. "When We Talk about Modernity," *The American Historical Review* 116:3 (2011), 715–26.

Tally, Jr., Robert T. *Poe and the Subversion of American Literature: Satire, Fantasy, Critique*. New York, NY: Bloomsbury, 2014.

Tang, Chenxi. *The Geographic Imagination of Modernity: Geography, Literature, and Philosophy in German Romanticism*. Redwood City, CA: Stanford University Press, 2008.

Tanner, Kathryn. *Jesus, Humanity and the Trinity: A Brief Systematic Theology*. Philadelphia, PA: Fortress Press, 2001.

Tausk, Victor. "On the Origin of the 'Influencing Machine' in Schizophrenia," trans. Dorian Feigenbaum, *Journal of Psychotherapy Practice and Research* 1:2 (1992), 184–206.

Taylor, Charles. *A Secular Age*. Cambridge, MA: Belknap Press, 2007.

Tennyson, Alfred Lord. *Idylls of the King*. London: Edward Moxon, 1859.

Terrell, Carroll Franklin. *A Companion to the Cantos of Ezra Pound*, vol. 2. Berkeley, CA: University of California Press, 1984.

Thomas, David and John Chesworth, eds. *Christian-Muslim Relations: A Bibliographical History*. Boston, MA: Brill, 2017.

Thomson, Iain. "Ontotheology." In *The Bloomsbury Companion to Heidegger*, eds. Eric S. Nelson and Francois Raffoul, 319–28. New York, NY: Bloomsbury Publishing, 2013.

Thorlby, Anthony. "Self-consciousness and social consciousness in literature." In *Aspects of History and Class Consciousness*, Vol. 30, ed. Istvan Meszaros, 173–91. New York, NY: Routledge, 2016.

Thorpe, Francis Newton, ed. *The Federal and State Constitutions, Colonial Charters, and other Organic Laws of the States, Territories and Colonies Now Heretofore Forming the United States of America*, Vol. III. Washington D.C.: Government Printing Office, 1909.

Todd, Emily. "Walter Scott and the Nineteenth-Century American Literary Marketplace: Antebellum Richmond Readers and the Collected Editions of the Waverley Novels," *The Papers of the Bibliographical Society of America* 93:4 (1999), 495–517.

Tolkien, J.R.R. *The Hobbit*. London: George Allen & Unwin, 1937.

Tondro, Jason. *Superheroes of the Round Table: Comics Connections to Medieval and Renaissance Literature*. Jefferson, NC: McFarland & Co., 2011.

Totten, Charles Adiel Lewis. *The Seal of History*, Vol. I. New Haven, CT: The Our Race Publishing Co., 1897.

Troyes, Chrétien de. *Perceval: The Story of the Grail*. Translated by Burton Raffel. New Haven, CT: Yale University Press, 1999.

Turner, Frederick Jackson. "The Significance of the Frontier in American History." In *Proceedings of the Forty-first Annual Meeting of the State Historical Society of Wisconsin*. Madison, WI: State Historical Society of Wisconsin, 1894.

Turner, John G. *They Knew They Were Pilgrims: Plymouth Colony and the Contest for American Liberty*. New Haven, CT: Yale University Press, 2020.

Twain, Mark. *The Adventures of Huckleberry Finn*. New York, NY: Harber & Brothers Publishers, 1904.

———. *The Adventures of Tom Sawyer*. Hartford, CT: American Publishing Company, 1876.

———. *The Complete Short Stories*. New York, NY: Everyman's Library, 2012.

———. *Connecticut Yankee in King Arthur's Court*. New York, NY: Harper and Brothers, 1901.

———. *Life of the Mississippi*. New York, NY: Harper Brothers, 1883/1917.

———. *No. 44, the Mysterious Stranger*. Berkeley, CA: University of California Press, 1969.

———. *Personal Recollections of Joan of Arc*. New York, NY: Harper, 1908.

———. *The Prince and the Pauper: A Tale for Young People of All Ages*. New York, NY: Harper & Brothers, 1917.

———. *Pudd'nhead Wilson*. New York, NY: Charles L. Webster & Co, 1894.

———. *Roughing It*. New York, NY: Signet Classics, 2008.

Tyerman, Christopher. *God's War: A New History of the Crusades*. Cambridge, MA: Belknap Press, 2006.

Ullyot, Jonathon. *Ezra Pound and His Classical Sources*. New York, NY: Bloomsbury Academic, 2022.

——. *The Medieval Presence in Modernist Literature: The Quest to Fail*. Cambridge: Cambridge University Press, 2016.

Ulph, Owen. "The Legacy of the American Wild West in Medieval Scholarship," *American West* 3:4 (1966), 50–2, 88–91.

Utz, Richard. "Academic medievalism and nationalism." In *The Cambridge Companion to Medievalism*, ed. Louise d'Arcens, 119–34. Cambridge: Cambridge University Press, 2016.

——. *Medievalism: A Manifesto*. Yorkshire: ARC Humanities Press, 2017.

——. "Residual Medievalisms: Historical Pageants in Eastern Bavaria," *The Year's Work in Medievalism* 31 (2016), 75–81.

——. "Three Vignettes and a White Castle: Knighthood and Race in Modern Atlanta." In *The United States of Medievalism*, eds. Tison Pugh and Susan Aronstein, 111–29. Toronto: University of Toronto Press, 2021.

Utz, Richard, ed. *Studies in Medievalism XIII: Postmodern Medievalisms*. Cambridge: D.S. Brewer, 2004.

Utz, Richard and Tom Shippey, eds. *Medievalism in the Modern World: Essays in Honour of Leslie J. Workman*. Turnhout: Brepols, 1998.

Vanderwerken, David L. "The Triumph of Medievalism in 'Pudd'nhead Wilson,'" *Mark Twain Journal* 18:4 (1977), 7–11.

Varoufakis, Yanis. *Technofeudalism: What Killed Capitalism*. Brooklyn, NY: Melville House, 2024.

Veblen, Thorstein. *The Theory of the Leisure Class*. New York, NY: The Macmillan Company, 1899.

Vento, Arnoldo C. *Mestizo: The History, Culture, and Politics of the Mexican and the Chicano*. New York, NY: University Press, 1998.

Verduin, Kathleen, ed. *Studies in Medievalism VI: Medievalism in North America*. Cambridge: D.S. Brewer, 1994.

Verhoevan, W.M. *James Fenimore Cooper: New Historical and Literary Contexts*. Amsterdam: Rodopi, 1993.

Viehmann, Martha. "Wests, Westerns, Westerners." In *A Companion to American Literature and Culture*, ed. Paul Lauter, 394–400. Hoboken, NJ: John Wiley & Sons, 2020.

Virginia House of Burgesses. *Charters of the Colony of Virginia*. Philadelphia, PA: Dalcassian Publishing, 2018.

Wade, Erik and Mary Rambaran-Olm. "What's in a Name? The Past and Present Racism in 'Anglo-Saxon' Studies?" *Old English to 1200* (YWES), 2022: 135–53.

Wallerstein, Immanuel. *The Capitalism World-System*. Cambridge: Cambridge University Press, 1979.

——. *The Modern World-System: Capitalist Agriculture and the Origins of the European World Economy in the Sixteenth Century*. New York, NY: Academic Press, 1974.

Warren, Michelle R. *Creole Medievalism: Colonial France and Joseph Bédier's Middle Ages*. Minneapolis, MN: University of Minnesota press, 2011.

Watson, Jay. *William Faulkner and the Faces of Modernity*. Oxford: Oxford University Press, 2019.

Watson, Jr., Ritchie Devon. *Normans and Saxons: Southern Race Mythology and the Intellectual History of the Civil War*. Baton Rouge, LA: Louisiana State University Press, 2008.

Weckmann, Luis. *The Medieval Heritage of Mexico*, Vol. 1. Translated by Frances M. López-Morillas. New York, NY: Fordham University, 1992.

——. "The Middle Ages in the Conquest of America," *Speculum* XXVI (1951), 130–41.

Wells, H.G. "The Chronic Argonauts." In *The Scientific Romances of H.G. Wells*, 1–31. London: Gollancz, 1933.

——. *The Time Machine*. London: William Heinemann, 1895.

Weston, Jessie Laidlay. *From Ritual to Romance*. Mineola, NY: Dover Publications, 1920/1997.

Weston, Jessie Laidlay, ed. *Sir Gawain and the Green Knight*. Cambridge, MA: Harvard University Press, 1900.

White, Jr., Lynn. "Dynamo and Virgin Reconsidered," *The American Scholar* 27:2 (Spring 1958), 183–94.

——. "The Legacy of the Middle Ages in the American Wild West," *Speculum* 40:2 (April 1965): 191–202.

——. "The Significance of Medieval Christianity." In *The Vitality of the Christian Tradition*, ed. G.F. Thomas, 87–115. New York, NY: Harper & Collins, 1944.

Whitman, Walt. *Passage to India*. New York, NY: Smith & McDougal, 1870.

Wilkerson, Isabel. *Caste: The Origins of Our Discontent*. New York, NY: Random House, 2020.

Willard, Charity Cannon. *Christine de Pizan: Her Life and Works*. New York, NY: Persea Books, 1984.

Williams, Peter. "The Varieties of American Medievalism" in *Studies in Medievalism* 1:2 (Spring 1982), 7–20.

Williams, Raymond. *Marxism and Literature*. Oxford: Oxford University Press, 1977.

Williams, Stanley. *The Spanish Background of American Literature*. New Haven, CT: Yale University Press, 1955.

Williamson, Edwin. *The Penguin History of Latin America, Revised Edition*. New York, NY: Penguin, 2009.

Wilson, Carter A. *Racism: From Slavery to Advanced Capitalism*. New York, NY: SAGE Publications, 1996.

Wilson, Diana de Armas. "Editor's Introduction." In *Don Quijote*, trans. Burton Raffel, vii–xvi. New York, NY: W.W. Norton & Co., 1995.

Wilson, Rob Sean. "Worlding as Future Tactic." In *The Worlding Project: Doing Cultural Studies in the Era of Globalization*, eds. Rob Sean Wilson and Christopher Leigh Connery, 209–23. Berkeley, CA: North Atlantic Books, 2007.

Wister, Owen. "The Evolution of the Cow-Puncher," *Harper's* (September 1895): 602–17.

——. *The Virginian*. New York, NY: Macmillan Co., 1902.

Wolmark, Jenny. *Aliens and Others: Science Fiction, Feminism and Postmodernism*. Iowa City, IA: University of Iowa Press, 1994.

Wood, Allen W. *Fichte's Ethical Thought*. Oxford: Oxford University Press, 2016.

Woodward, David. *Cartography in the European Renaissance*. Chicago, IL: University of Chicago, 2007.

Workman, Leslie J., ed. *Studies in Medievalism* IX, vol. 1. Cambridge: D.S. Brewer, 1997.

World of Warcraft. Developed by Blizzard Entertainment. Irvine, CA: Blizzard Entertainment, 2004-.

Wright, Roger. "Bilingualism and diglossia in Medieval Iberia (350–1350)." In *A Comparative History of Literatures in the Iberian Peninsula*, eds. Fernando Cabo Aseguinolaza et al., 333–50. Philadelphia, PA: John Benjamins Publishing, 2010.

———. *Late Latin and Early Romance in Spain and Carolingian France*. Leeds: Francis Cairns, 1982.

Young, Alexander. *Chronicles of the Pilgrim Fathers of the Colony of Plymouth from 1602 to 1625*. Boston, MA: Charles C. Little, 1844.

Young, Helen. *The Middle Ages in Popular Culture: Medievalism and Genre*. Amherst, NY: Cambria Press, 2015.

Zboray, Ronald J. "The Railroad, the Community, and the Book," *Southwestern Review* 71:4 (Autumn 1986): 474–87.

Zerubavel, Eviatar. *Terra Cognita: The Mental Discovery of America*. New Brunswick, NJ: Rutgers University Press, 1992.

———. *Time Maps: Collective Memory and the Social Shape of the Past*. Chicago, IL: University of Chicago Press, 2003.

Ziolkowski, Jan M. *The Juggler and the Medievalizing of Modernity: Tumbling into the Twentieth Century*. Cambridge: Open Books Publishers, 2018.

Zitkala-Ša. *American Indian Stories*. Mineola, NY: Dover Publication, 2012.

Index

Adams, Henry   61, 105, 114
Adorno, Theodor   143
Age of Exploration   17–20
Alhambra, The   69
Alhambra Decree, The   17
Anzaldúa, Gloria   12, 80–82
American Adam   94, 116, 141
Anglo-Saxonism   6, 11–12, 21, 56–72, 76–79, 94–97, 103, 119, 127–128
American Revolution   2, 55, 58
American Studies   3–9, 20–21, 74, 140
Anachronism   15, 88–89, 138, 143
Antimodernism   61, 108–109, 115, 147
Apophaticism   13–14, 94–96, 104
Aquinas, Thomas   94, 141–142
Ariosto, Ludovico   60
Arendt, Hannah   96
Arthur, King *see* Arthuriana
Arthuriana   41, 88, 99–100, 135
Aryanism   82
Augustine, St.   36, 142
Authenticity   2, 95, 105, 112–117, 138, 149

Barthes, Roland   29–30
Bartolomé de las Casas   31
Barataria, Island of   52
Bédier, Joseph   22
Belianís de Grecia   50–51
Bello, Andrés   2, 22, 64
Benjamin, Walter   15, 132, 143–144
Bill of Rights, U.S.   55
Binary oppositions   1–2, 7, 59, 63, 81, 95–96, 109, 113, 135
Bloom, Harold   115–116
Borderlands   12–13, 74–84
Bowling, Lawrence   113
Bradford, William   23
Brant, Sebastian   44

British colonial charters   9, 18–25
Brown, Norman O.   42
Bulfinch, Thomas   58–59
Bumppo, Natty   11, 62, 73, 77
Byrd, II, William   35

California Gold Rush   52, 70–71, 89
California, naming of   36–48
Caliphate, concept of   36–45
Capitalism   12, 16, 59, 123–127, 137, 145–147
Captivity narratives   10, 25–34
Cervantes, Miguel   10–12, 26, 36–37, 47–54, 55, 92–95, 109, 118–119, 136, 148
  Don Quixote   10–11, 15, 26, 35–37, 47–54, 55, 92–94, 109, 118, 148
Charlemagne   39–40
Chaucer, Geoffrey   58, 69, 100
Chivalric quest   35–36, 54, 151
Chivalric romance tradition   10–15, 30–37, 44–53, 66–67, 91, 113
Christian crusader ideology   10, 20, 26, 34
Christianity   27, 38, 52, 64, 99, 104, 107–109, 113, 116, 141
Christianization of the Saxons   107–109
Clemens, Samuel, *see* Twain, Mark
Columbus, Christopher   9, 17, 20, 36, 43, 50–51
Colonialism   1, 5–6, 9–12, 17–20, 53–54, 58–59, 96–97, 99
Coloniality of power   54
Conquistadors   31, 77
Conversos   54
Cooper, James Fenimore   11–12, 62–63, 70–72, 77, 100, 154
  Leatherstocking Tales   11, 61–63, 70, 72
Corrido, genre of   13, 80–82
Cortéz, Hernán   37–38

Index

Cosmographic shock, concept of 38–39
Cowboy, figure of 12, 76–82, 88, 148–149
Crusader cannibalism 30–32, 44–46
Crusades, The 10–11, 17–34
  First Crusade 19, 23, 30, 40, 56, 128
Crusader charters 9, 24–25

Dante 43, 98, 103
Deleuze, Gilles 16, 118–119, 144–147, 153–154
  Lines of flight 118, 144
  Nomadology 16, 136, 153–154
Democracy 2, 55, 96, 127, 153
Derrida, Jacques 143
  Metaphysics of presence 143
Development Studies 1, 6, 59, 104
Dialectics 96, 143–144
Diaz del Castillo, Bernal 37
Dickinson, Jonathan 25
Disney films 2, 31, 120, 135
Douglass, Frederick 31
Dreiser, Theodor 16, 144–147
  Sister Carrie 146

Early Modern Spain 36, 46, 52–53
Eilmer 88
El Cid, Song of 22, 40, 64
Eliot, T.S. 14, 98–109, 115, 116, 144, 151
  The Waste Land 14, 98–102, 103, 104–105, 109, 112, 151
Emerson, Ralph Waldo 58, 63–65, 77, 124
Enlightenment, The 1–2, 15, 122, 129, 141–144
Eriugena, John Scotus 104
Ethnonationalism 15–16, 18, 21–22, 59–60, 64–65, 72–73, 96, 101–102, 116, 118–119, 128, 133, 144, 148, 154
Eurocentrism 1, 53, 59

Fantasy literature 97, 131–134, 138

Faulkner, William 14–15, 109–119, 134, 136, 144, 147, 154
  Go Down, Moses 109–111, 147
  Sound and the Fury, The 111–118, 154
Feminism 41, 131–138
Fellahin Indians 150–154
Feudalism 16, 55–59, 91, 97, 122–128, 132, 135, 140–141, 145–146, 151, 153
Fichte, Johann Gottlieb 143–144
Fiedler, Leslie 16, 78–79, 140–145
Fisher King, myth of the 100–102
Fitzgerald, F. Scott 105–108
Foucault, Michel 86–87, 139
Frontier Thesis *see* Turner, Frederick Jackson
Freud, Sigmund 67–71, 96
Fugger, House of 48
Fury of Orlando, The 60

Game of Thrones, HBO series 14, 120–122, 129, 138
Gothicism 4, 8, 68, 70, 123
Grand narratives 1, 129
Granada 17, 20–21, 69, 83
Gramsci, Anthony 106–111
Guattari, Félix *see* Deleuze, Gilles

Hale, Edward Everett 37–44, 58
Hale, Sarah Josepha 80
Hawthorne, Nathaniel 70, 84–85
Hegel, Georg Wilhelm Friedrich 96, 143
Hemingway, Ernest 105–108
Historical periodization *see* Periodization
Historiography 1–6, 13, 17, 21–24, 56–59, 65, 83, 91, 107, 125–126, 133–138, 144
Holy Grail 11, 99–100, 113, 122, 151
Huxley, Aldous 102

Incest, motif of 71–72, 114–115
Industrialization 3, 85, 108–109
Insular imaginary 38, 46–47

Intersectionality   41, 80
Irving, Washington   49–50, 58, 69, 133–134
Islam   36, 40–45, 53, 127, 148
Islamic-Christian relations   53, 127–128, 148
Islamophobia   15, 26, 40, 46, 52–53, 116, 127
Isolario   46–47

James, Henry   4, 16, 144, 147–153
James I, King   18–19
Jamestown   31
Jefferson, Thomas   11, 56–57, 63, 65, 77, 150
Jesters   114
Jerusalem Delivered   60
Joan of Arc   91–94, 130
John, King   55

Kataphaticism   104
Kenner, Hugh
  Pound Era, The   98–99
Kerouac, Jack   16, 147–154
  On the Road   148–154
Ku Klux Klan   57

Lawrence, D. H.   12, 62–63, 71–72, 100, 115–118, 154
  Studies in Classic American Literature   12, 62–63, 71–72, 100, 154
Le Guin, Ursula K.   14–15, 131–139, 144, 154
  Hainish novels   14–15, 132–139
Leonard, Irving A.   10, 49
Longfellow, Henry Wadsworth   58–59
  Hiawatha, Song of   59
Lost Cause of the Confederacy   116

Magna Carta   11, 55–56
Magna Carta effect   56
Mad Trist   12, 66–68
Manifest Destiny *see* Western expansionism

Manifest Domesticity   79–80
Martin, George R.R.   14, 121
Martyr of Angleria, Peter   36
Marx, Karl   125–126, 145
Marx, Leo   84–85, 140
Mather, Cotton   25–26, 49, 75
Medieval/modern divide   1–6, 13–15, 21, 58–65, 81, 104, 114, 117, 129, 135–141
Medievalism Studies   2–9, 21, 64, 74, 99, 129, 141
Medievalisms
  Creole   22, 65, 95
  Definitions of   6–8
  Enlightenment   129
  Ethnonationalist   15–16, 64–65, 144
  Modernist   14, 99, 102, 107–110
  Organic   111–113, 118, 134
  Pedagogical   14, 106–116, 119
  Pluralization of   8
  Romantic   1–2, 60–63, 69, 127, 143
  Southern   4, 74, 146, 153
  Subversive   10–11, 15–16, 68, 131, 134, 144, 154
  Spectacular   14, 121–123, 130
Melville, Herman   69, 79
  Moby Dick   78–79, 118
Mestiza consciousness   80–82
Merlin   69
Merlin, character of   95
Middle Ages, definitions of   1–4
Miller, Perry   11, 35–37, 54, 140
de Montalvo, Garci Rodríguez
  Amadís de Gaula   36–38, 46–51, 74
  Las sergas de Esplandián   11, 36–50, 58
Moors   10, 12, 17, 20, 30, 37, 41, 45, 52, 69, 76–77, 82–83, 148, 150
Morgan, Edmund   58
Moriscos   54
Modernism   14, 98–99, 102, 110
Muslim American Studies   20
Myth and Symbol School   140–141

Nationalism   21–22, 42, 61, 79–80, 107

Index

Native Americans   10–12, 25–31, 36, 44–46, 52, 57–61, 76–82
  Genocide of   11, 18, 46, 52, 61, 70
  Representations as Moors   20–21, 150–154
New World Colonization *see* Colonialism
Norman Conquest of Britain   11, 40, 56
Northern bourgeoisie   115

Odyssey, The   103
Orientalism   7, 29, 99
Orlando Furioso see Fury of Orlando, The
Ottoman Empire   10, 26–33, 38, 46, 147, 150

Paganism   99, 104, 107–109
Patriarchy   15, 43, 61, 79, 94, 97, 115, 119, 127, 131–139
Periodization   1–2, 6–7, 74–76, 90
Pilgrims   22–25, 33–36, 48, 52, 56, 71, 83, 100
Pilgrims Progress   148
Plymouth colonists   19, 23–24
Pocahontas   31
Poe, Edgar Allan   11–12, 65–73
  "Fall of the House of Usher, The"   11–12, 66–72, 115–117, 119, 154
  "Gold-Bug, The"   11, 68–71
Postcolonial studies   2–6, 17, 22, 64, 124, 129
Pound, Ezra   14, 98–99
  Cantos, The   14, 98, 103–105, 109, 112
  "Seafarer, The"   103
Precaution   62
Proclus   94
Protestantism   75, 94
Pseudo-Dionysius   94–96
Puritans   11, 24, 35, 37, 49, 54, 75, 94

Quijano, Aníbal   54, 81

Racism   11, 14, 41, 57, 76, 82, 94, 97, 128, 145
  See also Ethnonationalism
Realism   13, 89, 94, 97, 115
Reconquista   17–20, 37–41, 48, 52, 83
Roland, Song of   39–44, 106
Romanticism   2, 13, 15, 42, 60–65, 104, 143–144
Rowlandson, Mary   10, 27–34

Sachsenspiegel   44–45
Schiltberger, Johann   26–34
Scholastic theology   15, 94, 105, 114, 143, 148
Science fiction   85, 88, 97, 132–139
Scott, Sir Walter   4, 15, 55, 60–62, 69, 95, 109–110, 118
  Ivanhoe   55, 70, 74, 89, 91
  reception in the U.S.   60–62
Settler colonialism   6, 43, 57–65
Shakespeare, William   58, 111
  Macbeth   111
Ship of Fools   44–45
Sir Gawain and the Green Knight   69
Slavery   11, 18, 31, 52, 58, 61, 84, 94
Smith, Henry Nash   5, 74, 78, 125, 140–141, 147
Smith, John   31, 71
Soja, Edward   46
Spanish Inquisition   17
Spatio-temporal fix   12–13, 147
Spenser, Edmund   60
  Faerie Queene, The   60
Spivak, Gayatri   148
Standardization of time   84–86
Stellinga   108–109

Tasso, Torquato   60
Thoreau, Henry David   84
Time travel   87–88
Tolkien, J. R. R.   108, 110
Trauma   7, 21, 70
Trinitarianism   141–143
Trojan War   51
Trump, Donald J.   57, 123–124, 127–128, 138

Trump Tower   123, 138
Tu Fu   105
Turner, Frederick Jackson   4–5, 12, 74, 80, 83–84, 88, 147
Twain, Mark   4, 13, 55, 75, 77–79, 88–97, 109, 112, 116, 118–119, 125, 136, 144, 146, 154
  Adventures of Huckleberry Finn, The   78–79, 89–94
  Adventures of Tom Sawyer, The   92, 93
  Connecticut Yankee in King Arthur's Court   88–90, 94–95, 115, 144
  Life on the Mississippi   4, 55
  Personal Recollections of Joan of Arc   91–94
  Prince and the Pauper, The   91

Uncanny, concept of   67–68, 73
Upanishads   105
Urban II, Pope   19

Vaquero, figure of   76–79, 149
Verisimilitude   29

Video games   120, 123
Voynich Manuscript   88

Wallerstein, Immanuel   49, 54, 81, 123
Warwick Castle   88, 110, 147
Western expansionism   4, 12, 18, 24, 58, 61–64, 71–72, 74–80, 83–84, 88–89, 151
Western, genre of   12–13, 76–77
Weston, Jessie L.   69, 99–100, 106, 108
Whitman, Walt   78, 150
Williams, Roger   49
World War I   108
World War II   102, 120
World-systems theory   48
Wister, Owen   12–13, 77–79, 148
  Virginian, The   13, 77–79

Yeats, William Butler   102

Zerubavel, Eviatar   38–39
Zitkala-Ša   31

Medievalism

I
Anglo-Saxon Culture and the Modern Imagination
edited by David Clark and Nicholas Perkins

II
Medievalist Enlightenment: From Charles Perrault to Jean-Jacques Rousseau
Alicia C. Montoya

III
Memory and Myths of the Norman Conquest
Siobhan Brownlie

IV
Comic Medievalism: Laughing at the Middle Ages
Louise D'Arcens

V
Medievalism: Key Critical Terms
edited by Elizabeth Emery and Richard Utz

VI
Medievalism: A Critical History
David Matthews

VII
Chivalry and the Medieval Past
edited by Katie Stevenson and Barbara Gribling

VIII
Georgian Gothic: Medievalist Architecture, Furniture and Interiors, 1730–1840
Peter N. Lindfield

IX
Petrarch and the Literary Culture of Nineteenth-Century France: Translation, Appropriation, Transformation
Jennifer Rushworth

X
Medievalism, Politics and Mass Media: Appropriating the Middle Ages in the Twenty-First Century
Andrew B.R. Elliott

XI

Translating Early Medieval Poetry: Transformation, Reception, Interpretation
edited by Tom Birkett and Kirsty March-Lyons

XII

Medievalism in A Song of Ice and Fire *and* Game of Thrones
Shiloh Carroll

XIII

William Morris and the Icelandic Sagas
Ian Felce

XIV

Derek Jarman's Medieval Modern
Robert Mills

XV

François Villon in English Poetry: Translation and Influence
Claire Pascolini-Campbell

XVI

Neomedievalism, Popular Culture, and the Academy: From Tolkien to Game of Thrones
KellyAnn Fitzpatrick

XVII

Medievalism in English Canadian Literature: From Richardson to Atwood
edited by M.J. Toswell and Anna Czarnowus

XVIII

Anglo-Saxonism and the Idea of Englishness in Eighteenth-Century Britain
Dustin M. Frazier Wood

XIX

Subaltern Medievalisms: Medievalism 'from below' in Nineteenth-Century Britain
edited by David Matthews and Michael Sanders

XX

Medievalist Traditions in Nineteenth-Century British Culture: Celebrating the Calendar Year
Clare A. Simmons

XXI

Old English Medievalism: Reception and Recreation in the 20th and 21st Centuries
edited by Rachel A. Fletcher, Thijs Porck and Oliver M. Traxel

XXII

International Medievalisms: From Nationalism to Activism
edited by Mary Boyle

XXIII

Old English Scholarship in the Seventeenth Century: Medievalism and National Crisis
Rebecca Brackmann

XXIV

Medievalism in Nineteenth-Century Belgium: The 1848 Monument to Godfrey of Bouillon
Simon John

XXV

National Medievalism in the Twenty-First Century: Switzerland and Great Britain
Matthias D. Berger

XXVI

Reinventing Medieval Liturgy in Victorian England: Thomas Frederick Simmons and the Lay Folks' Mass Book
David Jasper and Jeremy J. Smith

XXVII

Medievalisms in a Global Age
edited by Angela Jane Weisl and Robert Squillace

XXVIII

The Middle Ages in Computer Games: Ludic Approaches to the Medieval and Medievalism
Robert Houghton

XXIX

Medievalism and Reception
edited by Ellie Crookes and Ika Willis

XXX

Tennyson's Philological Medievalism
Sarah Weaver

Printed in the United States
by Baker & Taylor Publisher Services